Ulrike Abelein

User-Developer-Communication in Large-Scale IT Projects

Ulrike Abelein

User-Developer-Communication in Large-Scale IT Projects

The UDC-LSI method

Südwestdeutscher Verlag für Hochschulschriften

Impressum / Imprint
Bibliografische Information der Deutschen Nationalbibliothek: Die Deutsche Nationalbibliothek verzeichnet diese Publikation in der Deutschen Nationalbibliografie; detaillierte bibliografische Daten sind im Internet über http://dnb.d-nb.de abrufbar.
Alle in diesem Buch genannten Marken und Produktnamen unterliegen warenzeichen-, marken- oder patentrechtlichem Schutz bzw. sind Warenzeichen oder eingetragene Warenzeichen der jeweiligen Inhaber. Die Wiedergabe von Marken, Produktnamen, Gebrauchsnamen, Handelsnamen, Warenbezeichnungen u.s.w. in diesem Werk berechtigt auch ohne besondere Kennzeichnung nicht zu der Annahme, dass solche Namen im Sinne der Warenzeichen- und Markenschutzgesetzgebung als frei zu betrachten wären und daher von jedermann benutzt werden dürften.

Bibliographic information published by the Deutsche Nationalbibliothek: The Deutsche Nationalbibliothek lists this publication in the Deutsche Nationalbibliografie; detailed bibliographic data are available in the Internet at http://dnb.d-nb.de.
Any brand names and product names mentioned in this book are subject to trademark, brand or patent protection and are trademarks or registered trademarks of their respective holders. The use of brand names, product names, common names, trade names, product descriptions etc. even without a particular marking in this work is in no way to be construed to mean that such names may be regarded as unrestricted in respect of trademark and brand protection legislation and could thus be used by anyone.

Coverbild / Cover image: www.ingimage.com

Verlag / Publisher:
Südwestdeutscher Verlag für Hochschulschriften
ist ein Imprint der / is a trademark of
OmniScriptum GmbH & Co. KG
Heinrich-Böcking-Str. 6-8, 66121 Saarbrücken, Deutschland / Germany
Email: info@svh-verlag.de

Herstellung: siehe letzte Seite /
Printed at: see last page
ISBN: 978-3-8381-5163-2

Zugl. / Approved by: Heidelberg, Uni, Diss., 2015

Copyright © 2015 OmniScriptum GmbH & Co. KG
Alle Rechte vorbehalten. / All rights reserved. Saarbrücken 2015

User-Developer Communication in Large-Scale IT Projects

Advisor: Prof. Dr. Barbara Paech

2. Advisor Prof. Dr. Helen Sharp

To my Dad.

Zusammenfassung

Die Einbindung von Endbenutzern in der Softwareentwicklung wird bereits seit Jahrzehnten untersucht, und als essentiell für den Softwaresystemerfolg betrachtet. Die Einbindung von Endbenutzern kann zu positiven Effekten, wie zum Beispiel einer Verbesserung der Qualität aufgrund präziserer Anforderungen, der Verhinderung von teuren Systemfunktionen durch klarer Absprachen zwischen Entwicklern und Endbenutzern, der Schaffung einer positiven Einstellung zu dem Softwaresystem und einer effektiven Systemanwendung, führen. Trotz dieser Effekte binden große IT Projekte unter der Verwendung von traditionellen Entwicklungsmethoden die Endbenutzer häufig nur zu Beginn (Spezifikationsphase) und am Ende (Verifikations- und Validierungsphase) der Entwicklung ein oder haben überhaupt keine Endbenutzer-Entwickler-Kommunikation. Es werden allerdings auch endbenutzerrelevante Entscheidungen der Entwickler in den Zwischenphasen (Design- und Implementierungsphase) getroffen, diese werden selten zu den Endbenutzern kommuniziert. Die fehlende Kommunikation zwischen Endbenutzern und Entwicklern führt zu folgenden Effekten. Zum einen fühlen sich die Endbenutzer nicht in das Projekt integriert und haben eine geringe Motivation mitzuwirken. Zum anderen erkennen sie ihre gestellten Anforderungen im abgeschlossenen Softwaresystem nicht mehr wieder.

Deshalb untersuchen wir in dieser Arbeit, wie Endbenutzer-Entwickler-Kommunikation in der Design- und Implementierungsphase von großen IT Projekten verbessert werden kann, mit dem Ziel den Systemerfolg zu erhöhen.

Diese Arbeit folgt dem Technical-Action-Research-Ansatz mit den vier Phasen: Problemuntersuchung, Verfahrensentwurf, Entwurfsvalidierung und Implementierungsevaluierung. Zur Problemuntersuchung wurden eine systematische Mappingstudie (State-of-the-Art) sowie eine Befragung zur Endbenutzer-Entwickler-Kommunikation in der Praxis durchgeführt (State-of-Practice). Auf Basis dieser Information wurde die UDC–LSI Methode entwickelt (Verfahrensentwicklung) und anschließen über

Experteninterviews validiert (Entwurfsvalidierung). Am Ende wurde die UDC–LSI Methode in einer Fallstudie retroperspektivisch evaluiert (Implementierungsevaluierung).

Innerhalb dieser Arbeit präsentieren wir zuerst eine Metaanalyse von wissenschaftlichen untersuchten Effekten von Endbenutzereinbindung auf den Systemerfolg und erforschen bestehende Methoden zur erhöhten Einbindung der Endbenutzer in der Softwareentwicklung. Des Weiteren stellen wir die Ergebnisse der Expertenbefragung zum aktuellen Stand der Praxis von Endbenutzer-Entwickler-Kommunikation vor. Im Anschluss wird die UDC–LSI Methode und eine deskriptive Klassifizierung von endbenutzer-relevanten Entscheidungen vorgestellt. Darauf folgt die Experteneinschätzung der Methode, sowie die Ergebnisse der retroperspektivischen Validierung der UDC–LSI Methode in einem realen großen IT Projekt. Die Evaluierung zeigt, dass nach der Einschätzung der Projektbeteiligten die Methode einsetzbar ist (feasibility), positive Effekte auf den Systemerfolg hat (effectivness) und ein Einsatz wirtschaftlich wäre (efficiency). Zusätzlich würden die Projektbeteiligte die UDC-LSI Methode in diesem und zukünftigen Projekten einsetzen.

Abstract

User participation and involvement in software development has been studied for a long time and is considered essential for a successful software system. The positive effects of involving users in software development include improving quality in light of information about precise requirements, avoiding unnecessarily expensive features through enhanced aligment between developers and users, creating a positive attitude toward the system among users, and enabling effective use of the system. However, large-scale IT (LSI) projects that use traditional development methods tend to involve the user only at the beginning of the development process (i.e., in the specification phase) and at the end (i.e., in the verification and validation phases) or not to involve users at all. However, even if developers involve users at the beginning and the end, there are important decisions that affect users in the phases in between (i.e., design and implementation), which are rarely communicated to the users. This lack of communication between the users and developers in the design and implementation phase results in users who do not feel integrated into the project, are little motivated to participate, and do not see their requirements manifested in the resulting system. Therefore, it is important to study how user-developer communication (UDC) in the design and implementation phases can be enhanced in LSI projects in order to increase system success.

The thesis follows the technical action research (TAR) approach with the four phases of problem investigation, treatment design, design validation, and implementation evaluation. In the problem investigation phase we conducted a systematic mapping study and assessed the state of UDC practice with experts. In the treatment design phase, we designed the UDC–LSI method with experts, and we validated its design with experts in the design validation phase. Finally, in the implementation evaluation phase we evaluated the implementation of the method using a case study.

This thesis first presents a meta-analysis of evidence of the effects of UPI on system success in general and explore the methods in the literature that aim to increase UPI in software development in the literature. Second, we investigate the state of UDC practice with experts, analyzing current practices and obstacles of UDC in LSI projects. Third, we propose the UDC–LSI method, which supports the enhancement of UDC in LSI projects, and present a descriptive classification containing user-relevant decisions (and, therefore, trigger points) to start UDC that can be used with our method. We also show the validity of the method through an assessment of the experts who see potential for the UDC–LSI method. Fourth, we demonstrate the results of a retrospective validation of the method in the real-life context of a large-scale IT project. The evaluation showed that the method is feasible to implement, has a positive effect on system success, and is efficient to implement from the perspective of project participants. Furthermore, project participants consider the UDC-LSI method to be usable and are likely to use in future projects.

Danksagung

Dieser Arbeit ist geprägt von vielen Menschen, Ereignisse und Begegnungen. Im Besonderen möchte ich mich bedanken bei:
Mama und Papa für Ihre Liebe und Unterstützung, die es erst möglich gemacht hat Frau Doktor zu werden.
Meiner Schwester Stef für Ihre Liebe und immer offene Ohren, wenn es hart wurde.
Opa für seinen Stolz und die Geduld mir zuzuhören.
Dem ganzen Rest der Negele und Abelein Clans für Ihre Unterstützung.
Anita, Jos, Katha, Kerstin und Angie und allen meine Freunden für Ihre Unterstützung und Freundschaft.
Steffi H. und Joyce für dauerhaften Zuspruch und Joyce für Ihren Vergleich der Diss mit dem Baby.
Anna K. für das Bewusstsein, das es hart ist und die See-Geschichte.
Anna W. für die Hilfe bei den Korrekturen und bei den Interviews.
Stephan für den Glauben in mich und die Hilfe bei der Evaluierung.
Alex für die glückliche Zeit im letzten Schritt dieser Arbeit.

Barbara für viel Feedback, Vertrauen und Verständnis in schwierigen Situationen.
Helen für Ihren Glauben an meinen Inhalt und meine beste Veröffentlichung.
Gabi für viele gute Ideen und dass sie in einem meiner schwersten Momente für mich das war.
Dem Rest der AG für Feedback und Pausenunterstützung.
Florian und Silvia für den Zuspruch und den Tipp, die Diss in „a good mood" zu beenden.
Allen Experten für Ihre Zeit.
Gunter, Horst, Lydia, Manuel, Maria, Michael, Neha, Nico und Sven für die Unterstützung bei der Case Study.
Claus und Michael, sowie alle Mitarbeiter der sovanta AG für den netten Umgang im letzten Schritt dieser Arbeit.

Acknowledgements

This work has been influenced by many people, events, and encounters. In particular I extend my thanks to:
My mom and dad for their love and support, which made it possible for me to become a Ph.D.
My sister Stef for her love and always-open ears, even in hard times.
My grandpa for his pride in me and patience in listening to me.
The rest of the Negele and Abelein clans for their support.
Anita, Jos, Katha, Kerstin, Angie, and all of my friends for their support and friendship.
Steffi H. and Joyce for continuous encouragement and Joyce for her comparison of a dissertation with a baby.
Anna K. for the awareness that it is hard and the lake story.
Anna W. for her help through corrections and with the interviews.
Stephan for his belief in me and help with the evaluation.
Alex for the happy time in the last step of this work.

Barbara for a lot of feedback, trust, and understanding during my difficult times.
Helen for her belief in my content and my best publication.
Gabi for many good ideas and for being there for me in one of my most difficult moments.
The rest of the software AG for feedback and break support.
Florian and Silvia for the advice to finalize this work while remaining positive.
All experts for their time.
Gunter, Horst, Lydia, Manuel, Maria, Michael, Neha, Nico, and Sven for their time and support during the case study.
Claus, Michael, and all employees of the Sovanta AG for the pleasant environment in the last step of this work.

Table of Contents

PART I PRELIMINARIES — 16
  Chapter 1 Introduction — 18
    1.1. Motivation — 19
    1.2. Problem Statement — 21
    1.3. Contributions — 23
    1.4. Structure of this Thesis — 24
  Chapter 2 Foundations — 28
    2.1. Research Methodology — 29
    2.2. Glossary — 33
PART II PROBLEM INVESTIGATION — 40
  Chapter 3 Understanding the Influence of UPI on System Success (State of the Art) — 42
    3.1. Abstract — 43
    3.2. Introduction — 43
    3.3. Research Questions for the Systematic Mapping Study — 46
    3.4. Review Method of the Systematic Mapping Study — 47
    3.5. Included and Excluded Studies — 54
    3.6. Meta-Analysis of Statistical Surveys and Meta-Studies on the Effect of User Participation and Involvement on System Success — 56
      3.6.1. Aspects of UPI, Aspects of System Success, and Context Factors (RQ 1.1 and RQ 1.4) — 57
      3.6.2. Examples of Researched Aspects of System Success (RQ 1.1) — 58
      3.6.3. Correlations of Aspects of UPI and Context Factors with System Success (RQ 1.2, 1.3, and 1.7) — 63
      3.6.4. Overview of Positive and Negative Studies (RQ 1.3 and 1.4) — 67
      3.6.5. Number of Participants in Studies of Correlations of Aspects of UPI and Context Factors with System Success (RQ 1.3 and RQ 1.4) — 69
      3.6.6. Findings of the Meta-Analysis — 71
    3.7. Current Methods of Software Development or IT Project Management that Use User Participation and Involvement — 73
      3.7.1. Methods to Increase UPI in Software Development Projects (RQ 2.1) — 74
      3.7.2. Software Development Activities Affected by the Methods (RQ 2.2) — 74
      3.7.3. Targeted Aspects of UPI, Aspects of System Success, and Context Factors (RQ 2.3) — 75
      3.7.4. Validation Context of the Methods (RQ 2.4) — 76

3.7.5. Practices of the Proposed Solutions (RQ 2.4)	79
3.7.6. Findings of the Methods Analysis	80
3.8. Strengths and Weaknesses of the Systematic Mapping Study	92
3.9. Further Analysis	95
3.10. Summary of State of the Art	99
Chapter 4 User-Developer Communication in Large-Scale IT Projects	102
4.1. Abstract	103
4.2. Introduction	103
4.3. Research Questions for the State of Practice	105
4.4. Related Work on User-Developer Communication	106
4.5. Methodology of the Interview Series 108_Toc414370280	
4.5.1. Identification of Experts	108
4.5.2. Interview Process	111
4.5.3. Data Analysis	112
4.6. Results and Discussion	113
4.6.1. UDC in Large-Scale IT Projects (RQ 3.1)	113
4.6.2. Organizational Obstacles for UDC (RQ 3.2)	115
4.6.3. Reasons for and Consequences of Communication Gaps (RQ 3.3)	116
4.6.4. Overcoming Obstacles to the Implementation of UDC and the Reasons for Communication Gaps (RQ 3.4)	118
4.7. Threats to Validity	123
4.8. Summary of the State of Practice	124
Chapter 5 A Descriptive Classification of User-Relevant Decisions in Large-Scale IT Projects	126
5.1. Abstract	127
5.2. Introduction	127
5.3. Research Questions for the Descriptive Classification	128
5.4. Background	129
5.5. A Classification with Which to Structure User-Relevant Decisions	129
5.6. Results of the Expert Interview Series	132
5.6.1. Validation of the Classification (RQ 4.1)	132
5.6.2. List of Examples (RQ 4.2)	134
5.7. Summary of the Descriptive Classification	145
PART III TREATMENT DESIGN	146
Chapter 6 Requirement for the UDC-LSI Method	148
6.1. Abstract	149
6.2. Introduction	149

6.3. Conceptual Framework of the UDC-LSI method	150
6.4. Requirements for the UDC-LSI Method	152
6.5. Findings from Interviews and Existing Methods	153
6.6. Summary of the Requirements for the UDC-LSI Method	155
Chapter 7 The UDC-LSI Method to Enhance User-Developer Communication in Large-Scale IT Projects	158
7.1. Abstract	159
7.2. Introduction	159
7.3. The UDC-LSI Method	160
7.3.1. Part 1 – Set up the Communication Structure	163
7.3.2. Part 2 – Train Developers on Capturing Decisions or Changes	164
7.3.3. Part 3 – Set up How Decisions Will Be Traced	165
7.3.4. Part 4 – Define the Means of Communication	165
7.3.5. Operationalization	166
7.4. Use Cases for the Descriptive Classification	167
7.5. Summary of the UDC-LSI Method	170
PART IV DESIGN VALIDATION AND IMPLEMENTATION EVALUATION	*172*
Chapter 8 Expert Assessment of the UDC-LSI Method	174
8.1. Abstract	175
8.2. Introduction	175
8.3. Research Questions for Design Validation	176
8.4. Potential of the UDC-LSI	176
8.4.1. Assessment of the UDC-LSI Method (RQ 5.1)	177
8.4.2. Extensions of the UDC-LSI Method (RQ 5.3)	179
8.4.3. Implementation Feasibility and Obstacles to the Implementation of the UDC-LSI Method (RQ 5.2)	181
8.5. Discussion of the Design Validation	183
8.6. Summary of the Expert Assessment	189
Chapter 9 Evaluation of the UDC-LSI Method: the iPeople Case Study	192
9.1. Abstract	193
9.2. Introduction	194
9.3. Case Study Design	195
9.3.1. Research Questions, Goals, and Hypotheses	197
9.3.2. Case Selection	202
9.3.3. Research Method	205
9.4. Understanding the Current Status of the Project (As-is Study)	206
9.4.1. Design and Data Collection Procedure	206
9.4.2. Results	209
9.4.3. Summary of the As-is	234

9.5. Applying the UDC-LSI Method in Practice (Simulated Instantiation)	235
9.5.1. Design and Data Collection Procedure	235
9.5.2. Adaptation Process	236
9.5.3. Results	242
9.5.4. Summary of the Simulated Instantiation	254
9.6. Evaluation of the Application of the UDC-LSI Method	254
9.6.1. Design and Data Collection Procedure	255
9.6.2. Results	259
9.6.3. Discussion	283
9.7. Threats to Validity	286
9.7.1. Construct Validity	286
9.7.2. Internal Validity	288
9.7.3. External Validity	288
9.7.4. Reliability	289
9.5. Summary of the Case Study	289
PART V. SUMMARY	*294*
Chapter 10 Conclusion and Outlook	296
10.1. Major Findings of this Thesis	297
10.1.1. Contribution to Theory	300
10.1.2. Implications for Practice	301
10.2. Limitations	302
10.3. Future Work	303
Index of Tables	305
Index of Figures	307
References	310
APPENDIX	*324*
APPENDIX I: Further Data to Systematic Mapping Study	326
APPENDIX II: Further Data to Expert Interview Series	352
APPENDIX III: Further Data to Case Study	360

PART I
PRELIMINARIES

17

Chapter 1
Introduction

"Definiteness of purpose is the starting point of all achievements."

W. Clement Stone

1.1. Motivation

The complexity and scale of customer-specific software systems increase constantly (Kanungo & Bagchi, 2000). Most customer-specific software systems are developed in large-scale IT (LSI) projects, and such projects that customize commercial off-the-shelf (COTS) software are becoming more common than individual developments (Austin & Nolan, 1998). These projects tend to be complex because of the required customization for company-specific processes. LSI projects involve many stakeholders whose differing goals often lead to conflicting opinions and requirements, but the resulting software system is supposed to be consistent with all stakeholders' desires. Users are an important source of information, as they are familiar with the work and the context that the software system should support (Hendry, 2008). In particular, the knowledge and expectations of users on the business side must be integrated into software-development projects in order to ensure a successful project (Esteves et al., 2003).

Even though UPI is essential for system success (Harris & Weistroffer, 2009), the change in complexity and scale requires specific attention on how to include users throughout the software development process. A summary from Harris and Weistroffer (2009) names advantages of this approach, including improved quality resulting from precise requirements and the prevention of unneeded, expensive features. Furthermore, users who feel involved in a software system are likely to have a positive attitude toward the system, to perceive it as useful, and to be satisfied with the system (McGill & Klobas, 2008). As the level of user acceptance and understanding of the system rises, the system will be used more effectively. The increased participation in decision-making also leads to a more democratic organizational culture.

However, many large-scale IT project still do not involve users in the software development process adequately, which can decrease the changes in system success and increase the likelihood that the project is finished on time and on budget because of quality issues. In particular, LSI projects often use traditional project management and software development methods like the waterfall model (Austin & Nolan, 1998; Alleman, 2002), which often results in a low level of user participation. If users are involved at all, the involvement takes place only in the early (specification) or late (validation and verification) phases of the traditional software development cycle (Iivari et al., 2010; Ives & Olson, 1984). In the specification phase most projects rely on the one-way transfer of specification artifacts, while backward communication of decisions and their rationale after the requirements are elicited occurs rarely in those projects (Al-Rawas & Easterbrook, 1996).

Involving users in large-scale customer-specific IT projects has three clear advantages. First, in comparison to new or evolutionary development of systems for a mass market, the prospective users are available within the company as are the developers who work long-term on such systems. Second, most large-scale customer-specific IT projects use standard systems that have best-practices functionality built in, so the technical challenges are not as important as the need to involve users because of their specific context knowledge. Third, in enterprises that implement these large-scale systems, both users and IT developers have an interest in achieving system success because the users' work will depend on the resulting system, and IT personnel want to improve how they are perceive by the business domains.

The effects of UPI on system success have been studied widely and for a long time (e.g., McKeen et al., 1994; Cavaye, 1995; McGill & Klobas, 2008; Harris & Weistroffer, 2009; Kujala, 2003; Ives & Olson, 1984). While there are many approaches to increasing UPI in software development, the implementation of those approaches, especially in LSI projects, remains limited. In addition, the focus of many approaches is on the early and late phases of software development (Taylor & Kujala, 2008; Majid et al., 2010), although many important decisions are made in the design and implementation phases, when user requirements are translated into system requirements (Abelein et al., 2012). In fact, none of the existing approaches even focuses on *communicating* user-relevant decisions in the design and implementation phases.

We argue that it is important to UPI to determine how user-developer communication (UDC) can be enhanced in LSI projects that use traditional methods in customer-specific software development. Hence, this work focuses on an analysis of the problem of UDC in customer-specific LSI projects.

1.2. Problem Statement

LSI projects that still use traditional software development methods seek to benefit from the advantages of these methods, including a high level of stability and clear agreement on price, timeline, and scope (Fowler & Highsmith, 2001). However, the drawbacks include long development cycles (Fowler & Highsmith, 2001), as the translation from user requirements to system requirements often leads to considerable interpretation and misunderstanding and a low level of UDC. These long cycles have three primary effects on users: First, users do not feel integrated into the project since they are involved only at the beginning of the project, when they are asked for their requirements (McGill & Klobas, 2008). Second, because of a high level of transformation and a long time span between elicitation and validation, users often do not see their requirements implemented when they are consulted again during the acceptance phase (Doll & Torkzadeh, 1989). Third, users tend not to be motivated to participate in IT projects if they are not informed about progress or decisions. These effects lead to their being unlikely to accept the system in LSI projects. In addition, frustration and inefficiency result from the lack of communication between users and developers (Bjarnason et al., 2011).

A typical process (**Figure 1**) for a project that uses traditional methods is comprised of four activities: specification, design, and implementation; verification and validation; rollout (of the system in several business units); and evolution (Sommerville, 2004). The specification activity can be separated into the sub-activities of feasibility study, elicitation and analysis of requirements, specification of requirements, and validation of requirements (Sommerville, 2004). The users are often involved at the beginning of the specification activity (Alleman, 2002), and when there is a requirements engineer, the users communicate with him or her. The requirements engineer then finalizes the documents of the specification activity and communicates with the architects or developers (Sommerville, 2004). However, this communication is often transactional, that is, it consists of little more than handing over documents. After the developers and architects complete the design and implementation of the software, communication to the tester occurs, and although the tester role can be fulfilled by users, such is not the case for all LSI projects. In fact, in most cases, the user is not involved again until the rollout and software evolution activity, so there is a long period between the users' involvement in the specification activity and the users' involvement in the validation activity.

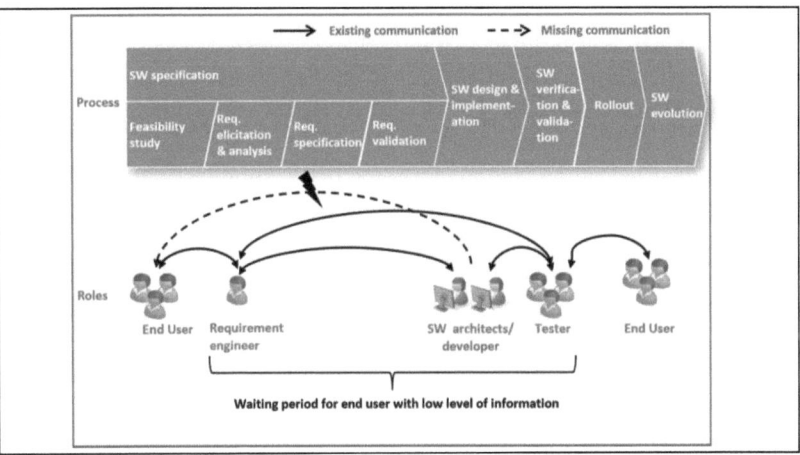

Figure 1: Characteristics of the Traditional Software Development Process

Given these effects and this common process, it is important to understand the influence of UPI on system success, to identify which existing methods increase UPI in software development and how they do it, and to determine how UDC can be enhanced in LSI projects to improve the likelihood of system success.

This thesis targets three primary goals related to UDC in large-scale software development projects:
- Analyze the status of user participation and involvement (UPI) in software development to clarify the effects of existing methods.
- Design a new method to enhance UDC in the design and implementation phase of LSI projects that use traditional development methods.
- Evaluate the new method's effects on system success (i.e. user satisfaction, ease of use, system use, project's time and budget, system quality, and data quality).

1.3. Contributions

We make four contributions to the body of knowledge on UDC in LSI projects. First, we use a meta-analysis of empirical evidence to provide an overview of the *state-of-the-art knowledge* that clarifies the influence of UPI on system success. UDC is one aspect of UPI, which we focus on in the method design. However, we wanted to study the overall effect of UPI in order to understand the effects in a broader manner. Thus, we analyze eighty-six studies to show that most UPI has a positive effect on system success, particularly on user satisfaction and system use. In addition, we show that existing methods for increasing UPI in software development projects have been validated in a public sector project. We also investigate the *state-of-practice* of UDC in LSI projects by interviewing twelve experts on the current practices and obstacles for implementation of UDC in LSI projects, finding that most projects feature limited communication between users and developers. In order to figure out what needs to be communicated to the users, we also collect *examples of user-relevant decisions for a descriptive classification*.

Our second contribution is to use these analyses to present the *UDC-LSI method*, which supports LSI projects that use traditional methods in customer-specific software development projects in their use of UDC.

Third, we *validate the potential and the structure* of the UDC-LSI method through a series of semi-structured interviews with twelve experts in LSI projects and improve our method according to their suggestions.

Fourth, we show the *usability and utility of the UDC-LSI* method by means of a retrospective use of the method in a real-world large-scale IT project. Project participants made positive assessments of the method's feasibility, revealed positive effects on system success in particular as they relate to user satisfaction, and indicated that the benefits of implementing the method outbalanced the effort required and that they would use it in the future.

1.4. Structure of this Thesis

This thesis is structured in five parts and ten chapters. Parts II–IV are structured based on the technical action research (TAR) approach (chapter 2.1.). An overview of the structure and the according research questions and results is shown in **Figure 2**.

Part I, the preliminaries, is comprised of the introduction, which explains the motivation for the thesis topic and describes the problems, contributions (Chapter 1), and methodology, the last of which includes the research questions and a glossary to explain important terms (Chapter 2).

Part II provides the problem investigation, in which we present the results of our systematic mapping study (Chapter 3) and the state-of-practice of UDC in LSI projects (Chapter 4),) and the descriptive classification for end-user-relevant decisions (Chapter 5). .

In Part III, the treatment design, we present the requirements of the UDC-LSI Method (Chapter 6) and the UDC-LSI Method (Chapter 7).

Part IV, design validation and implementation evaluation, presents the expert evaluation of the UDC-LSI method (Chapter 8) and the results of the iPeople case study (Chapter 9).

The thesis concludes with a summary in Part V, where we discuss major findings, limitations, and future work (Chapter 10).

Much of the content of this thesis is based on the author's publications, which have gone through a peer-review process.

Table 1 indicates the areas of the thesis in which these publications are used and where they are not cited separately in order to increase readability.

Table 1: The Author's Published Papers Used in the Thesis

Publication	Research questions Addressed	Used in chapter(s)
Abelein, U. 2013a. Developer-User Communication in Large-Scale IT Projects. *In: Doctoral Symposium of the 19th International Working Conference on Requirements Engineering: Foundation for Software Quality (REFSQ'12), Essen (Germany)*		Abstract, Introduction
Abelein, U. and Paech, B. 2013c. Understanding the Influence of UPI on System Success - a Systematic Mapping Study. *Empirical Software Engineering* [online]. In press.	RQs 1 & 2	3
Abelein, U. et al. 2013b. Does Involving Users in Software Development Really Influence System Success? *Software, IEEE, 30(6), pp. 17–23.*	RQ 1	-
Abelein, U. and Paech, B. 2014. State of Practice of User-Developer Communication in Large-Scale IT Projects: Results of an Expert Interview Series. *In: 20th International Working Conference on Requirements Engineering: Foundation for Software Quality (REFSQ'14), Essen (Germany).*	RQ 3	4
Abelein, U. and Paech, B. 2013b. A descriptive classification for user-relevant decisions of large-scale IT projects. *2013 6th International Workshop on Cooperative and Human Aspects of Software Engineering (CHASE)* [online], pp. 137–140.	RQ 4	5

Abelein, U. and Paech, B. 2012. A proposal for enhancing user-developer communication in large IT projects. *In: Proceedings of the 5th International Workshop on Cooperative and Human Aspects of Software Engineering (CHASE 2012) at the ICSE 2012 Zurich, June 2nd* [online].	RQ 4	5

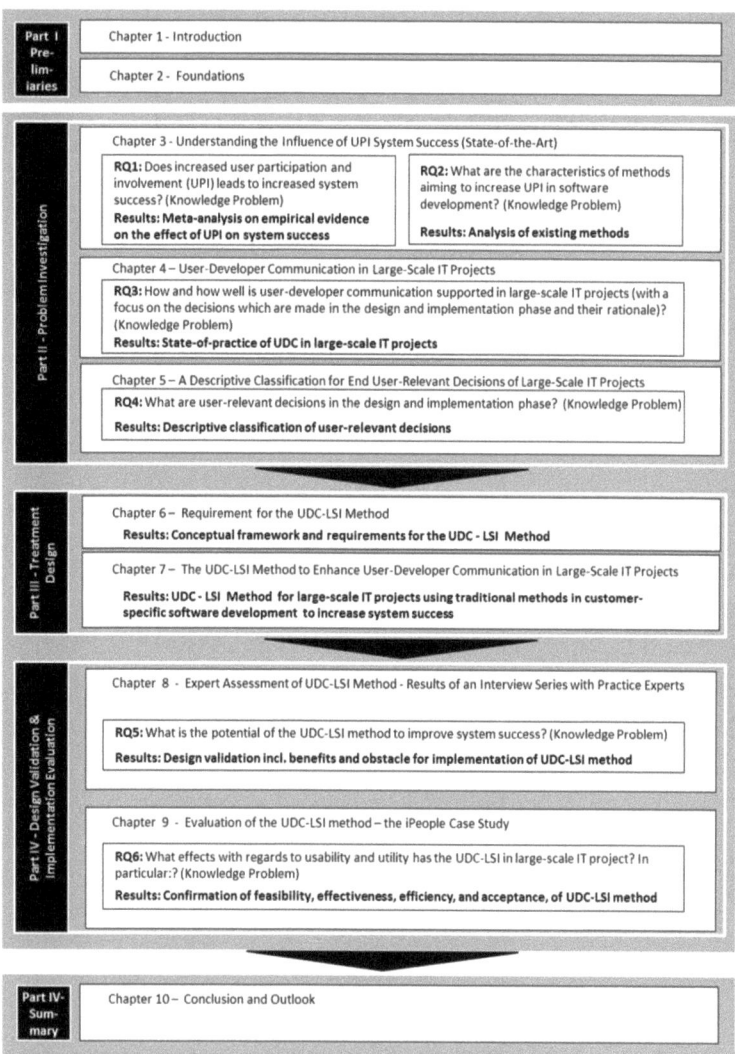

Figure 2. Structure and Contributions of the Thesis

Chapter 2
Foundations

"First, have a definite, clear practical ideal; a goal, an objective. Second, have the necessary means to achieve your ends; wisdom, money, materials, and methods. Third, adjust all your means to that end."

Aristotle

2.1. Research Methodology

This research follows the TAR methodology, which combines design science with action research (Wieringa & Moralı, 2012). Fuller and McHale (1967) introduced the term "design science" as "a systematic form of designing." Hevner, March, Park, and Ram (2004) then described design science as seeking "to create innovations that define the ideas, practices, technical capabilities, and products through which the analysis, design, implementation, management, and use of information systems can be effectively and efficiently accomplished."

Wieringa and Moarah (2012) described the TAR in terms of its cycles: the researcher's engineering cycle, the researcher's empirical research cycle, and the client's engineering cycle. We completed the researcher's engineering cycle and three researcher's empirical cycles in the thesis. Wieringa and Moarah (2012) emphasized the importance of distinguishing between practical problems (the "difference between actual state of the world and the world as desired by some stakeholder") and knowledge problems (the "difference between what stakeholders know about the world, and what they would like to know"). In TAR there is always a practical problem to be solved in the center, but nested knowledge problems must also be solved. The practical question we researched in this thesis can be stated as:

How can UDC in LSI projects that use traditional methods in customer-specific software development be enhanced to increase the likelihood of system success?

TAR consists of four phases: problem investigation, treatment design, design validation, and implementation evaluation. We explain our research according to these phases. An overview of the research cycles is presented in

Figure 4.

Problem investigation

We start with the problem investigation by researching the relevant phenomena and existing solutions. The first four research questions are:

- *RQ1 - Does increased UPI lead to increased system success in LSI projects?*
- *RQ2 - What are the characteristics of the existing methods in the literature that seek to increase UPI in software development?*
- *RQ3 - How and how well is UDC supported in LSI projects (with a focus on the decisions made in the design and implementation phase and their rationale)?*
- *RQ4 - What are the user-relevant decisions in the design and implementation phase?*

To answer RQs 1 and 2, we enter the first empirical research cycle. We conduct a systematic mapping study in order to identify the state-of-the-art knowledge on the influence of UPI on system success using a meta-analysis of empirical evidence, in particular structural equation models (SEM). A meta-analysis comprises statistical methods for contrasting and combining results from different studies in the hope of identifying patterns among study results. The term "structural equation model" refers to a combination of two things: a "measurement model" that defines latent variables using one or more observed variables, and a "structural regression model" that links latent variables together (Evans, 2008).

We also analyze existing methods that seek to increase UPI in software development projects. To answer RQ 3, we start our second empirical research cycle with a series of semi-structured expert interviews. We analyze the current practices in and obstacles to implementation of UDC in LSI projects. In addition, we identify with experts what should be communicated to users, i.e. user-relevant decision and collect examples of user-relevant decisions and classifying them descriptively.

Treatment Design

Based on the results of analysis of existing methods and the knowledge of the state-of-the-practice, we develop the conceptual model, the requirements and the four parts with task of the UDC-LSI method to enhance UDC in LSI projects.

In order to measure UDC, we build on the model of Mohr and Nevin (1990), who define communication model based on its frequency, direction, modality, and content. Frequency refers to the amount of time that communication occurs between the involved parties. Direction describes the democratic aspect of communication, that is, the extent to which one party exerts power over the other(s). Modality refers to how information is transmitted. For example, it may apply to cues like whether the communication takes place face-to-face or whether it is possible to provide immediate feedback (Kristensson et al., 2011). Content refers to what is being transmitted during the communication [25].

Design Validation

To validate the design of our UDC-LSI method, we ask the following research question:

- RQ 5 - *What is the potential of the UDC-LSI method to improve the likelihood of system success by means of UDC in LSI projects?*

We answer this question also in our second empirical research cycle through interviews, where we validate the potential and structure of the UDC-LSI method. Then we use the suggestions in the interviews to improve our UDC-LSI method.

Implementation Evaluation

To evaluate the utility and usability of the UDC-LSI method, we raise the following research question:

- *RQ 6 – What effects on the resulting system's usability and utility does the UDC-LSI have on LSI projects?*

To answer these questions we started the third empirical research cycle, which includes a client helper cycle, by conducting a case study to evaluate the use of the UDC-LSI method in a real-world large-scale IT project. The goal of the case study was to determine the utility and usability of the UDC-LSI method by validating the method in a real-world practical context retrospectively. We studied the as-is status of the iPeople project, simulated an instantiation of the method by describing detailed processes and examples, and evaluated that instantiation with the project participants with regard to the method's utility ((i.e., feasibility, effectiveness and efficiency) and usability (i.e., acceptance). To measure acceptance of the method, we used the technology acceptance model (TAM). Several theoretical models can be applied to study user acceptance and usage, but the most widely applied is the TAM (Venkatesh, 2000). The TAM, which was adapted from the Theory of Reasoned Action (TAR), defines a conceptual framework (**Figure 3**) that includes perceived usefulness (U), defined as "the prospective user's subjective probability that using a specific application system will increase his or her job performance within an organizational context"; perceived ease of use (E), which refers to "degree to which the prospective user expects the target system to be free of effort" (Davis et al., 1989); and behavioral Intention (BI), that is "jointly determined by the person's attitude toward using the system (A)and perceived usefulness (U)."

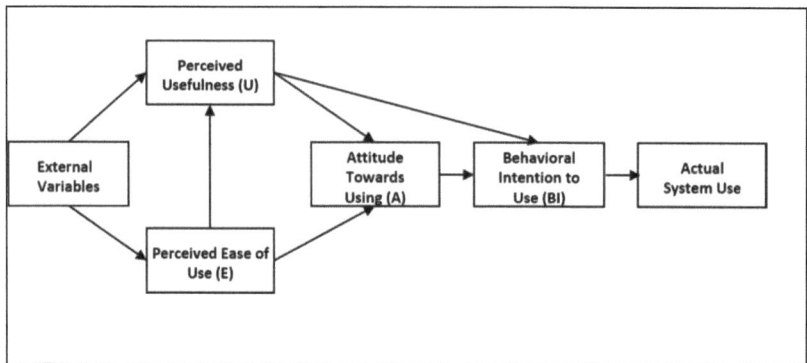

Figure 3: Conceptual framework of the Technology Acceptance Model (Davis et al., 1989)

2.2. Glossary

In this chapter we define important terms used throughout the thesis.

Agile development: Agile or lightweight development approaches have evolutionary and incremental life cycles and use iterative development and intensive stakeholder involvement. These methods embrace unstable business needs and use flexible development and short implementation cycles to mitigate risks (Berger, 2011). Examples are the Dynamic System Development Methodology, SCRUM, and Extreme Programming (XP) (Hope & Amdahl, 2011). Some of these approaches demand that users be on site and require continual feedback to the user.

Approaches to User Involvement and Participation: There are many approaches to UPI in literature and practice. We will introduce the main approaches (participatory design, user-centered design, ethnography, and contextual design). The major difference between those approaches is how active the users are and whether they actually participate in decision-making (Kujala 2008). Participatory design (PD), originated in Scandinavia, emphasizes democracy and skill enhancement, but efficiency, expertise, quality, commitment and buy-in also have been named as motives (Kujala 2003). It is therefore essential, that users are part of the decision-making process, e.g., in workshops or through prototype evaluation. User-centered design comes from the research area of human-computer-interface (HCI). It puts the user, instead of technical needs, into the center of design. Therefore, the designers focus on the users' context (Kujala 2003). In this approach, users are normally not involved in decisions concerning the design; here, other methods such as task analysis are used. Ethnography targets the social aspects of human cooperation and uses observations or video-analysis, thus users are involved rather passively. Contextual design focuses purely on the context of use for the system and methods, such as the contextual inquiry, which combines observing and interviewing (Kujala 2003).

Aspects of System Success in Software Development: System success is controversial and difficult to measure (Harris & Weistroffer, 2009). We want to include all aspects of system success that were named in identified papers, categorized them in areas like user satisfaction, ease of use, system use, system quality, data quality, and project completed on time and on budget. We emphasize the broadness of success in this thesis, so we define system success as "whether the IT project and the resulting system has achieved its objectives."

Customer-specific software development: customer-specific software development refers to projects that develop software that is specifically designed and programmed for an individual customer, including projects that involve customization of standard software packages. These projects should be considered separate from projects that develop market-driven software and end-consumer-software for a mass market.

Data Quality: The degree to which the data's characteristics, such as accuracy, consistency, and availability (Zeffane et al., 1998), satisfy stated and implied needs when used under specified conditions (ISO 25012).

Ease of Use: The degree to which a user expects using the system to be free of effort (Amoako-Gyampah, 2007). Ease of use also refers to system friendliness (Wixom & Todd, 2005).

Large-scale IT projects (LSI projects). We define LSI projects as those that fulfill two or more of the following characteristics: a large number of users (more than 1000 users), system rollout in multiple countries or business units, a large budget (more than 1 million EUR), and project duration of at least one year (twelve calendar months).

Project on Time and on Budget: Project efficiency and effectiveness in terms of schedule, budget, and work quality (Chang et al., 2010).

Rapid application development: Rapid application development consists of the phases of requirements planning, user design, construction, and cutover. Its main advantage is development speed, as the short cycles ensure a close match of the system with the business needs.

System Quality: A structured set of characteristics that include the functional suitability, reliability, usability, performance efficiency, compatibility, security, maintainability, and portability of a system (ISO 9126-1, 2011).

System Use: The frequency with which users use the developed system (Hartwick et al., 2001).

Technology Acceptance Model (TAM): The TAM, a commonly used model to measure system success, focuses on *system use* (Davis et al., 1989), which is mainly influenced by the user's perception of the system's *ease of use* and *usefulness*. The perceived usefulness, that is, the degree to which the users perceive the system as favorable (Wixom & Todd, 2005), is often referred to with the term *user satisfaction*.

Traditional Methods: Traditional development approaches, such as the waterfall model, normally require the determination of a complete, consistent, and accurate list of system requirements before design and implementation start (Berger, 2011). Even though this approach leads to thorough documentation of system requirement, the documentation is often not given to the users. Therefore, users are typically involved only in the requirements definition and the validation process. Traditional project management and software development methods are characterized by clear phases of development (specification, design and implementation, validation and verification, rollout, and evolution) and typically feature a low level of UPI in the design and implementation phase. The advantages of these traditional methods are stability and clear agreements, but the drawbacks include long development cycles after the requirement definition until system validation.

User-Developer Communication (UDC): UDC is a specific form of user participation that we define as communication, evaluation, and approval activities between users and IS (Hartwick & Barki, 1994) and the frequency, content, and direction of that communication (Kristensson et al., 2011). We include all communication between the users and developers as well as communication that is mediated through project management. "Users" include all users from the (business) organization who use the new system and their managers (Carmel et al., 1993). "Developers" include all IT personnel, such as designers, architects, coders, and IT managers, who are involved in the software development project.

User Participation and Involvement (UPI): User participation and involvement are widely studied in fields like information systems, human-computer interaction, and requirements engineering. The terms "user participation" and "user involvement" are often used interchangeably, but some publications distinguish between them. This thesis uses the two definitions of Barki and Hartwick (1994), so we define user involvement as a "psychological state of the individual, defined as the importance and personal relevance of a system to a user" and user participation as "behaviors and activities users perform in the system development process." User participation takes place when the user takes an active part in the development or design process (Hope & Amdahl, 2011). Even though we define user participation and user involvement separately, both influence system success (McGill & Klobas, 2008). In addition to the distinction between user participation and user involvement, Hartwick and Barki (1994) identified several context factors for UPI, such as the characteristics of the system and organizational factors. Various aspects of user involvement, such as a user's motivation or attitude toward the system, have also been identified.

User-Relevant Decisions: We define user-relevant decisions as decisions that are made by IT personnel in the design and implementation phase of software development and are of interest to the users or their managers. We argue that a user-relevant decision becomes a trigger point to start communication.

User Satisfaction: The degree to which the users perceive the system and the mechanics of interaction as favorable (Wixom & Todd, 2005). The Technology Acceptance Model describes user satisfaction as perceived usefulness.

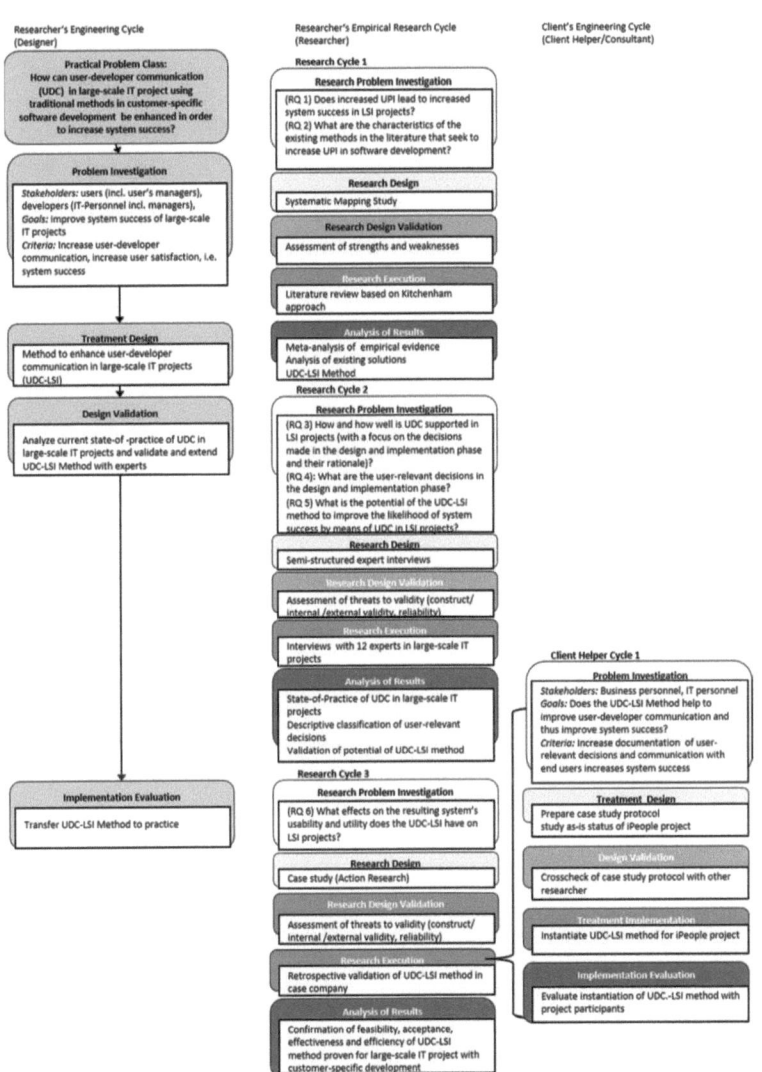

Figure 4. Research Cycles of the Thesis Based on Design Science

PART II
PROBLEM INVESTIGATION

41

Chapter 3
Understanding the Influence of UPI on System Success (State of the Art):

A Systematic Mapping Study

"Twenty years from now you will be more disappointed by the things that you didn't do than the ones you did do, so throw off the bowlines, sail away from safe harbor, and catch the trade winds in your sail. Explore, dream, discover."

Mark Twain

3.1. Abstract

Context: User participation and involvement in software development are considered to be essential for a successful software system. Three research areas—requirements engineering, information systems, and human aspects of software engineering—study these topics from various perspectives. We think it is important to analyze UPI comprehensively in software development to encourage further research in this area.

Objectives: We investigate the evidence on effects of UPI on system success and identify the methods that are available in the literature.

Methods: A systematic mapping study yielded 3,698 hits, from which we identified 289 unique papers. The author of this thesis culled these papers based on inclusion and exclusion criteria, while the supervisor of this thesis validated the selection. Finally, 58 of the 289 papers—22 statistical survey and meta-study papers and 36 methods papers—were selected.

Results: Based on the empirical evidence from the surveys and meta-studies, we developed a meta-analysis of structural equation models, demonstrating that most papers showed positive correlations between, on one hand, aspects of development processes (including user participation) and human aspects (including user involvement) and, on the other hand, system success. The analysis of the proposed solutions from the method papers revealed a wide variety of UPI practices for most activities involved in software development.

3.2. Introduction

UPI in software development are considered essential for system success (Harris & Weistroffer, 2009). Users are an important source of information, as they are familiar with the work and the context that the software system should support (Hendry, 2008). A review from Harris and Weistroffer (2009) names several advantages of UPI: improved quality because of precise requirements; the prevention of unneeded, expensive features; users' positive attitude toward, greater satisfaction with, and positive perception of the system (McGill & Klobas, 2008). As the level of user acceptance and the users' understanding of the system rises, the system will be used more effectively. In addition, the increased participation in decision-making leads to a more democratic organizational culture. All of these benefits can increase the likelihood that a software system will be successful.

In general, there are three research areas that study aspects of UPI: information systems, human aspects of software engineering, and requirements engineering. So far, the topic of UPI in software development has been researched primarily in the information system field. Iivari (2004) explains that such is the case because of the distinctive activities in information systems development, where the alignment of information technology (IT) artifacts and organizational and social context is crucial. This field of research studies primarily the empirical dependencies between UPI and system success. Most of the studies analyzed here use structural equation models (SEM) to present the identified aspects of UPI and system success, as well as correlations between them.

This topic has not received much attention in the field of software engineering, as evidenced, for example, by the fact that neither user participation nor user involvement is mentioned in the SWEBOK (Iivari et al., 2010). However, the relatively new field of human aspects of software engineering seeks to support the people involved in software development processes and considers that many defects in software are the results of human mistakes (Hazzan & Tomayko, 2004). Furthermore, requirements engineering, as a subfield of software engineering, concentrates on eliciting requirements from users and other stakeholders in order to clarify the functionality a software system should fulfill (Sommerville, 2007).

Even though many studies state the positive effects of UPI on system success, some identify contradictory results (e.g., Cavaye, 1995; Olson &

Ives, 1981). In addition, there are still problems with UPI in software development projects. Large-scale projects that use traditional software development methods in particular use UPI on a limited basis (Alleman, 2002).

As the effects of UPI on system success, as well as methods of UPI have been studied for a long time, there are several meta-studies on UPI (McKeen et al., 1994; Cavaye, 1995; McGill & Klobas, 2008; Harris & Weistroffer, 2009; Kujala, 2003; Ives & Olson, 1984). Bano and Zowghi (2013) also systematically reviewed the relationship between user involvement and system success in parallel with our study, so that work is not included in our meta-analysis. However, we include a discussion of how this study extends and differs from our work in the strengths and weaknesses section of this chapter.

None of the meta-studies on UPI provides a comprehensive overview that combines qualitative and quantitative data and considers both the information systems field and the software engineering field. Therefore, we conducted a systematic mapping study based on the guidelines of (Kitchenham & Charters, 2007) in the field of UPI. The strength of this systematic mapping study is the wide scope in which we consider the influence of UPI in software development: We analyzed statistical surveys and meta-studies and synthesized their correlation data in a meta-analysis, and complemented our study with a description of various methods from which we analyzed and identified suggested practices. We analyzed the results of fifty-eight scientific papers in this systematic mapping study and used secondary data from six additional meta-studies on the effects of UPI.

This chapter is partially literally based on the author's peer-reviewed paper (Abelein & Paech, 2013b), published in the *Journal of Empirical Software Engineering*. For reasons of readability, we do not reference this paper in chapters 3.3–3.10.

In chapter 3.3., we sketch out the reasoning behind the study and the motivations for our research questions. Then chapter 3.4. describes our research method and process, and chapter 3.5. describes the studies that we included and excluded. In chapter 3.6., we present our results from the surveys and meta-studies and chapter 3.7.shows the results of the analysis of the methods papers. In chapter 3.8., we discuss the results, along with their strengths and weaknesses, and we describe some further analysis in 3.9.. We conclude with a summary in chapter 3.10.

3.3. Research Questions for the Systematic Mapping Study

In order to encourage further research on aspects of UPI and methods of UPI in software development, we investigate two areas. First, we seek to strengthen confidence in existing evidence that UPI has a positive effect on system success, to identify studies with statistical evidence that have been published so far, and to identify the aspects of UPI and system success the evidence on context factors that have already been studied. This effort will help researchers to ensure that new methods have a positive effect and help to identify which aspects of UPI are important to include in developing new methods. As empirical studies on these effects have been done primarily in the area of IS, this identification effort can be most valuable for researchers in the software engineering domain. Second, we seek to synthesize existing methods of UPI in software development in order to identify gaps and help practitioners to find a suitable method. Therefore, we seek to answer the following research question:

RQ1: Does increased UPI increase system success?

In order to give a comprehensive overview of the existing evidence and help follow researchers to understand the underlying details in a systematic matter, we broke this research question down into four sub-questions:

- RQ 1.1 Which aspects of UPI and system success have extant studies already addressed?
- RQ 1.2 Which correlations between the aspects of UPI and system success have been studied?
- RQ 1.3 What are the characteristics of these correlations (percentage of studies reporting positive or negative correlations, variation, and number of participants involved)?
- RQ 1.4 What further evidence on context factors and their correlations with the aspects of UPI and system success have been reported?

RQ2: What are the characteristics of the methods that aim to increase UPI in software development?

- RQ 2.1. What methods exist to increase UPI in software development projects?
- RQ 2.2. Which activities of software development are affected by these methods?
- RQ 2.3. Which context factors and which aspects of UPI and system success do these methods influence and target?
- RQ 2.4. On what validation context and proposed solutions do these methods report?

3.4. Review Method of the Systematic Mapping Study

In this chapter, we explain the steps in our review method and refer to our exclusion criteria. (Detailed definitions of the inclusion and exclusion criteria are found in chapter 3.5.) In order to answer the research questions listed in chapter 3.3, we conducted a systematic mapping study. Following the recommendation of Kitchenham and Charters (2007), a systematic mapping study should have the following characteristics:

- C1 – a defined search strategy
- C2 – a defined search string based on a list of synonyms combined by ANDs and ORs
- C3 – a broad collection of search sources
- C4 – a strict documentation of the search
- C5 – quantitative and qualitative papers analyzed separately
- C6 – explicit inclusion and exclusion criteria
- C7 – paper selection checked by two researchers.

Our systematic mapping study followed all of these requirements, which we indicate with "Cx" in the following steps of our review method and in chapter 3.5.

We analyzed the surveys and the methods papers in two parts. Branch A includes the statistical survey papers that report the correlations between UPI and system success (RQ 1), and branch B includes the methods papers that suggest forms of UPI in software development (RQ 2). We reviewed the papers according to a structured, defined search strategy (C1) with an initial three-step phase (generation of a search string, identification of research, and first exclusion round) and a two-step refinement phase (second exclusion round, consolidation of results) for each branch. An overview of the research method, including the data of the results, is shown in Figure 5.

STEP 1 – Generation of the Search String

Papers that are relevant to our research questions had to cover the key terms for UPI in software projects: "user," "participation and involvement," and "information technology" or "software engineering." To identify commonly used synonyms of these terms, we reviewed six sources (Al-Rawas & Easterbrook, 1996; Bjarnason et al., 2011; Curtis et al., 1988; Maalej & Pagano, 2011; Maalej et al., 2009; Sutcliffe et al., 1999), and based on this review, developed a search string consisting of four terms (C2): a collection of various synonyms for users, synonyms for "participation and involvement," "participatory design" as defined by the Scandinavian School (e.g., Kujala et al., 2005), and another frequently used synonym for UPI. All of these terms had to appear in the title of the paper in order to increase the likelihood of identifying relevant research. Given the number of sources we considered, searching the abstracts in addition to the titles would have led to too many hits. We used the fourth term to ensure that the research was in the context of IT or software engineering, so this term was not restricted to the title but could appear anywhere in the full text of the paper. The final search string is illustrated in Figure 4.

STEP 2 – Identification of Research

We sought to create a comprehensive picture of the area of UPI, so we used three kinds of sources (electronic sources, general databases, and reference search) in three domains (IT, business, and communication) (C3). We searched three domains in order to find studies from differing perspectives and research areas for our review. The socio-technical perspective was covered by the IT domain, the management science perspective by the business domain, and the social science perspective by the communication domain.

To identify appropriate research, we searched with our search string (defined in step 1) in domain-specific publication sources. We used the sources *IEEE, ACM,* and *Springer Link* for the IT domain; *MIS Quarterly* and *Harvard Business Review* for the business domain; and the *European Journal of Communication* and the *Research Journal of Communication* for the communication domain. We also wanted to ensure that studies from less dominant sources were included in our review, so after the search in domain-specific sources, we included four databases that cover all domains: *Web of Science, Science Direct, Business Source Premier,* and *Scopus*.

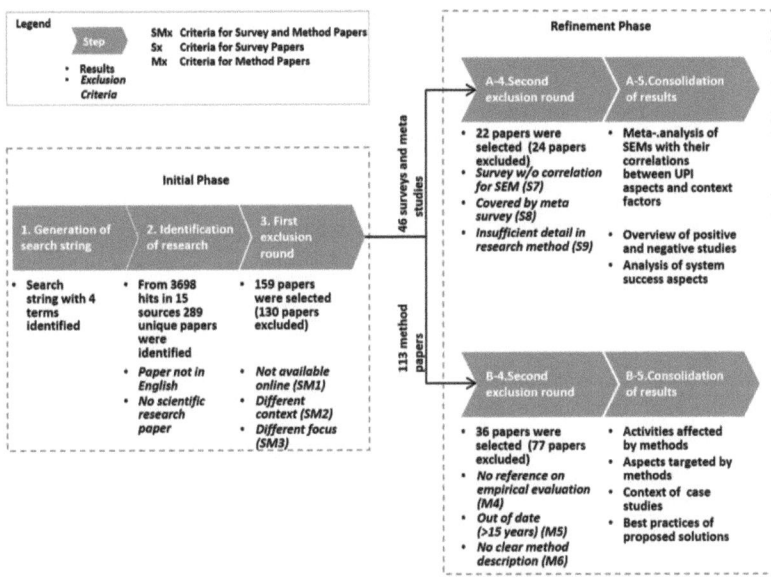

Figure 5: Research Method for the Systematic Mapping Study

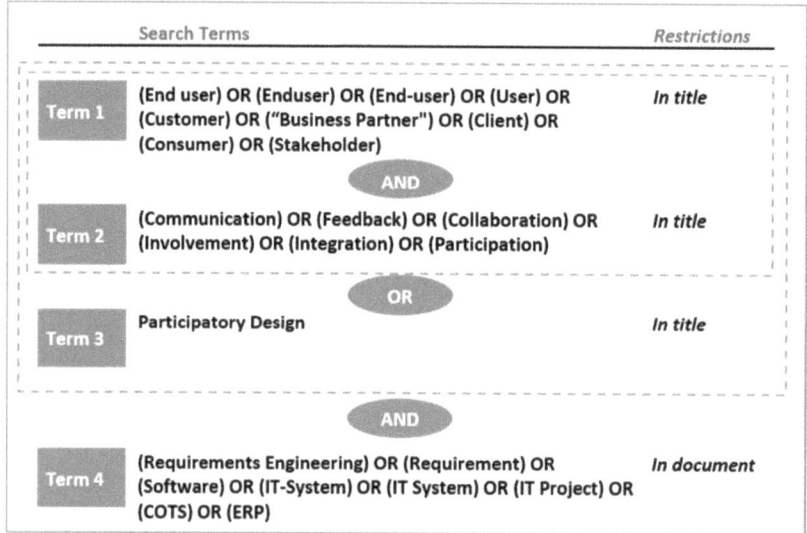

Figure 6: Derived Search String for the Systematic Mapping Study

In addition, we did a reference search in Al-Rawas and Easterbrook (1996) with Google Scholar, as this paper is on our initial research topic of communication of requirements in software development and is frequently cited. We also looked at sources that specialize in UPI: *Information Technology & People Journal*, *Participatory Design Conference Proceedings*, and the *Scandinavian Journal of Information Systems*. As these sources are specific to the topic of user participation or involvement, the search string defined in step 1 would not necessarily identify all relevant papers in them, so we adapted the search string for these sources to more general terms and searched for "software engineering," or "system engineering, "software development," or "system development" in titles, keywords, or abstracts. This series of searches retrieved 3698 hits (3393 with the search string, 97 in the reference search, and 208 in sources that specialize in UPI) in these fifteen sources.

Following the Kitchenham & Charters' (2007) recommendation, we made initial selections based on hits in publication titles and abstracts, which led to 289 unique publications (250 with the search string, 11 in the reference search, 28 in sources that specialize in UPI). An indication of the validity and the wide coverage of the source selection is the increased number of duplicates in the databases that were searched later; for example, the search in the *Business Source Premier* resulted in 433 papers that had already been identified. For an overview of the hits and the relevant and unique papers per source, see Figure 7 (C4).

STEP 3 – First Exclusion Round

As 289 publications are too many for a thorough analysis, we conducted a first exclusion round based on the abstract, introduction, and conclusion sections of the papers. We included the conclusion section, as the quality of IT and software engineering abstracts is not high. In the first exclusion round, we excluded papers if they were out of the context of software engineering or development—for example, some papers considered UPI in civil engineering or in the development of health care products—and papers in software engineering whose focus was not UPI. Finally, we excluded four papers that could not be accessed online or in an offline library. In total we excluded 130 papers. The remaining 159 papers were separated into the two branches: A (46 papers) for statistical surveys and B (113 papers) for methods of UPI.

STEP 4 – Second Exclusion Round

Twenty-four papers in branch A were removed from our selection in the second exclusion round because they did not report clear correlations that were usable for the meta-analysis of SEM, they were covered by one of the meta-studies, or the description of the research method was not sufficient, suggesting a threat to validity.

We excluded seventy-seven papers in branch B because they did not provide an empirical evaluation of their methods; the research was out of date in terms of software and development processes, which have changed significantly in the last fifteen years; or there was no clear description of the method used.

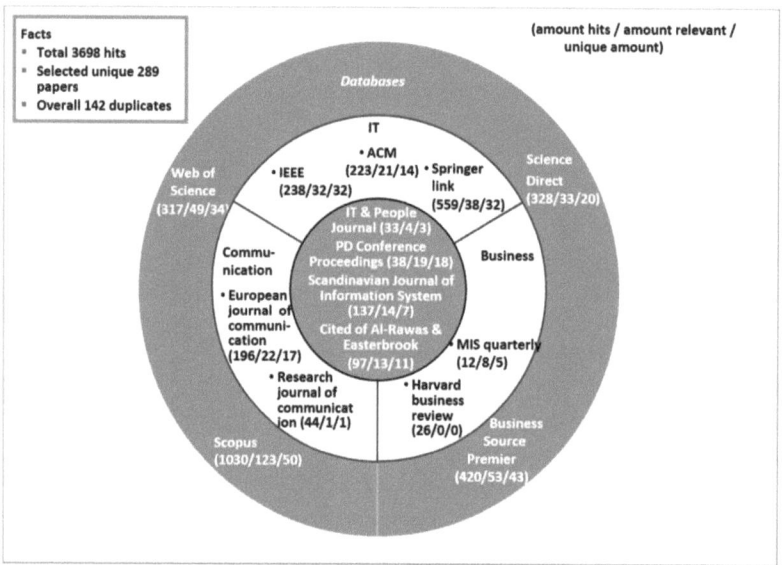

Figure 7: Sources and Hits in the Identification of Research Step

STEP 5 – Consolidation of Results

We synthesized the two branches (surveys and methods papers) separately (C5) and compared the results in the categories and subcategories of aspects of UPI and context factors (chapter 6.2.). We summarized the twenty-two papers that statistically examined the effects of UPI on system success (branch A) in a meta-analysis of SEMs and present an overview of positive and negative studies. We analyzed the thirty-six methods papers (branch B) in terms of the affected activities in software development, the targeted aspects of UPI, and their validation context and developed an overview of

UPI practices according to the solutions suggested in the papers. The results of the various analyses are presented in chapter 3.6. and 3.7.

3.5. Included and Excluded Studies

We defined explicit inclusion and exclusion criteria in order to derive our set of studies (C6) and get a comprehensive picture of UPI's influences in the area of software development. Therefore, we included every paper that either statistically investigated how UPI correlates to system success or described a validated UPI method for use in software development. In addition, we included only scientific research papers that were published in English and that were not excluded by any of the exclusion criteria described below. The supervisor of this thesis reviewed a sample (about 10%) of the list of included and excluded papers to determine the validity of the results (C7).

In the list of nine exclusion criteria that follows, "SM" refers to criteria that are valid for both survey papers and methods paper, "S" refers to criteria that are only valid for only survey papers, and "M" refers to criteria that are valid only for methods papers.

SM1 – Not available in libraries or online
Of the 289 papers that have been rated as relevant, based on title and abstract, four could not be retrieved from any (online or offline) library to which we had access. Two of them were published in very small conferences and were therefore neglected.

SM2 – Out of context
Papers that describe research on UPI, but within a different context than software engineering, e.g., a different industry such as health care products

or a different business function such as marketing were excluded. We excluded 41 papers based on that criterion.

SM3 – Different focus
Papers that describe research on users in the context of software engineering and development, but with the focus on a different area than UPI, e.g., improvements of usability of user interfaces, integration of business processes or project portfolio selection, were excluded. We excluded 85 papers based on this criterion.

M4 – No empirical validation
Methods papers which did not evaluate their work in a case study and/or a survey were excluded. We excluded 29 papers based on this criterion.

M5 – Out of date (published more than 15 years ago)
Only for methods papers, we argue that software and development processes have significantly changed within the last 15 years. Therefore, papers that were published before 1997 were excluded. (Kitchenham & Charters, 2007) also suggested such a exclusion criterion.

M6 – No clear description of methods
We excluded thirty-two method papers that did not describe a clear method for UPI, such when the paper described only high-level lessons learned.

S7 – Survey without correlations for meta-analysis of SEMs
We excluded twelve survey papers that did not describe how UPI correlates with system success, as they could not be used for the meta-analysis.

S8 – Covered by meta-study
We excluded eleven survey papers that were covered by one of the six meta-studies, but we included all the available correlation data of these studies for the meta-analysis of SEMs. This exclusion criterion prevents multiple use of the same data, which would bias our results (Kitchenham & Charters, 2007).

S9 – Insufficient details in the research method
We excluded one paper that did not provide sufficient details about the research method used, as Jorgensen et al. (2005) suggested. In this case, the paper did not clearly describe the people who were interviewed.

Figure 8 provides an overview of the number of papers included and excluded from our analysis.

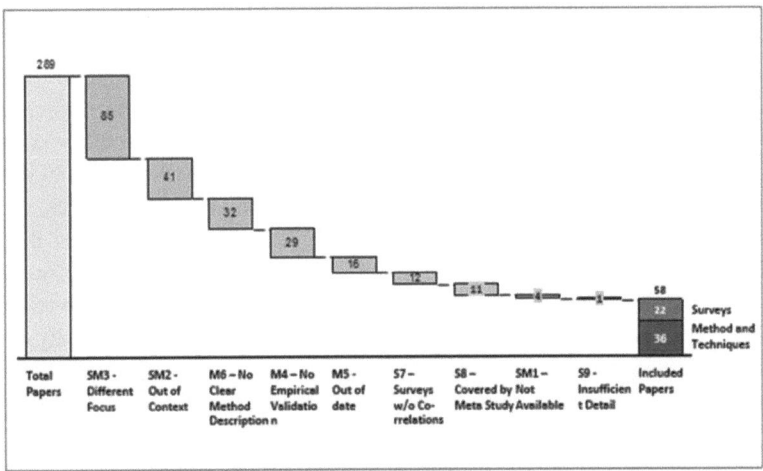

Figure 8: Excluded and Included Papers Based on Exclusion Criteria

3.6. Meta-Analysis of Statistical Surveys and Meta-Studies on the Effect of User Participation and Involvement on System Success

As Kitchenham and Charters (2007) suggested for quantitative studies, we combined the data from the surveys using meta-analytic techniques to increase the likelihood of detecting real effects that individual, smaller studies cannot. In particular, we sought to determine whether *increased UPI leads to increased system success (RQ1)?*

We extracted the SEM and/or the correlations from the eighteen surveys as well as the six meta-studies, from which we extracted the data from another sixty-four surveys described in those studies. In total, we used data from eighty-six unique studies for the overview SEM. To answer our RQs 1.1, 1.2, 1.3, and 1.4, we extracted the researched aspects of UPI and system success and other context factors, as well as the statistically significant correlations between two aspects of UPI or context factors. In addition, we extracted the number of participants in each survey wherever possible. In the rare case that we did not find paper to which a meta-study referred, we used 1 or -1 as a replacement for the correlation value but did not consider that value in the variation of correlations. If we could not find the number of participants, we ignored the study for the analysis. We analyzed the context factors that influence UPI or system success (RQ 1.4) as a side product of our main research question (RQ 1), so we integrated these results into the subsection on RQ 1.1, 1.2, and 1.3. From a statistical perspective, correlations usually do not have a direction, as they are a dimensionless measure between two values, but it is common practice to set up hypotheses with directed links and then interpret the results in the most likely direction. We used the directed links that the analyzed paper suggested for our analysis.

3.6.1. Aspects of UPI, Aspects of System Success, and Context Factors (RQ 1.1 and RQ 1.4)

In order to determine which aspects of UPI and system success and which related context factors existing studies have addressed, we developed a classification of the more than two hundred aspects of UPI and the context factors the studies used. We structured these aspects of UPI and system success, and context factors into five main categories: development process and human aspects for aspects of UPI, system attributes and organizational factors for context factors, and one category for aspects of system success. They were defined by a top-down approach. We defined the subcategories using a bottom-up approach, beginning with the 231 research aspects of UPI named in the studies.

The *development process* category includes all aspects of UPI that involve active participation or communication, as well as the roles and responsibilities of the people involved in software development. We combined various aspects of UPI that occur on a psychosocial level, such as the participants' attitudes or beliefs, in the *human aspects* category. We classified context factors based on the software system in the *system attributes* category. In the same way, we summarized the availability of various resources into the *organizational factors* category. The last category, *system success*, is comprised of various aspects of system success, such as user satisfaction, system use, and system quality (Hwang & Thorn, 1999). **Table 2** provides detailed definitions of each category and subcategory.

3.6.2. Examples of Researched Aspects of System Success (RQ 1.1)

All of the reviewed studies researched system success in software development in various ways. Some papers used existing conceptual models, such as the TAM (Davis et al., 1989), with its aspects of "perceived ease of use" and "usefulness". However, not all papers used predefined models. Various terms have been found for "user satisfaction," which is the aspect of TAM used most often. "Project on time and on budget" has also been used in various ways, such as in "process satisfaction" or simply "project success." **Table 3** presents examples of originally studied aspects of system success, while **Table 54** in the Appendix lists which papers studied which aspects of system success.

After the data extraction (researched aspects of UPI and aspects of system success, context factors, significant correlations between two aspects or UPI or system success, and number of participants), we classified the papers' 231 aspects of UPI and system success and context factors into our subcategories and categories. Then we counted the number of unique studies for each category and subcategory, which gave us an answer to RQ 1.1 (Figure 5). As one study could examine several subcategories of a category, the sum of the unique papers in all subcategories is not the same as the number of unique papers in that category.

Table 2: Definitions of Categories and Subcategories

Aspects/Factors	Category/Subcategory	Definition
Aspects of UPI	**Development Process**	**Activities of project participants (i.e., users, developers) that contribute to the system development**
	User Participation	Behavior and activities users perform in system development process, such as being the leader of the project team, having responsibility for the overall success of the system, and being responsible for selecting hardware or software, estimating costs, or requesting funds (Hartwick & Barki, 1994).
	User-Developer Communication	Communication, evaluation, and approval activities that take place between users and IS staff (Hartwick & Barki, 1994); the frequency, content, and direction of that communication (Kristensson et al., 2011).
	Mode of Development	Depending on which roles are mainly responsible for development, the development process can vary; for example, the system can be developed by developers, by end-users directly, or in a cooperative way between these groups (Zeffane et al., 1998).
	Human Aspects	**Attitudes or beliefs of project participants**
	User Involvement	Psychological state of the individual, defined as the importance and personal relevance of a system to a user (Hartwick & Barki, 1994); the degree of users' perceptions of their sense of ownership toward the system (Wu et al., 2006).
	Users' Motivation	A rationally calculative perspective that an individual's involvement in an activity arises from his/her desire to obtain rewards, including the instrumentality of creating opportunity and improving conditions of work (Chang et al., 2010).
	Users' Intention to Use	A function of attitudes toward a behavior and subjective norms (i.e., influence of people in one's social environment); has been found to predict actual behavior (Hunton & Beeler, 1997).

	Users' Attitude toward the System	Affective or evaluative judgment of users toward the system, that is, the extent to which users feel the system is good or bad (Lin & Shao, 2000; Barki & Hartwick, 1994).
	Users' Ability in IT Projects	The users' ability, such as that gained through previous experience, to participate as members of the systems development team and accomplish the goals of the project (Chang et al., 2010).
	Users' Beliefs about Developers	Users' attitudes and beliefs regarding developers' behavior, such as whether they take the users seriously (Amoako-Gyampah & White, 1993) and whether the decision process is fair (Harris & Weistroffer, 2009; Hunton, 1996).
	Developers' Attitude toward Users	Attitude of the systems developers toward the users, such as whether users are treated with dignity and whether they are informed (Amoako-Gyampah & White, 1993; Gefen et al., 2008).
	Disagreement/ Conflict	Divergence of opinions and goals that can lead to conflicts, as well as their resolution possibility (Barki & Hartwick, 1994).
Context Factors	**System Attributes**	**Attributes and challenges of the to-be-developed system**
	Complexity	Complexity of the organizational task(s) being supported by the systems project under study (McKeen & Guimaraes, 1997) as well as the ambiguity and uncertainty that surround development of that system (Lin & Shao, 2000).
	Uncertainty	Extent of the business environment and management's stability and resulting conflicting requirements (Emam et al., 1996; McKeen et al., 1994).
	Organizational Factors	**Influences on the project that come from the organizational context of the IT projects**
	Top Management Support	Support through recognition and timely decisions of high-level managers (Rouibah et al., 2008).
	Organizational or Managerial Culture	Shared assumptions that guide actions in organizations, such as harmony-oriented or control-oriented cultures (Bai & Cheng, 2010); management style can be distinguished as people- or task-oriented (Lu & Wang, 1997).

	Availability of Resources	The presence of project resources, such as a system plan, project mission and goals, and training (Amoako-Gyampah & White, 1993).
Aspects/Factors	**Category/ Subcategory**	**Definition**
Aspects of System Success	System Success	Assessment, whether the IT project and the resulting system has achieved its objectives.
	User Satisfaction	The degree to which users view of the system and the mechanics of interaction are favorable (Wixom & Todd, 2005).
	Ease of Use	The degree to which a user expects using the target system to be free of effort (Amoako-Gyampah, 2007); system friendliness and handling (Wixom & Todd, 2005).
	System Use	Frequency with which users use the developed system (Hartwick & Barki, 1994).
	System Quality	A structured set of characteristics, such as the functional suitability, reliability, usability, performance efficiency, compatibility, security, maintainability, and portability of a system (ISO 9126-1, 2011).
	Data Quality	The degree to which the characteristics of data satisfy stated and implied needs when used under specified conditions (ISO 25012); for example, the accuracy, consistency, and availability of data in the system (Zeffane et al., 1998).
	Project in Time and Budget	Project efficiency and effectiveness in terms of schedule, budget, and work quality (Chang et al., 2010).

Table 3: Aspects of System Success

Subcategory	Examples of Original Aspects of System Success
User Satisfaction	End-user computing satisfaction, end-user satisfaction, information satisfaction, outcome satisfaction, perceived system usefulness, perceived usefulness, system acceptance, system satisfaction, usefulness, user assessment, user information satisfaction, user satisfaction
Ease of Use	Perceived impact on work, system friendliness
System Use	Intention to use, system impact, system usage, time spent using
System	Accessibility, accuracy, completeness, flexibility, perceived system

Quality	quality, product success
Data Quality	Appropriateness of format, availability of historical data, data accuracy, data consistency, data sufficiency
Project on Time and on Budget	MIS project success, overall success, process satisfaction, project completion, project performance, project success, successful implementation

3.6.3. Correlations of Aspects of UPI and Context Factors with System Success (RQ 1.2, 1.3, and 1.7)

We counted the number of unique studies for each correlation between two categories to help answer the research questions:
- RQ 1.2 Which correlations between the aspects of UPI and system success have been studied?
- RQ 1.3 What are the characteristics of these correlations (percentage of studies reporting positive or negative correlations, variation, and number of participants involved)?
- RQ 1.4 What further evidence on context factors and their correlations with the aspects of UPI and system success have been reported?

Figure 9 provides an overview of the meta-analysis of SEMs. Each box represents a category with the corresponding subcategories in bullets. After each (sub) category the number of unique studies is stated in brackets. Each correlation is depicted as an arrow and labeled with the number of studies, where # is the number of studies that considered that correlation. Each correlation between two categories is labeled with a number in a circle. In addition to the number of studies, **Table 4** specifies the split between positive and negative studies and the variation in the correlations.

Findings on the Category Level

Categories: Regarding the aspects of UPI, most of the eighty-six studies examine aspects of the categories of development process (71%), human aspects (49%), and system success (87%) and investigate correlations among these categories. The context factors of system attributes and organizational factors play only a minor role in empirical research (fewer than a dozen studies), while user participation (75% of all aspects of development process) and user involvement (49% of all human aspects) are the most researched subcategories, and user satisfaction is the most common success factor (51% of all aspects of system success).

Correlations between categories: Most of the studies show positive correlations between aspects of UPI and aspects of system success. Only 10 percent (14 of 1146 links) of the correlations are negative, which is in line with Hope and Amdahl (2011), Hendry (2008), Harris and Weistroffer (2009), and McGilland Klobas (2008).

Considering the correlations in **Figure 9**, the most frequently researched link (50 studies) is the link from the development process category to the system success category (1). However, three of the correlations are negative. The second most frequently studied link is that between human aspects and system success (31 studies) (2). Even though 87 percent of these correlations are positive, four studies measured a statistically significant negative correlation. Some studies address the link between development processes and human aspects (3), research begun by Hartwick and Barki (1994), who distinguished between the definition of user participation as an active part that the user performs in software development and user involvement as the cognitive part of cooperation with users. Seven studies addressed the cognitive aspects of cooperation with the user and the correlation between these aspects of cooperation (4). Even though all of the studies showed a positive correlation, some showed small values, indicating a low correlation, with the low end of the range of the correlations at 0.03. Nine studies examined the effect of organizational factors like top management support as a context factor for system success and revealed positive correlations, from 0.04 to 0.57 (5).

Seven studies addressed the correlation between aspects of the development process, such as that between user participation and UDC (6). Moreover, the studies found that some interdependencies between the various system success factors were minor (0.06 significant correlation), but others found a strong correlation of 0.85 (7). Three studies did not directly focus on the effect of organization factors on system success but on the effect of organizational factors on aspects of the development process (8), addressing questions like whether projects with significant top management support have higher user participation than other projects and/or whether there is more UDC in such cases.

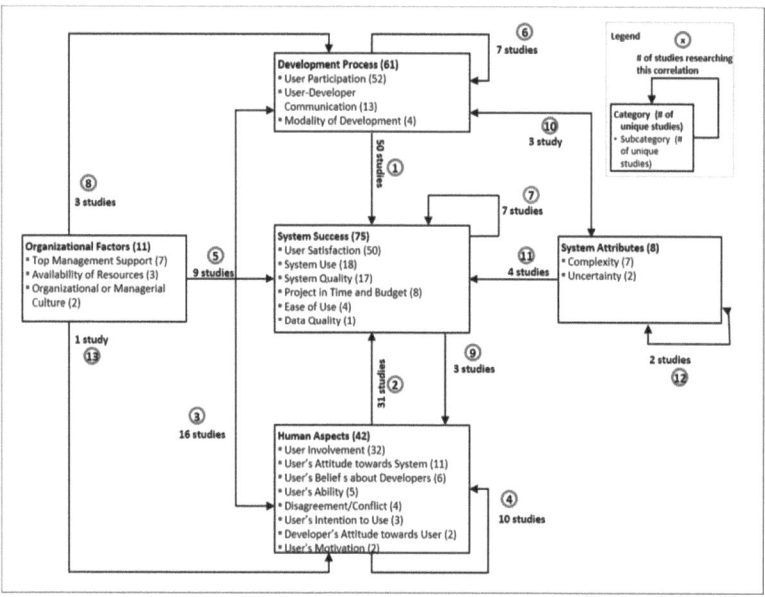

Figure 9: Structural Equitation Model (SEM) of Surveys and Meta-Studies

One would tend to assume all studies considered the effects of human aspects on system success (9), but three studies also sought to determine whether system success depends on human aspects. The attributes of the context factor system have actually been studied more thoroughly with regard to negative effects on the development process category than positive. Most people would agree that it is more difficult to develop a complex and uncertain system than a simple one (10), so these four studies sought to determine whether complexity has an effect on user participation or UDC. One of the four studies that researched the link between system attributes and system success showed a negative effect of system attributes on factors of system success (11). Given that it is more difficult to implement a complex and uncertain system than a simple one, it is also more difficult to lead it to success, so this negative link is easy to understand. Two studies also addressed the connection between uncertainty and complexity (12), and one study showed a negative link from organizational factors to human aspects (13).

Table 4: Number of Positive and Negative Studies and Amount of Variation

Link	# Positive Studies	# Negative Studies	Variation of Correlations
1	47	3	-0.47 – 0.69
2	27	4	-0.18 – 0.64
3	13	3	-0.97 – 0.93
4	10	0	0.03 – 0.75
5	9	0	0.04 – 0.57
6	7	0	0.27 – 0.85
7	7	0	0.06 – 0.85
8	3	0	0.17 – 0.36
9	3	0	0.24 – 0.93
10	3	0	0.17 – 0.36
11	1	3	-0.30 – 0.28
12	2	0	0.53 – 0.53
13	0	1	-0.22 – -0.22
Sum	132 (90%)	14 (10%)	-0.97 – 0.93

3.6.4. Overview of Positive and Negative Studies (RQ 1.3 and 1.4)

In order to study the overall positive effect of UPI on system success, we separated the positive and negative studies (see **Table 4**)
We structures the studies based on the correlations of one category (category 1) to another category (category 2) (see **Table 54** in the Appendix). Most studies show positive correlations from aspects of UPI to system success, but we defined a study as negative if it reported one negative correlation. Therefore, if one study tested two correlations of development processes (e.g., user participation and UDC) with aspects of system success, and one of the correlations was positive and the other negative, the study was counted as a negative study. We wanted to prevent any concealment of negative results, also known as the publication bias (Kitchenham & Charters, 2007). When we reference a study from a meta-study, we name the meta-study reference and the original reference in brackets.

The first negative study, Barki and Hartwick (1994), showed that an increase in user participation can correlate negatively with the possibility of conflict and disagreement in the project team, a reasonable finding, as an increase in active cooperation between users and developers will also increase the potential for conflict. Of the two studies covered in the Cavaye's (1995) meta-survey, Kim and Lee (1991) showed a negative link from user participation to the users' attitude toward the system, and Robey and Farrow (1982) cited two negative correlations, one between user participation and perceived influence and one between user participation and conflict resolution. Both negative correlations can be explained by the fact that increased participation can also increase users' expectations.

Tait and Vessey (1998), also cited by Cavaye (1995), found a negative correlation between user participation and user satisfaction. Zeffane et al. (1998), cited in Harris and Weistroffer's (2009) meta-survey, found a negative relationship between the aspect mode of development and data quality. The authors determined that, depending on who has the main responsibility for development (e.g., the user or the developers), the data quality could be influenced negatively because users may lack technical competence. Heinbokel (1996), cited in Kujala's (2003) meta-study, reported negative correlations between user participation and four factors that we clustered on the aspect of project on time and on budget. This finding is reasonable, as participation binds the resources of a project.

Moreover, four studies associated human aspects with negative system success. Two studies, Amoako-Gyampah and White (1993) and Amoako-Gyampah (2007), revealed negative correlations between the developer's attitude towards the user and system success and between the user's intention to use and system success. Doll and Torkzadeh (1991), cited in McGill and Klobas (2008), described a negative link of users' desired level of involvement with user satisfaction, but the correlation of 0.03 is low. In addition, Zeffane et al. (1998), cited in Harris and Weistroffer's (2009) meta-study, stated that human aspects like involvement in the functional design or the system definition have a negative effect on system success factors like data quality. This result might be due to users' lack of technical knowledge.

Amoako-Gyampah and White (1993) determined that the context factor availability of resources—specifically, the availability of a project plan—has a negative influence on user involvement, perhaps because such plans do not encourage flexible involvement, so they do not improve the users' psychological state concerning the system. We expected the last three negative studies of the correlation between system attributes and system success, Emam et al. (1996), Palanisamy and Sushil (2001), and Yetton et al. (2000), to be negative because it is clear that a system that is complex and uncertain is more likely to prevent system success than to increase it.

3.6.5. Number of Participants in Studies of Correlations of Aspects of UPI and Context Factors with System Success (RQ 1.3 and RQ 1.4)

Another characteristic analyzed in the correlations is the number of participants involved in each study (RQ 1.3). Studying this factor helps to increase the credibility of the finding that increased UPI increases system success. In order to inspect the correlation on a subcategory level, we used the cumulative number of participants as the relevant factor, arguing that a significant correlation that is validated by more participants has more credibility and indicates a higher research interest than does a correlation validated by fewer participants.As the number of correlations between each pair of subcategories would be too high for this report, we identified seven links about which more than 1000 participants were asked. Only one study of these seven links showed a negative correlation, so we did not separate positive and negative studies. **Figure 10** provides an overview of the links.

Findings on the Subcategory Level

As shown in **Figure 10**, in the measure "cumulative number of participants," the relationship between user involvement and user satisfaction has the highest credibility, so we conclude that the interference of the individual's psychological state, defined as the importance and personal relevance of a system to a user (Hartwick & Barki, 1994), with his or her satisfaction is relevant to researchers. As 3,980 participants in the study stated positive results, this result is also a strong argument for answering RQ 1. The correlation between user participation and user satisfaction has also been researched intensively (4,476 participants). As none of the studies showed a negative correlation in this relationship, we have evidence that an increase in user participation increases the users' satisfaction with the system. The dependency between user satisfaction and system use was the focus of four studies and 1,604 participants. In addition, if the system is easier to use, users are more satisfied.

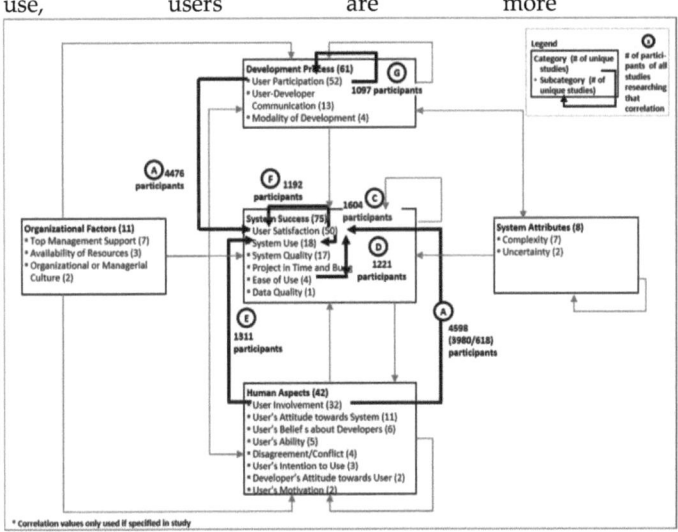

Figure 10: Overview of Links in Studies with the Most Participants (on

the Subcategory Level)

A total of 1,311 participants revealed positive correlations between user involvement and system use. Considerable research has been done on the interdependencies to achieve user satisfaction, such as research on the correlation between system benefits perceived by users and user satisfaction and that between information satisfaction and user satisfaction. The question concerning what is relevant in order to understand user participation has also been a research focus, as in Barki and Hartwick's (1994) separation between hands-on activities and overall responsibility.

3.6.6. Findings of the Meta-Analysis

Finding 1 - UPI is an important research topic (RQ 1.1 and 1.4). The 231 aspects of UPI addressed in the 86 studies show that UPI has been studied on a broad scale in several research areas. The variety of aspects of UPI in the categories of human aspects and development process, the various context factors, and the various aspects of system success show that this field is complex to measure and the various influences difficult to define. In addition, the fact that we found 86 studies that researched the effects of UPI on system success shows that the field is important for researchers and practitioners.

Finding 2 - Aspects of UPI have positive effects on system success (RQ 1.2, 1.3, and 1.4). Given the vast number of positive correlations of aspects of UPI with system success, we conclude that, even though the results are not completely consistent, there is evidence of a robust and transferable effect (Kitchenham & Charters, 2007). Most surveys researched the effect on system success of aspects of UPI from the development process category or the human aspects category, but it is remarkable how many studies undertook the study of various interdependencies among the other categories or subcategories. User satisfaction seems to be the most appropriate variable with which to measure system success, but this choice could also be biased by the researchers, as they tend to have a human focus when studying UPI.

Finding 3 - Most studies with negative correlations were published more than ten years ago (RQ 1.3 and 1.4). We identified only fourteen studies that described any negative correlation between aspects of UPI and system success or between context factors and system success. Overall, we can see that most of the studies with negative results are old; only one study was originally published in the last ten years. In addition, some of the negative correlations can be explained through the researched aspect or context factor; for example, the system attribute complexity is expected to decrease system success. Furthermore, the correlation values of more than half of the remaining studies are under 0.2. Four of the negative studies report negative correlations between aspects of UPI and context factors, such as between development process and human aspects, suggesting that these negative correlations do not influence the positive effects of UPI on system success. Apart from that, we counted studies as negative even if they presented only one negative correlation, and most of them also show other positive results.

Finding 4 - Large variations in correlations show the complexity of measuring and studying UPI (RQ 1.3 and 1.4). The analysis of the correlation data of 86 studies shows a large variation for most links between aspects of UPI, aspects of system success, and context factors, indicating that there is still no clear conceptual model for measuring the effects of UPI. Therefore, additional research in the area of UPI and its effects is needed.

Finding 5 - UPI has a positive effect on user satisfaction and system use (RQ 1.3 and 1.4). Overall, the triangle of user involvement, user participation, and user satisfaction is dominant in this field of research. Based on the values of the correlations, the correlation between user satisfaction and system use is studied frequently, so it is relevant for UPI research. An indicator of the broadness of UPI in research is the number of participants that were involved in validating the effects on a subcategory level. The fact that more than 1000 participants from various studies agreed on positive correlations on a subcategory, while only one study reported a negative correlation, indicates the validity of the identified correlations. The analysis showed that users who participate in software development are more satisfied with the system than those that do not participate. The same is true for users who are more involved compared to those who are less involved. Therefore, we conclude that UPI has a clear positive effect on user satisfaction. In addition, the analysis showed that more satisfied users use the system more frequently than less satisfied users do, so we conclude that an increase in UPI increases system use, which is a measure for system success. As there is a positive correlation between ease of use and user satisfaction, we also conclude that, if a system is easy to use, the users are more satisfied than they are if a system is not easy to use.

Summary of findings for RQ 1. We conclude that the answer to our first main research question, whether increased UPI increases system success, is positive, as shown by our meta- analysis. Therefore, research and work in the area of UPI in software development is beneficial and should be continued. However, the variety of aspects of UPI and context factors that we derived from the studies indicates that there is still no common conceptual model with which to measure and evaluate these effects. Although we did not focus our meta-analysis specifically on the context factors that influence UPI, they did not play an important role in our studies, so more research on the influencing factors in specific contexts is required. Furthermore, the large variation in the identified correlations indicates the need for more sophisticated empirical studies on the effects of UPI.

3.7. Current Methods of Software Development or IT Project Management that Use User Participation and Involvement

To determine the *characteristics of the methods that aim to increase UPI in software development (RQ 2)*, we used a variation of the line of argument synthesis (Kitchenham & Charters, 2007) by first analyzing the individual papers with regard to their targeted issues, their validation contexts, and their proposed solutions. We identified thirty-six papers that described methods of UPI (RQ 2.1) and, using the set of studies as a whole, analyzed which activities in software development are affected by these methods (RQ 2.2). In order to compare the methods papers to the surveys and meta-studies, we identified which aspects of UPI, aspects of system success, and context factors (on a category and subcategory level) are influenced and targeted by the method papers (RQ 2.3). Seeking background on the existing research, we analyzed the contexts (development methods, industry, and software system) in which these methods were validated (RQ 2.4). Finally, we derived an overview of practices, including examples of methods, and ordered them according to the activities in software development (RQ 2.4).

3.7.1. Methods to Increase UPI in Software Development Projects (RQ 2.1)

We selected thirty-six papers that identified methods by which to increase UPI in software development. (See summaries of the papers in the Appendix in **Table 57**.) This analysis revealed a broad variety in this research area. A list of all method papers can be found in the Appendix in **Table 53**.

3.7.2. Software Development Activities Affected by the Methods (RQ 2.2)

Intending to determine the variety and breadth of the methods, we did a first analysis of the activities in software development that are mainly affected. We used the activities based on Sommerville (2007), who suggested that the general activities of all software processes are software specification, software design and implementation, software validation and verification, and software evolution. In addition, planning and project management is a critical activity, as software development is always subject to the budget and schedule constraints set by the organization that is developing the software.

Figure 11 provides an overview of the methods studies, structured by the activities in software development. Thirty-three percent of the papers considered all or several activities of software development as they relate to

UPI. In addition, eleven percent of the methods referred to influencing the planning and project management setup. Almost a fifth (19%) of the methods focused on the early steps of software development (i.e., software specification and requirements engineering), which is in line with Kujala (2008), who heavily promoted early user involvement. Four studies specifically focused on requirements engineering, and three took a broader view of software specification. Eleven percent focused on the design and implementation activity. Only one paper (3%) focused on the verification and validation activity. Finally, twenty-two percent of the papers focused on the software evolution activity.

3.7.3. Targeted Aspects of UPI, Aspects of System Success, and Context Factors (RQ 2.3)

We analyzed both quantitative studies (surveys and meta-studies) and qualitative studies (methods papers) in our systematic mapping study and integrated the results of those two branches to determine which aspects of UPI, aspects of system success, and context factors were targeted and influenced by the methods used. An overview of which methods papers targeted which category and subcategory is given in the Appendix in Table 9.

The development process (94% of all studies), human aspects (81%), and system success (100%) are the categories most influenced by the methods that were used in these papers. On the subcategory level, 69 percent of the studies discussed methods that targeted or influenced UDC, whereas only twenty-three percent of the surveys studied the influence of UDC. The mode of development is also important, as nearly a third (31%) of the methods are influenced by responsibility for development. In the human aspects category, user involvement was the subcategory most influenced by the methods, but the developers' attitude toward users is the second most targeted subcategory, with 39 percent of the methods targeting this human aspect. System attributes and organizational factors were not influenced significantly by the methods used, but system success was targeted by all papers, with system quality the most important target for 92 percent of the methods. In addition, system quality is the single goal for 18 percent of the papers in pursuit of system success. User satisfaction is the second most frequently targeted (53% of the studies), but this system success factor is most often used in a combination with other factors.

3.7.4. Validation Context of the Methods (RQ 2.4)

Seeking to show in what context most of the studies were validated, we analyzed the validation context for each methods paper by extracting which UPI method or development method was used in the papers. If a paper named a method for UPI, we preferred that method over the development method. We also looked at the industry and the software systems in which the proposed methods were validated. **Figure 12** shows the distribution of UPI and the development methods. While four papers that did not name a clear method, 31 percent of the papers used agile development methods in their validations, while 25 percent used PD methods. In contrast to agile methods are the heavyweight methods, such as the waterfall approach used in 17 percent of the papers.

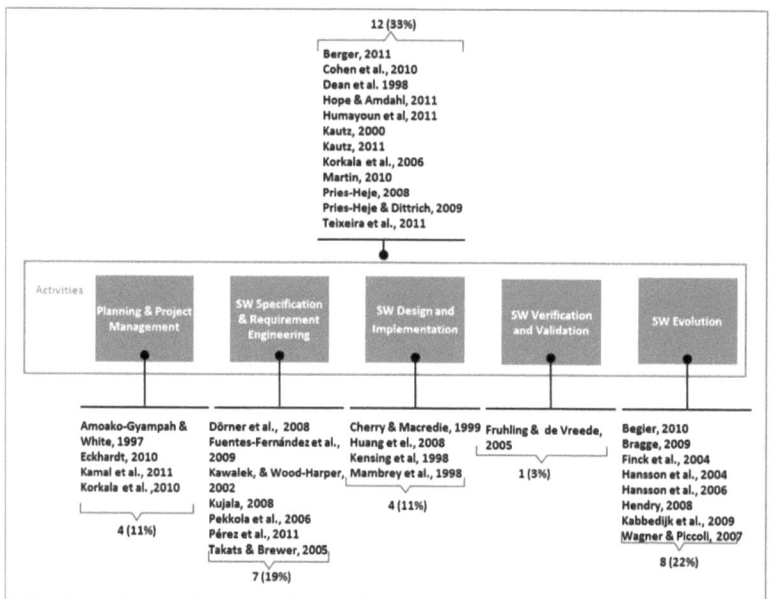

Figure 11: Methods Studies Classified by the Software Development Activities Affected

The UPI methods, user-centered design and PD, are similar methods but differ from other methods in their rationale for why users should be involved. PD emphasizes democracy and skill enhancement (Kujala, 2008). Therefore, users must not only be part of the design process but also be involved in the decision-making. Other approaches, such as user-centered design, focus mostly on gaining varied information from users, so the users' context is important for the software system design, but users do not necessarily have a say in the final decisions (Kujala, 2008). Five case studies use user-centered development methods, and one paper uses the rapid application development method where, similar to the agile methods, the focus is on a fast-running application with a prototype-like approach (Dean et al., 1998).

In addition the methods used in validation, some other context-related information about the case studies was analyzed. Forty-two percent of the papers used a public environment for their validation, including case studies in public administration, defense, and educational organizations. Only 14 percent used more than one case study in more than one industry.

Regarding the software systems for validation researched in the case studies, the area of information systems was by far the most frequently used, with 72 of the studies. Thirty-six percent of the papers did not specify the software system, but some gave specific system descriptions (17% enterprise systems, 14% enterprise resource management systems, and 6% expert systems).

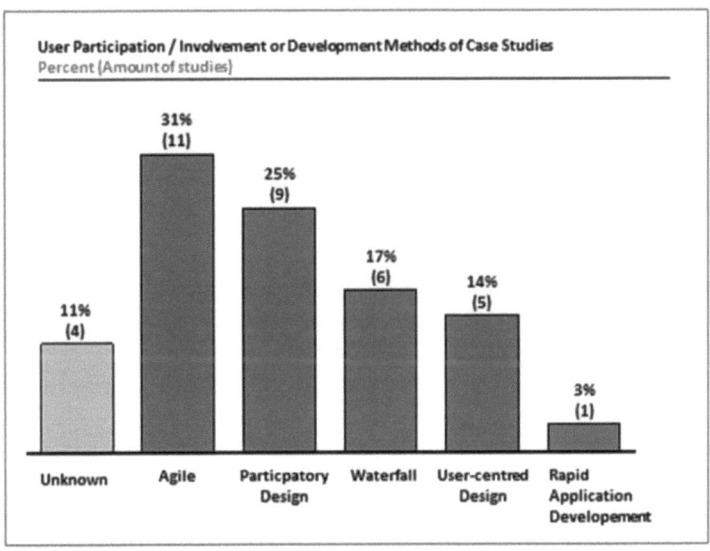

Figure 12: Development Methods of Case Studies

3.7.5. Practices of the Proposed Solutions (RQ 2.4)

Finally, we analyzed the solutions proposed in the thirty-six methods papers. We used a reciprocal translation, an approach to qualitative synthesis (Kitchenham & Charters, 2007) that can be used if all studies address a similar topic. In this approach, researchers provide an additive summary by "translating" each case into each of the other cases. We used this approach to structure the practices according to the software development activities (planning/project management, software specification and requirements engineering, software design and implementation, software verification and validation, and software evolution). Furthermore, we distinguished between what needs to be done (practices) and how it is done (examples for UPI). There are practices for UPI for every activity (see

Table 5), so there are many methods available in the research. The planning and project management activity reveals the most frequently used practices. We separated the practices into the three major identified categories (set-up of communication structures, set-up of project management, and set-up of project environment) and found that most of the suggested practices are grouped into the set-up of communication structures category. However, most examples of the "clarify the project visions based on users' needs" practice, which is part of the project management category. We identify only one example for UPI in the method papers that supports the set-up of the project environment. For the software specification and requirements engineering activity, we identified several practices, but there is a wider variety of examples of how to include users in the activity of software development. To increase the UPI in the design and implementation activity, many of the identified practices and examples are based on PD (e.g., Cherry & Macredie, 1999) or the agile approaches (e.g., Kautz, 2000).

Therefore, the suggested practices and examples are mostly part of a broader approach throughout the whole software development process. For the verification and validation activity, we identified only four practices and two examples to increase UPI. This result is unexpected, as validation is an activity that requires checking whether a system meets the users' expectations (Sommerville, 2007). Practices and examples of how to involve users should be more common in the research. We identified several practices and examples to increase UPI in the software evolution activity, an indication that more software projects are being developed and are dependent on user feedback for new releases. Not every item on this list of practices is meant to be applied in one project; instead, practices should be selected from the list. **Table 5** contains a summary of the practices.

3.7.6. Findings of the Methods Analysis

Finding 1 - All software development activities are affected by methods (RQ 2.2). The analysis of affected software development activities revealed that many methods focus on all activities of software development, which shows an attempt by most researchers to take a comprehensive approach. A clearer focus on one activity might help in the implementation of UPI in real software development projects. Even though it is important to involve users early in the process (Taylor & Kujala, 2008; Majid et al., 2010), many important decisions are made when translating user requirements into system requirements, which happens in the design and implementation activity (Abelein et al., 2012). Contradicting Majid et al. (2010), only one method focuses on the software verification and validation activity, but the practices of the proposed solutions show that most of the methods that focus on all activities include validation activities in their solutions. In addition, we did not anticipate so many methods that focus on software evolution. Perhaps most users start to get interested in a software system only when they are directly affected by it, which is normally after the first deployment of the system (Wagner & Piccoli, 2007). Furthermore, most software development today is evolutionary development, which explains the high number of methods that affect the software evolution activity.

Table 5: Proposed Solutions from the Methods Papers

When?/ Activity	What? / Practice for UPI	How? / Examples of UPI
Planning and Project Management	Set up communication structures.	
	Clarify roles of users and mediators, such as usability experts, design evaluators, geek interpreter, and boundary spanners, to reduce communication barriers (Amoako-Gyampah & White, 1997; Hope & Amdahl, 2011; Eckhardt, 2010; Humayoun et al., 2011; Korkala et al., 2010).	25 item skill set for boundary spanner (Eckhardt, 2010). Role descriptions for customer's apprentice, customer pairing, customer boot camp (Martin et al., 2010).
	If distributed development prevents using an on-site customer, define a person to play the role of the user and ensure daily communication (Korkala et al., 2010).	
	Set up asynchronous communication in case face-to-face communication is infeasible because of distributed environment.	
	Identify right users (Amoako-Gyampah & White, 1997; Kujala, 2008; Kamal et al., 2011)	Stakeholder analysis (Kamal et al., 2011).

When?/ Activity	What? / Practice for UPI	How? / Examples of UPI
Planning and Project Management	**Set up communication structures.**	
	Keep people informed and give them timely feedback (Amoako-Gyampah & White, 1997; Begier, 2010a).	Charts in meeting rooms (Amoako-Gyampah & White, 1997). Email listserv (Korkala et al., 2010).
	Use shared representations to mediate communication between professional groups (Pries-Heje & Dittrich, 2009).	
	Set up project management.	
	Ensure project manager's visibility (Amoako-Gyampah &and White 1997)	
	Set up development plan based on the user's need/input and share with users (Dean et al., 1998; Kautz, 2000).	User survey (Dean et al., 1998).
	Clarify the project vision with a high-level concept based on users' needs (ideally with users on site) (Cohen et al., 2010; Takats & Brewer, 2005; Kensing et al., 1998).	Workshop with structured agenda using a Group Solve pattern to produce a one-page description of the vision and a one-page logical architecture (Takats & Brewer, 2005). Big Picture Up-Front Workshop (Martin, 2010).

When?/ Activity	What? / Practice for UPI	How? / Examples of UPI
		Presentation rounds/hearings with organizational units (Kensing et al., 1998).
		Initial analysis of the organization's own documents
Planning and Project Management	Use a globally available project management tool with daily project status for all participants (including users) (Korkala et al., 2010).	
	Have an ERP competence center to mediate between users and external IT experts (Pries-Heje & Dittrich, 2009).	
	Set up project environment.	
	Use incremental project lifecycle with iterative development (Berger, 2011).	
	Collocate user and developer (Berger, 2011; Kautz, 2000)	Joint Application Development (JAD) workshops (Berger, 2011).
Software Specification and	Have IT professionals work for some time in the users' organization in order to understand the needs and observe existing practices (Pries-Heje & Dittrich, 2009).	
	Visit users in their own environment and explore their needs (Kujala, 2008; Martin et al., 2010; Teixeira et al., 2011).	Contextual and sociotechnical analysis (Kawalek & Wood-Harper, 2002).
		Focus group and direct

		observations (Teixeira et al., 2011).
	Describe the current situation (Kujala, 2008).	Task hierarchy, scenario, and user-needs table within field studies (Kujala, 2008).
		Strategic analysis (Kensing et al., 1998).
When?/ Activity	What? / Practice for UPI	How? / Examples of UPI
	Identify user-dependent scenarios (Pérez et al., 2011).	
Software Specification and Requirements Engineering	Guide the user representative from the analysis of business needs to the identification of system requirements (Dean et al., 1998).	
	Conduct requirements analysis face to face with users (Korkala et al., 2006; Takats & Brewer, 2005).	Paper-based prototypes (Korkala et al., 2006).
		Activity theory requirements engineering (Fuentes-Fernández et al., 2009).
		Focus groups and card-sort methods (Humayoun et al., 2011).
		Heavily facilitated workshops using "be visual" and "forced rank" patterns (Takats & Brewer, 2005).
	Use software support to elicit requirements while the user is using a prototype.	Infrastructure probes (Dörner et al., 2008).
		Domain-specific visual language (Pérez et al., 2011).
		Multi-methodological information system

		development approach that uses prototyping (Pekkola et al., 2006).
	Have a thorough requirements specification (for off-the-shelf systems) as a basis for the contract (Pries-Heje, 2008).	
When?/ Activity	What? / Practice for UPI	How? / Examples of UPI
Software Design and	Involve on site customers in requirements and story-card prioritization in design approval (Kautz, 2011).	
	Take users' existing practices as the starting point for the design process (Cherry & Macredie, 1999). Let users articulate their requirements through prototypes that can be iteratively modified (Cherry & Macredie, 1999). Allow users to experiment with various work scenarios (Cherry & Macredie, 1999).	Cooperative prototyping (Cherry & Macredie, 1999).
	Have structured brainstorming sessions to transform general characteristics into a common design strategy for both users and developers (Cherry & Macredie, 1999).	Future workshop (Cherry & Macredie, 1999; Kensing et al., 1998).
	Develop a vision for the overall change in design and anchor the vision in management and the steering committee, the technical and organizational implementation team, and the users.	Visits to similar work places (Kensing et al., 1998). Design workshops (Kensing et al., 1998).

When?/ Activity	What? / Practice for UPI	How? / Examples of UPI
	Have designers visit the workplace and have contact with users (Mambrey et al., 1998).	Osmosis (interviews, user workshops, active user services, and simply being present at the workplace) (Mambrey et al., 1998).
	Let skilled spokespersons of users participate in development work (Hope & Amdahl, 2011; Berger, 2011).	Dynamic system development methods work (Hope & Amdahl, 2011). Paper prototypes (Humayoun et al., 2011). User advocacy (Mambrey et al., 1998).
Software Design and Implementation	Allows consideration of alternative work processes by playing them out and confronting the problems created (Cherry & Macredie, 1999).	Organizational gaming (Cherry & Macredie, 1999).
	Plan the content of the next iteration with users on site (Korkala et al., 2006).	Planning games (Kautz, 2000), Mobile-D (Korkala et al., 2006).
	Evaluate the design with users through quick evaluation methods and improve the design based on prototype evaluation (Humayoun et al., 2011).	Evaluation experiments run from within the development environment with UEM and TaMUlator tools (Humayoun et al., 2011).
	Have weekly feedback meetings with onsite customers during working software presentations (Kautz, 2011).	

	Use an iterative design process with task analysis, scenario design, design implementation, and usability testing and evaluation (Huang et al., 2008).	Brainstorming, focus groups, mockups, and usability quiz (Huang et al., 2008).

When?/ Activity	What? / Practice for UPI	How? / Examples of UPI
Software Design and Implementation	Develop iterations and get feedback quickly from the users through testing the software versions (Teixeira et al., 2011).	eXtremProgramming (XP) (Teixeira et al., 2011).
	Allow change requests for the software design from onsite users in weekly feedback loops (Kautz, 2000).	Re-calibration workshops (Martin et al., 2010).
	Allow necessary customizations to the system (for off-the-shelf systems) (Pries-Heje, 2008).	
Software Verification and Validation	Use prototypes for evaluation with users (Dean et al., 1998; Humayoun et al., 2011; Cohen et al., 2010).	Heuristic evaluation, question-asking protocol, and performance measurement (Humayoun et al., 2011).
	Let users evaluate modules, supported by automated tools.	
	Let on site user representatives collect feedback and proposals for improvements from other users based on the working software (Kautz, 2000; Martin et al., 2010).	"Road shows" from onsite users to other users (Kautz, 2000; Martin et al., 2010; Kautz, 2011).
	Prepare and perform an acceptance test with onsite customers (Kautz, 2011).	

	Use prototypes for evaluation with users (Dean et al., 1998; Humayoun et al., 2011; Cohen et al., 2010).	Heuristic evaluation, question-asking protocol, and performance measurement (Humayoun et al., 2011).
When?/ Activity	What? / Practice for UPI	How? / Examples of UPI
Software Evolution	Encourage users to suggest new features asynchronously (Bragge, 2009).	Feedback function within the system (Bragge, 2009). Mailing lists with the active participation of developers (Hendry, 2008). User questionnaires (Begier, 2010a). Electronic web interface for feedback and proposals (Hansson et al., 2004).
Software Evolution	Obtain feedback from users concerning system limitations, faults, and proposals for future development through various channels (Hansson et al., 2006). Use support as a channel for feedback and change proposals (Hansson et al., 2006). Keep track of user feedback (Hansson et al., 2006).	Support calls, user meetings, courses, the website, and newsletter (Hansson et al., 2006). Customer relationship management tools (Hansson et al., 2006).

	Exchange information and feedback about the ongoing development (Finck et al., 2004).	Discussion forum in groupware system (Finck et al., 2004).
	Give users an incentive to express problems and ideas about system usage (Finck et al., 2004).	
	Inform users through a facilitator about the design decisions of the next release based on requirements from the discussion forum (Finck et al., 2004).	
	Set up a synchronous feedback session with user groups (Kabbedijk et al., 2009).	IT helpdesk (Bragge, 2009; Hansson et al., 2004). Virtual group support systems.
	Set up usability workshops with users.	Customer participation sessions with idea feedback and user suggestions (Kabbedijk et al., 2009; Hansson et al., 2004). Thinklets (Fruhling et al., 2005).
	Acknowledge that users have limited interest before "go-live" and involve them afterward (Wagner & Piccoli, 2007).	

Finding 2 - Methods for UPI target the same categories as the surveys but differ on the subcategory level (RQ 2.3). At first look, there are similarities between the aspects of UPI the surveys address and those the methods address. However, many more methods focus on communication between user and developer and the responsibilities for development than survey papers. Furthermore, many of the methods aim to improve the developers' attitude toward the user, the users' attitude toward the system, and the users' motivation, but the surveys did not investigate these issues extensively, perhaps because it is difficult to measure human attitudes empirically. Even so, doing so is an important goal for a method. In line with the surveys' results, the methods did not closely target the context factors of system attributes and organizational factors, but we also did not focus our mapping study on such context factors. In general, complexity appears to be more important for system success than is the uncertainty of the system. Among the organizational factors, 22 percent of the method papers targeted the subcategory of top management support, which shows that convincing managers of the importance of UPI methods is central to a method's successful implementation. Therefore, we suggest empirical validation of that effect. In addition, the methods focus on system quality, the measure most frequently used for system success, whereas the surveys focus on user satisfaction. This finding indicates that authors who suggest new methods still have functional or technical views on system success.

Finding 3 - Most methods were validated in a public environment (RQ 2.4). The methods' validation contexts were primarily agile environments. This finding is not unexpected, as the lightweight methods become widespread in software development and are focused on the user based on principles of the agile manifesto (Beck et al., 2001). In the analysis of the validation context, we found that many papers used a public sector environment for their validation, perhaps because access to these organizations is easier. Nevertheless, it is important to validate new methods in various environments, such as large companies and organizations in the private sector. Further research should also validate new methods in more than one case study. Most researched software systems for validation were information systems, perhaps because information systems focus on the support of everyday operations of human beings, for which UPI is more important (Singh & Kotzé, 2003).

Finding 4 – There is a broad variety of practices in all software activities derived from the methods' solutions (RQ 2.4). The structured overview of practices with examples of UPI shows that there are suggestions for each software development activity. Most of the practices are grouped in the planning and project management activity. In line with the analysis of the targeted aspects, of UPI there is a focus on communication structures. Various papers suggest determining the right users to be involved and the setup of structures for how and when to communicate with them, keep them informed, and give them feedback. Nevertheless, besides some role descriptions, the papers suggest only a few concrete methods, which frequency differs from that of the software specifications and requirements engineering activity, where there are many methods for ensuring participation because of the active research field of requirements engineering. Even though only four studies focused on the design and implementation activity, we extracted some suggestions for practices. Most of the papers keep the development and design content flexible, such as through mid-iteration communication or iteration planning with the users. The suggested participation methods have a connection to agile methods but also suggest completely new approaches, such as the evaluation experiments that run within the development environment (Humayoun et al., 2011). Finally, many specific participation methods for collecting feedback from the user, either asynchronously or synchronously, have been identified in the software evolution activity.

Summary of findings for RQ 2. The analysis of characteristics of methods that aim to increase UPI in software development shows that many approaches have been developed, although most have been evaluated in small projects in the public sector area. The relative absence of evaluation in large projects and in private companies and organizations might explain why UPI is still not widespread in these contexts. Nevertheless, our meta-analysis shows a clear positive effect of UPI on system success, so methods related to ensuring UPI are of value for software development projects. Therefore, further research on methods to increase UPI specifically targeted to large projects in private companies is required.

3.8. Strengths and Weaknesses of the Systematic Mapping Study

This chapter identifies the strengths and weaknesses of our study; describes the differences between this study and the other identified meta-studies, as well as to another systematic literature review; discusses the benefits of our study; and explains threats to validity.

The six meta-studies that we identified in our systematic mapping study each had a different focus or approach than that of our systematic mapping study. Harris and Weistroffer's (2009) study analyzed twenty-eight empirical studies but summarized them on only a descriptive basis and did not quantitatively evaluate the results. Kujala (2003) also combined qualitative and quantitative data but focused on the early steps with regard to requirements management, so the paper did not address the whole software development process. McKeen et al. (1994) is a good study regarding the various context factors of user participation, but it focuses solely on empirical studies. Such is also the case for Cavaye (1995) and Ives and Olson (1984), both of which seek to resolve some contradictory results regarding the effect of UPI. Furthermore, all three studies were published almost twenty years ago. McGill and Klobas' (2008) meta-study is a useful overview, but it focuses on a user-developed system, a constraint we did not use in this paper.

A clear strength of our systematic mapping study in comparison to the identified meta-studies is the wide range with which we considered the influence of UPI in software development. We included statistical surveys and meta-studies to increase confidence in the effects of UPI on a quantitative basis and complemented this approach with a description of various methods from which we analyzed and derived practices. We also used a wide range of sources from three domains, and the 3,698 hits of our search string indicates the richness of the research from which we chose our studies. In total, we use the results of fifty-eight scientific papers in this systematic mapping study and also consider results in the six meta-studies about the effects of UPI.

In parallel with our work, Bano and Zowghi (2013) conducted a systematic literature review of the relationship between user involvement and system success using a similar search string consisting of synonyms for users, involvement, and software development and a mixture of search strategies. Their electronic sources for the IT domain are identical to those in our study, but they used other databases. They also used specific sources of management science journals and DBLP publication profiles of highly cited researchers but did not include journals for PD and communication in their search. Given these differences in the search strategy and inclusion criteria, the sets of identified papers have some overlap but also major differences: Forty-one of the eighty-seven studies analyzed in Bano and Zowghi (2013)are included in our work. In line with our results, Bano and Zowghi (2013) confirms the positive effects of user involvement on system success and argues that UPI is a complex phenomenon that is difficult to measure. This alignment supports our finding that UPI has a positive effect on system success, particularly since the reviews analyzed different studies to a degree. However, the goals of Bano and Zowghi (2013) and our work differ. Bano and Zowghi (2013) researched the relationship of user involvement to system success with respect to controversial results, analyzed the historical development of this relationship, and studied the differences in the characteristics of the existing evidence. Their finding of an increase in positive effects in recent decades is evidence that extends our results. Furthermore, Bano and Zowghi (2013) focused on analyzing current knowledge on the relationship between user involvement and system success, while we focused on a deeper understanding of the aspects of UPI considered in existing evidence, following a meta-analytical approach. We seek to determine practices in existing methods in order to reveal the current research status and to enable new methods that will increase UPI.

There are several possible threats to our study's validity. First, the author of this thesis, a first-year Ph.D. student at the time, was primarily involved in the selection process. Because of the large number of hits from our search string, the initial round of selection was based only on titles and abstracts. The decision concerning which papers were relevant was solely made by the author of this thesis, which could indicate a certain degree of subjectivity and be a threat to internal validity. However, as we retrieved such a large number of duplicates from our sources that we are convinced that the selection was consistent with the defined criteria. The fact that the author of this thesis was a first-year Ph.D. student who had just started his research in UPI helped to ensure that the selection was not biased. For the selection following the initial selection, we defined clear exclusion criteria and stated the reason for exclusion in a protocol. The supervisor of this thesis then checked the protocol on a random sample (about 10% of the results) for validity based on the reason for inclusion or exclusion and a check of the paper itself. By following the approach of Kitchenham & Charters (2007) with a strict process and clear inclusion and exclusion criteria and by means of the supervisor's validation check, we hope to have reduced the bias in the study.

Another possible systematic bias derives from the possibility that authors used other terms for UPI that we did not cover in our search string. We tried to reduce this risk by using synonyms and by including the common term "participatory design" as an alternative; however, it is still possible that we missed some useful studies. In addition, UPI in software development is not a mainstream research topic, so some publications may appear in places not covered by our sources. Therefore, the IS community in particular suggests using backward and forward snowballing instead of a search string as a search strategy (Jalali & Wohlin, 2012). Instead, we tried to overcome this possible defect by including sources like *Participatory Design Conference proceedings, Information Technology & People Journal*, and the *Scandinavian Journal of Information System*s. However, we used some part of backward snowballing, as we did reference searches for the papers (Al-Rawas & Easterbrook, 1996) and the six meta-studies.

Another possible weakness of our approach could be that we excluded methods papers that were published more than fifteen years ago but used survey papers that were published more than fifteen years ago. Although this approach might seem inconsistent, software and development processes have changed significantly, so methods developed more than fifteen years ago are not relevant for this study. While such could also be the case for survey papers, the statistical correlations are more general and should be used.

3.9. Further Analysis

A historical analysis of all fifty-eight papers plus the sixty-six papers that were references in the meta study shows that the topic of UPI has been consistently studied over the last five decades; the first paper was published in 1959 (Figure 9). There was an increase in published surveys until 1997, with some dips in the '80s. From 1997 onward, we also included the method papers—method papers published prior to 1997 were excluded based on the exclusion criterion M5—but there was a clear decrease from 2000 to 2005, when research interest in UPI increased again. A particularly high number of method papers were published in the last five years. In line with our findings, based on our research questions, this analysis shows that, even though the topic of UPI in software development has been considered for a considerable length of time, there still is no clear solution concerning how to implement UPI in practice. Therefore, research on methods to increase UPI in various contexts is required.

We also sought to identify trends of terminology in the research area of UPI (**Figure 14: Historical Analysis of Important Terms**

. "User participation" and "user involvement" were mentioned in about the same number of titles, so our approach of combining them to the term UPI is useful. However, "user involvement" was more prominent in the early 1990s, while "user participation" has been more popular since then. This could also be an indication that active participation of users has been proven to be more effective. User satisfaction, the most common aspect of system success, was not mentioned in many titles, suggestions that it is a commonly used measure for system success but not an important term in the area of UPI. Especially after 1997, when we started to include the method papers, "communication" and "collaboration" appeared frequently in the titles, which is in line with our analysis of practices from the method papers and strengthens our assumption that UPI depends significantly on communication between the involved stakeholders.

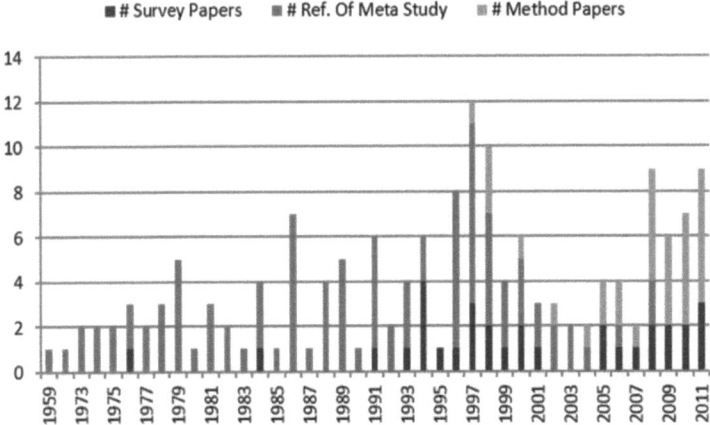

Figure 13: Historical Analysis of the Number of Surveys and Method Papers

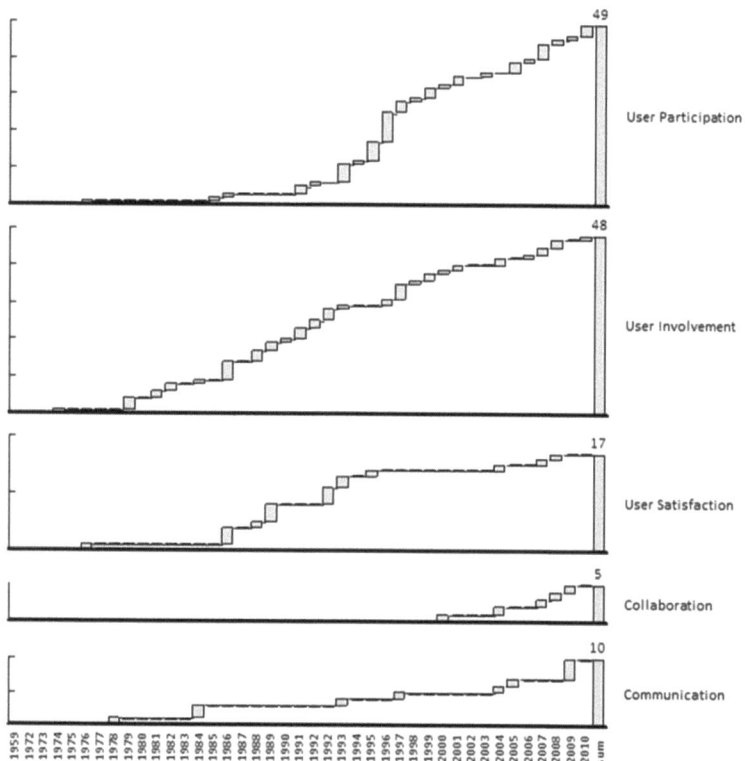

Figure 14: Historical Analysis of Important Terms

Another important contribution of this chapter is the classification of the aspects of UPI into development process, human aspects, system attributes, organizational factors, and system success. The analysis revealed that **UPI is an important research topic,** as it has been researched in a broad manner by various research areas (RQ 1.1 and 1.4). This classification can support other researchers in studying the aspects of UPI and be used as a starting point from which to develop a common conceptual model for aspects of UPI, aspects of system success, and context factors.

We first analyzed thirty-six papers' targeted issues, validation contexts, and proposed solutions (RQ 2.1). (For a summary of each paper, see Table 5 in the Appendix.) An important finding is that **all software development activities** (planning and project management, software specification and requirements engineering, software design and implementation, software verification and validation, and software evolution) **are affected by the method used,** but only a few methods focus on the design and implementation activity (RQ 2.2). This insight can support other researchers in the identification of existing research gaps for methods that aim to increase UPI.

Another important contribution of this chapter is the structured overview of practices with examples of methods that use them. The overview shows **that there is a wide variety of practices derived from the solutions in all software activities** (RQ 2.4). Most of the practices are grouped into the planning and project management activity, which includes all activities that are required for the entire project. In line with the analysis of targeted aspects of UPI there is a focus on communication structures. The overview is particularly helpful for practitioners who want to use existing practices and methods to increase UPI in software development. The review of the state-of-the-art research in ways to increase UPI in software development projects can also be valuable to other researchers. The comparison between aspects of UPI researched by the surveys and the targeted aspects of UPI from the methods reveals that **methods for increasing UPI target categories that are similar to those the surveys target** (RQ 2.3). However, they do have a greater focus on UDC and the user's motivation. In addition, they target mostly the success factor of system quality, which differs from the survey papers that tend to focus on user satisfaction. The analysis of the validation context revealed that **most methods were validated in a public environment** (RQ 2.4). Therefore, we encourage other researchers to validate new methods in private organizations.

Overall, we conclude that the systematic mapping study shows a positive correlation between various aspects of UPI and system success but that there is still no common conceptual model with which to measure and validate this effect. This includes a positive effect from UDC to system success. Furthermore, the analysis of aspects of UPI indicated only minor focus on organizational factors and system attributes. However, large IT projects in big companies are heavily influenced by factors like the complexity of the system and the organization's managerial culture, so it might be beneficial to emphasize these aspects of UPI in a new method. In addition, the study reveals that only a few methods focus on UPI and UDC in the software design and implementation activity, even though many important decisions are made in the course of this activity. Given that many of the methods target users' motivations; this aspect should also be included in the method design. In line with Ives and Olson (1984), user satisfaction is a critical factor that increases system acceptance and use, which increases the system's value. Therefore, a new method should target user satisfaction as a measure of success that is as important as system quality.

3.10. Summary of State of the Art

This chapter described a systematic mapping study that examined the influence of UPI on system success. We followed the guidelines of Kitchenham and Charters (2007), defining our research question, conducting a structured identification of research based on a search string, defining clear inclusion and exclusion criteria, and analyzing the resulting fifty-eight papers with regard to our research questions.

The objectives of the study were to determine whether an increase in UPI increases system success and to identify the characteristics of methods that increase UPI in software development projects.

We used meta-analytical techniques to validate the effect of UPI, extracting the researched aspects of UPI, correlation data, variation, and number of participants for validation from eighty-six studies. The most important finding is that most of the derived correlations had a positive effect on system success, so we concluded that **aspects of the development process and human aspects have a positive effect on system success** (RQ 1.2, 1.3, and 1.4). Most of the fourteen studies with negative correlations have only a few negative correlations and do not question the main correlations between aspects of UPI and system success. In addition, we found that **most studies with negative correlations were published more than ten years ago** (RQ 1.3 and 1.4). These results increase the confidence that UPI is beneficial to system success, which is an important finding for attempts to increase UPI in software development. The number of participants involved in the studies indicates the breadth and profundity of this research area. This finding shows that **UPI has a positive effect on user satisfaction and system use** (RQ 1.3 and 1.4). Nevertheless, the **large variation in correlations shows the complexity of measuring and studying UPI** (RQ 1.3 and 1.4).

In the next chapter, we present the state of practice on UDC in LSI projects, in order to also understand the perspective of practitionniers on the issue of UDC in LSI projects

Chapter 4
User-Developer Communication in Large-Scale IT Projects:
Results of an Expert Interview Series

"Life is what happens to you while you're busy making other plans."
John Lennon

4.1. Abstract

Context: User participation in software development is considered to be essential for successful software systems. A lack of direct communication between users and developers can cause serious issues in LSI projects.

Objective: This chapter seeks to identify current practices in UDC in LSI projects, the factors for, and consequences of communication gaps, and what experts suggest to prevent them.

Method: We conducted a series of semi-structured interviews with twelve experts who work on the coordination of business and IT in a total of sixty-nine LSI projects.

Results: The analysis of our interviews showed that direct UDC is limited and that there is no commonly used method for the UDC in the design and implementation activity. The interviews helped to identify current practices and issues resulting from a lack of communication and the need for a method that would enhance UDC in LSI projects.

4.2. Introduction

In the last chapter, we extracted the state-of-the-art literature on UPI and found that it is an important, well-studied research topic. We concluded that UPI has a positive effect on system success. In particular, there is a positive correlation between UDC and system success.

For example, Amoako-Gyampah and White (1993) found a positive correlation between the level of communication between the users and the IS team and user satisfaction as a measurement for system success. In addition, Hartwick and Barki (2001, 1997) and Barki and Hartwick (1994) studied the dependencies between the user-IS relationship and UPI and confirmed that users' informal and formal communication with the IS team and senior management significantly influences the management of a software project and the system design, but not necessarily satisfaction with the system. McKeen et al. (1994) investigated the contingency factors of user satisfaction and found that UDC is an independent predictor of user satisfaction. There are several ways to support UPI in software development projects (chapter 3.7), and the analysis of proposed solutions showed the importance of how structures are set up to enable communication using these methods (Abelein & Paech, 2013b). For example, several authors suggested clarifying users' and mediators' roles to reduce communication barriers (Amoako-Gyampah & White, 1997; Hope & Amdahl, 2011; Eckhardt, 2010; Humayoun et al., 2011; Korkala et al., 2006). We also have not found a method that supports UDC in the design and implementation phase of software development.

Begier (2010) mentioned that it is important to keep people (e.g., users, stakeholders) informed and to give them timely feedback. Particularly in the design and implementation phase, Kautz (2011) suggested having weekly feedback meetings with onsite customers during the presentations of working software. Several research studies on agile methods have targeted communication problems in software development projects (e.g., Hope & Amdahl, 2011; Takats & Brewer, 2005).

However, we have seen from our experience as management consultants for IT projects that many LSI projects still use traditional methods, such as the waterfall approach. Therefore, we seek to identify the current practices of LSI projects with a focus on projects that use traditional development methods.

Other studies on communication issues and structures (e.g., regular meetings or workshops) in software development projects include Bjarnason et al. (2011), Stapel et al. (2011), and Marczak et al. (2007), although none of these studies focused on UDC in LSI projects. The research on UDC in LSI projects has provided only limited empirical insights from practitioners, but it is important to consider practitioners' perspectives on the communication between users and developers and why they think it is difficult to implement processes that ensure effective cooperation between the two parties. Capturing this perspective is essential for the design of methods to improve UDC in LSI projects.

This chapter is built Abelein and Paech (2014), published in the proceedings of the *International Working Conference on Requirements Engineering: Foundation for Software Quality* and nominated for the "best paper" award. We do not reference the paper in the discussion that follows for reasons of readability.

This chapter is structured as follows. In chapter 4.3 and 4.4.. we motivate the research questions and present related work. Chapter 4.5. explains the interview method and data about the interview partners. We present the results and the discussion on the state of practice of UDC in LSI projects in chapter 4.6., and chapter 4.7. describes the threats to validity. The chapter concludes with a summary in chapter 4.8.

4.3. Research Questions for the State of Practice

So far, the research on UDC in LSI projects has provided only limited empirical insights from practitioners, although it is important to consider their perspectives on communication between users and developers and why they think it is difficult to implement processes that ensure effective cooperation between the two parties. Capturing this perspective is essential in designing methods to improve UDC in LSI projects. Other studies on communication issues and structures (e.g., regular meetings or workshops) in software development include Bjarnason et al. (2011), Stapel et al. (2011), and Marczak et al. (2007). However, none of these studies focused on UDC in LSI projects.

We conducted series of interviews with experts in LSI projects to determine the answer to RQ 3.

RQ 3 - *How and how well is UDC supported in LSI (with a focus on the decisions made in the design and implementation phase and their rationale)?* In particular:
- RQ 3.1: Do users and developers communicate in LSI projects?
- RQ 3.2: What are the organizational obstacles that prevent LSI projects from implementing UDC?
- RQ 3.3: What factors might cause communication gaps between users and developers, and what are the consequences of these communication gaps?
- RQ 3.4: What do experienced practitioners suggest to overcome the obstacles to the implementation of UDC and to eliminate the factors that cause communication gaps?

4.4. Related Work on User-Developer Communication

Here we present empirical studies that have explored communication in various software development projects or settings. None of the studies presented focuses on the communication from the developer to the users in LSI projects, but we compare their results to ours and discuss similarities in chapter 4.6. Bjarnason et al. (2011) empirically studied communication gaps in terms of their root causes and effects with practitioners in a large company that develops market-driven software. However, the study focused on the communication of requirements, and as the context was market-driven software development, the results did not include communication with customers, that is, the users of the software. Stapel and Schneider (2012) proposed an approach to managing knowledge on communication and information flows in global software projects and identified poor communication as a main obstacle to successful collaboration. However, they focused on distributed development settings and not on LSI projects. Marczak et al. (2008) explored information flow patterns in requirement-dependent social networks. In particular, they studied communication and coordination in cross-functional teams that work on the same or on interrelated requirements. However, they addressed only the communication among IT personnel and did not study the communication of IT personnel with the users. Finally, Gallivan and Keil (2003) studied the UDC process in a software project that failed despite of a high level of user involvement and found that communication gaps occurred because the developers were not informed about the underlying reasons for the users' not accepting the software system. Their results are based on only one project, so their insights are from a limited perspective.

4.5. Methodology of the Interview Series

4.5.1. Identification of Experts

We developed role descriptions for IT personnel and business users (**Table 6**) to ensure that our interview partners were experts in LSI projects. As we want to interview those with experience in projects that used traditional methods, we searched for experts who had been involved in projects that did not use or apply agile methods. As consultants are typically not involved in the whole IT project timeline, we set a minimum time of three months of participation. We used role descriptions together with some explanation about our research area and the goals of the interviews to contact primarily interview partners with whom the author of this thesis as well as her supervisor had existing relationships.

Table 6: Role Descriptions for Experts

IT Personnel (Developer, Architect, Designer)	Business Personnel
Involved in more than one LSI project with at least one of the following characteristics: large number of users, multiple countries, business units involved, large budget, project duration at least one year, such as an ERP implementation). Ideally, no use of agile development methods. Involved in the project for at least three months (for consultants).	
Had a leading role in the development/ implementation/ customizing of an LSI project. Involved in discussions with users during the project or in change-request management after go-live.	Had a leading role in the requirement analysis, concept development, or project management in an LSI project. Involved in defining requirements and discussions with developers during the project and/or involved in the change request process after go-live.

We identified and attained twelve experts for our interview series. During the interviews, we realized that it is not always possible to separate the IT and business roles completely, so we included a third category (business and IT). We asked our interview partners to classify themselves in the domains of "business" (one expert), "business and IT" (six experts), or "IT" (five experts).

The interview partners' educational backgrounds were wide-ranging (**Figure 15** and **Figure 17**). Five interview partners' highest level of education was Ph.D. and six partners' highest level of education was a Master of Science (MSc). The twelfth interview partner had been working in software development for the last twenty-five years. The interviewees' study backgrounds covered seven areas, half IT-related subjects (computer science and IT).

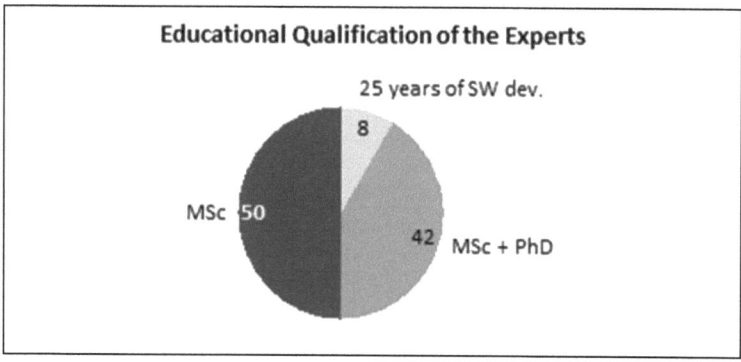

Figure 15: Overview of the Experts' Educational Qualifications

The experts' varied industries and roles in their companies ensured we would hear opinions on the UDC-LSI method from a variety of angles. Six experts were employed by IT or management consultancies, four experts worked in large organizations' IT departments, and two experts worked for software or IT service providers (**Figure 16**). All experts had a leading role in their companies that enabled them to have a broad overview of IT projects (**Figure 17**).

Ranging from two to fifteen LSI projects, the interview partners averaged experience in six LSI projects in various roles during the course of their carriers (e.g., developer, project manager, architect, requirement engineer, consultant, quality manager) (see **Table 7**).

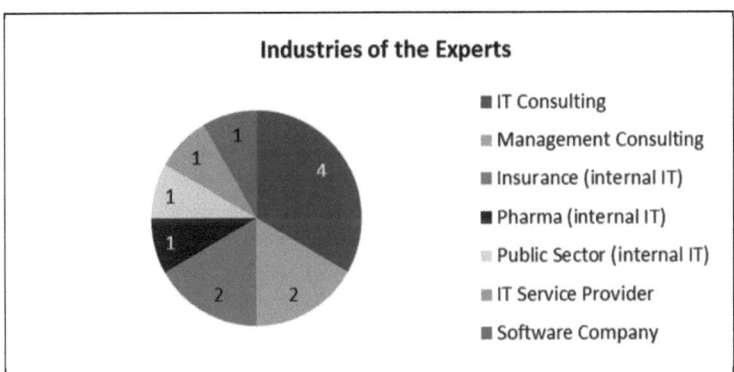

Figure 16: Overview of the Experts' Industries

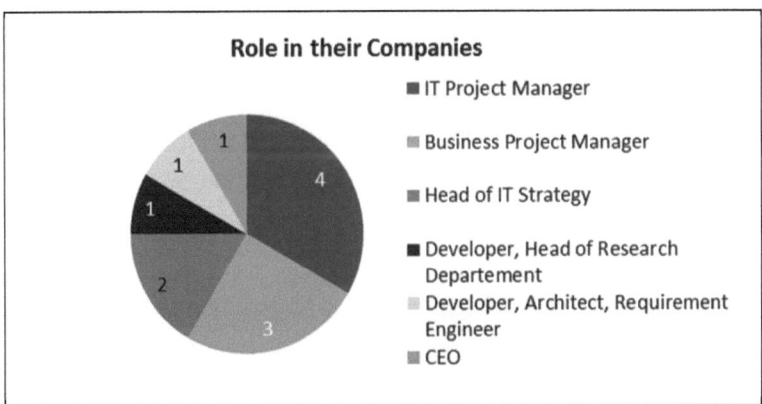

Figure 17: Overview of the Experts' Roles in their Companies

We asked the interview partners about the main characteristics of the experts' LSI projects, including:
- Development system
- Industry
- Project duration
- Project volume in million EUR
- Number of users
- Amount of rollout units
- Development method
- Role/task of expert

Even though the experts could not always identify all of these characteristics for each of their projects, either because the data was not documented or for confidentiality reasons, we were able to record the full list of characteristics for forty-four projects. (See Appendix II **Table 58**.)

4.5.2. Interview Process

Four interviews were conducted in person and eight via telephone. During the interviews, we explained the problems of LSI projects that use traditional software development methods (chapter 1.2) and the purpose of our research on UDC. We structured the interviews in three parts: First, we asked the interviewee about his or her experience in LSI projects (questions 1 - 8 of the questionnaire in the Appendix). Second, we discussed the classification of user-relevant decisions and collected examples from the experts (questions 8 - 13 of the questionnaire in the Appendix (see chapter 3.1). Third, we explained the UDC-LSI method and discussed the possible extensions, benefits, and feasibility of implementation (questions 14 - 20 of the questionnaire in the Appendix) (see chapter 8.3.). As we used a semi-structured setup, we did not always follow this order of the questions but used an open discussion format.

4.5.3. Data Analysis

The average time required for an interview was ninety minutes (range 44 - 125 minutes). In total, we collected about eighteen hours of interview recordings (**Table 7**). All interviews were recorded with the permission of the interviewees and transcribed for analysis purposes.

The results of the second part of the interviews (interview questions 8 - 13) was used to develop a descriptive classification of user-relevant decisions (Abelein & Paech, 2013a) (chapter 2.3). We coded the interviews to help us analyze the results (Saldana, 2009). We built a code tree based on our research questions with descriptive codes and extended and reorganized the code tree in two cycles of coding (Saldana, 2009). Since we used the software MaxQDA, we could also do cross-interview or cross-code analysis (e.g., between the usefulness and the benefits of the UDC-LSI method).

Table 7: Overview of Interview Time

Interview Number	Interview time [min]	Experience of expert [# of projects]
1	91	15
2	87	6
3	115	3
4	44	3
5	125	5
6	88	6
7	71	2
8	108	3
9	78	4
10	81	14
11	90	5
12	97	3

Sum	1075	69
Average	90	6
Minimum	44	2
Maximum	125	15

4.6. Results and Discussion

This chapter describes the results of the interviews on current communication structures (e.g., meetings, reports, workshops) in LSI projects. We use tables to show the descriptive codes and the corresponding number of occurrences in the interviews. (For a detailed explanation, see chapter 4.5.3.) Each subsection first presents the results and the table and then discusses them and compares them to the existing literature. To answer our research questions, we determined whether the interview partners experienced UDC in LSI projects (chapter 4.6.1.). We also report on organizational obstacles (chapter 4.6.2.), factors for communication gaps, and the consequences of these communication gaps for the IT projects (chapter 4.6.3.). Finally, we describe the experts' ideas for overcoming these obstacles and reasons for communication gaps (chapter 4.6.4.).

4.6.1. UDC in Large-Scale IT Projects (RQ 3.1)

We asked all interview partners what communication took place within their projects and who communicated with whom in the project. Only three experts reported on projects in which communication between users and developers took place, and two of these three experts also participated in projects where there was no direct communication between these parties. Hence, eleven experts told us about LSI projects that did not include direct communication between developers and users (Table 4). Less than one-fifth of the sixty-nine projects in which our experts were involved featured communication between users and developers.

Nevertheless, some projects had other forms of UDC, such as communication between the IT consultant and the users, communication between the architect and the users, and communication between the requirements engineer and the expert users (not users but business personnel with broad context knowledge or a management role). Even though our analysis of existing methods for using UPI in the systematic mapping study (see chapter 3.7.) indicated that the method affects all activities of software development, we learned from our interview partners that, in practice, most of the communication is done in either the early or the late activities of software development (i.e., in specification or acceptance).

Table 8: Experts' Experience with Direct Communication Between Developers and Users

Experts' Experience with UDC in LSI Projects	# of Experts[1]
Communication between developers and users	3
No communication between developers and users	11
Other forms of communication with users	
Communication between IT consultant and users	3
Communication between architect and users	2
Communication between requirements engineer and expert user	2

1 Number of interviewees who mentioned an experience with UDC, mapped to descriptive code

Based on our experts' experiences, we conclude that there is no direct communication between developers and users in most LSI projects. This result is in contrast to those of Chang et al. (2010), who found that the presence of mutual influence among IT staff and users, which enables open and direct communication and coordination, is significantly associated with project performance. However, their context was not that of LSI projects. The reported communication between requirements engineers and expert users is in line with Kanungo and Bagchi (2000), who suggested moving user participation upstream in the implementation process and using representatives of user groups. The finding that most of the communication is done either in the early or the late activities of software development shows a lack of communication in the middle of the development, that is, in the design and implementation activity. Even though the literature contains suggested methods for including communication in the middle of the development (see chapter 3.7.) –for example, Kautz (2011) and Korkala et al. (2006) suggested having weekly feedback meetings with onsite customers during working software presentations or at least mid-iteration communication with users—our findings show that such methods are limited in practice.

4.6.2. Organizational Obstacles for UDC (RQ 3.2)

We identified four obstacles, of which three concern the users or access to them (**Table 9**). We discussed the topic of organizational obstacles with half of the experts, but the other experts did not mention any organizational obstacles. Of those who did, two experts mentioned that users are not a homogeneous group but are a collection of user groups or business units with often differing opinions and organizational power in the company. In such cases developers (and other IT personnel) faced the challenge of mediating between these groups. Other experts mentioned that it was difficult to find user representatives with the right qualifications and knowledge to participate in an IT project, perhaps because such users tend to be important to the business operations and are unlikely to be made available for tasks in IT projects. One expert mentioned that sometimes the real users are not identified during the project, so the developers and other IT personnel could not contact them even if they wanted to. Finally, one expert reported that no mediators were available to establish and uphold the relationship between the users and the developers.

Table 9: Organizational Obstacles for Implementing Communication with Users

IDD	Organizational Obstacles (Descriptive Code)	# of
O1	Different opinions between user groups	2
O2	Getting the right user representatives for LSI projects	2
O3	No contact to users/users unknown	1
O4	Lack of local mediators	1

Obstacles O1 and O2 correspond with the findings of Bjarnason et al. (2011), who also identified as root causes for communication gaps the scale effects that result from complex products and large organizations and gaps between roles over time through distributed environments. Even though Bjarnason et al.'s (2011) study used a setup that included no direct contact with users, these obstacles also seem to be present for UDC. Obstacle O4 is supported by the findings of Marczak et al. (2008), who studied communication and coordination in cross-functional teams that work on the same or interrelated requirements. Marczak et al. (2008) found that the power of information flows lies with a few key members who control the flow of information between dependent networks. Our findings indicate that such is also the case for UDC.

4.6.3. Reasons for and Consequences of Communication Gaps (RQ 3.3)

Table 10: Reasons for and Consequences of Communication Gaps

ID	Reasons for communication gaps (Descriptive Code)	# of Instances
F1	Lack of motivation of developers or users	4
F2	Lack of a common language between business and IT	4

F3	Lack of appreciation between business and IT	1
	Consequences of communication gaps (Descriptive Code)	**# of Int.**
C1	Misunderstanding of requirements	8
C2	Ad-hoc changes required because of unclear requirements	3
C3	Increased implementation costs	3
C4	Increased test effort because of rework	1

We identified three reasons for and four consequences of communication gaps (**Table 10**). According to the interviewees, common reasons for communication gaps are lack of motivation from either the users or the developers and the lack of a common language between the business and IT side. Another reason, which is related to the first two reasons, is lack of appreciation between these two sides. The consequences that the interviewees most frequently named is the misunderstanding of requirements, that is, when developers either interpret requirements incorrectly or users do not specify requirements on a sufficiently detailed level. This latter consequence often leads to the need for ad-hoc changes or "scope creep" during implementation. Increased implementation costs or test efforts were also named as consequences of communication gaps.

The results of RQ 3.3 show that the consequences are severe, as misunderstandings and ad-hoc changes have an impact on cost and schedule of the project. The factor F1 is similar to Bjarnason et al.'s (2011) identified effect of "low motivation to contribute to requirements work," and F2 is a commonly known issue in IT projects. However, the factor F3, missing appreciation, has not yet been described, and the actions required in order to improve appreciation between IT and business are different from those required in overcoming the barriers of a common domain language. The identified consequences C1 and C2 are in line with Bjarnason et al.'s (2011) effect, described as "problems with the system requirements specification." C3 and C4 are similar to Bjarnason et al.'s (2011) effect of "wasted effort." However, our results show that the experts stated a clear connection of communication gaps with increased implementation costs and a higher test effort. In addition, consequences C1, C2, C3, and C4 correspond with the benefits of UPI (see chapter 3.6.), such as improved quality resulting from precise requirements and the prevention of expensive features.

4.6.4. Overcoming Obstacles to the Implementation of UDC and the Reasons for Communication Gaps (RQ 3.4)

The experts suggested a total of twelve approaches to overcoming the reasons for communication gaps obstacles to communication. We classified these approaches into three categories: user-centered approaches, developer-centered approaches, and organizational approaches. We mapped them to the identified reasons for communication gaps and organizational obstacles wherever possible and identified similar approaches from the literature (chapter 3.7.) (see **Table 11**).

We placed five ideas into the category of user-centered approaches. The first idea is to show the users prototypes (often called "proofs of concept"). One expert described a successful project in which the software was highly complex, so the project members wrote down all requirements in large workshops and then invited two vendors to build prototypes before the design and implementation activity began. The users were highly involved in this activity, as the vendors presented the status of the prototype in regular meetings with them. At the end of the proof-of-concept activity, a prototype that demonstrated about 80 percent of the system's functionality, had been built and was aligned with the users' needs. The vendor selected for implementation could proceed with implementing the rest of the requirements, integrating the prototypes into the system's landscape, and building the data structures. Even though this is a promising approach, the expert mentioned that it would be difficult to implement in LSI projects like an ERP implementation because those systems' functionality is too wide for a prototype approach. Nevertheless, two other experts suggested showing users mockups or even integrating users as beta customers into the software development process by showing them running prototypes. The idea of using prototypes is not new and has been described in the literature (e.g., Cohen et al., 2010; Dean et al., 1998; Humayoun et al., 2011). However, the detailed description of how such an approach was used in a real-life IT project can be helpful for the research community to understand the implementation in a real-world project.

Another suggested approach, one that is similar to the prototype approach, is to do house tours with running software. The difference from the proof of concept approach is that, after about half of the actual implementation time, the project team presents the running software to business units and users. This approach allows small, timely changes to be made to the system based on user feedback and helps to manage users' expectations. Kautz (2011) and Martin et al. (2010) described a similar approach as "road shows" and suggested having onsite users conduct them with other users.

One approach to overcome the lack of common language between business and IT was to explain the added value of the system to the users by means of posters, result descriptions, and meetings with the users.

One expert also mentioned including users in the rollout and change management planning process, which would integrate users more closely into the project. We could not identify a similar approach in the literature, so these may be new ideas that would be particularly useful in the design of a new method.

Table 11: Ideas for Overcoming Obstacles to Communication and Reasons for Communication Gaps

Category	Ideas (Descriptive Code)	# of Instances	Literature	ID	Reason/Obstacle Addressed
User-centered approaches	Developer presents user interface prototypes or proofs of concept to users.	3	Cohen et al., 2010; Dean et al., 1998; Humayoun et al., 2011	O2	Difficult to get the right user representatives for LSI projects
	Developer holds house tours in business units with running software.	1	Kautz, 2011; Martin et al., 2010	F2	Lack of common language between business and IT
	Developer describes added value to users to increase acceptance.	1	n/a		
	Developer provides incentive system for the participation of business users.	1	Finck et al., 2004	F1	Lack of motivation among developers or users
				O2	Difficult to get the right user representatives for LSI projects
	Developer involves users in the organization of rollout and change management.	1	n/a	O2	Difficult to get the right user representatives for l projects
Developer-centered approaches	Developers mediate between user groups.	2	Eckhardt, 2010	O1	Differing opinions between user groups
				O4	Lack of local mediators
				F2	Lack of common language between business and IT
				F3	Lack of appreciation between business and IT
	Developers take end-to-end feature responsibility.	1	n/a	F2	Lack of common language between Business and IT

	Developer writes informal description of how to implement requirements.	1	n/a	
	Developer justifies all technical decisions with functional need.	1	n/a	
Organizational approaches	Developer uses test data early in the project.	2	Teixeira et al., 2011	n/a
	Developer uses agile methods like frequent review meetings.	2	e.g., Kautz, 2011; Korkala et al., 2010	
	Developer defines usability guidelines to avoid detailed user interface discussions.	1	n/a	

The last suggestion in the user-centered category, to create an incentive system for business users, had been in the mind of one of our interview partners for years. The expert wants to overcome the users' lack of motivation and the difficulty in getting the right user representatives. In the expert's opinion, one issue is that users are not rewarded by promotions or increased pay for working IT projects in addition to their usual daily work. This lack of appreciation leads to low interest and low involvement on the part of the user. Finck et al. (2004) presented a similar idea in suggesting an incentive system for the software evolution activity after the system's first rollout.

Four ideas were suggested in the category of developer–centered approaches. Especially in response to the obstacle of differing opinions between user groups, two experts recommended that developers mediate between user groups. As the opinions of user groups (e.g., the finance and the marketing department) often differ, the developers must solve the resulting communication gap by helping to resolve their disagreement.

One interview partner referred to the lack of appreciation between business and IT and the lack of common language between business and IT by explaining that "most (non-IT) users do not think in structures.... Thus, the IT personnel need to learn to talk in examples to explain their structure, even though it is not relevant to them." Therefore, this expert suggests always having someone in the project who has experience with the to-be-implemented business domain to fulfill the mediator role. The general idea of clarifying roles and mediators is described in the literature (e.g. Eckhardt, 2010), but the idea to assign this role to a developer is new. To address the lack of common language between business and IT, one expert suggested giving end-to-end feature responsibility for each developer; that is, you do not need a developer who is responsible for one technical crossover area, such as database or user interface (UI), but a developer who is responsible for the implementation of one use case, including the UI, the business logic, the database, and the interfaces.

A similar approach is to oblige the developer to write an informal description of how to implement a given requirement so the users can understand information related to implementation. This informal description must be aligned with the users before the implementation begins. Doing so would also help to mitigate all four of the consequences of communication gaps delineated above. In order to address the lack of a common language, developers could justify all technical decisions with a functional need. For example, the need for another database could be justified only because it provides a higher service level for the business unit, not because of a developer's narcissistic technical preferences. Three of the developer-centered approaches have not yet been described in the UPI literature, so these suggestions should be part of future work on methods to improve UDC.

Three ideas were offered in the category of organizational approaches. The use of test data early in the software development process gives users a chance to challenge the logic and the quality of the system. One expert suggested using extreme test data to provoke situations where complications can occur, while another suggested having usability tests with real data as early as possible in a large-scale IT project, which Teixeira et al. (2011) also suggested.

Another suggested approach was to use agile methods, such as weekly or monthly meetings (often called sprint meetings) with user representatives. However, the same expert reported that such meetings had not been a success, which the expert attributed to the too finely grained level of the meetings (on the bug-tracker level), which was too detailed for the users, whose attention wandered quickly. These meetings had been held via telephone conference, which the expert indicated was not the ideal setting, as many participants did not pay attention in the long meetings. The literature has described agile methods, including a high level of feedback from the users, extensively (e.g., Kautz, 2011; Korkala et al., 2010).

In addition, one expert mentioned that, while it is important to involve users by offering workshops or showing them prototypes, they should also get clear guidelines for the UI, as several unnecessary discussions about screen details occur in meetings with users. The expert also mentioned that the lack of such guidelines this can have negative implications for the project.

We conclude that the experts' ideas address all of the reasons for communication gaps (F1 – F3) and all of the organizational obstacles (O1, O2, O4), except obstacle O3, the lack of access to users. Even so, the experts did not report a successful, sustainable solution to overcome the communication gaps in LSI projects, particularly in the design and implementation phase.

4.7. Threats to Validity

We analyzed threats to validity based on the scheme suggested by Runeson et al. (2012).

Construct validity – As described in the research method section (chapter 4.5.), the interviews were semi-structured so the interviewees and the interviewer could influence the direction of the discussion, rather than being tied to an explicit list of questions. Eight interviews were conducted via telephone, which excludes the possibility of interpreting visual cues. We mitigate the threat that we would not be able to understand the experts fully. We mitigated that threat by recording the so we could replay them in the case of poor acoustic reception.

Internal validity – We relied on our personal relationships to identify the experts, an approach that can present a threat to internal validity. However, only three of the experts knew the interviewer before the interviews.

External validity – A possible threat to external validity is that we interviewed only twelve experts. However, the experts' backgrounds covered a broad range, and all had been involved in at least two LSI projects. Therefore, we are confident that our results show a broad overview of communication structures in LSI projects and can be transferred to other projects outside the experience of our interviewees.

Reliability – One person conducted the interviews and performed their coding. This approach ensured the consistency of the interviews and their analysis, but it can also be a threat to the reliability, as another researcher could interpret the results differently.

4.8. Summary of the State of Practice

In this chapter, we reported on the results of an interview series with experienced practitioners in LSI projects. We conducted twelve semi-structured interviews, transcribed them, and coded them with descriptive codes based on our research questions. Our experts described experiences from sixty-nine diverse LSI projects. In the context of our larger research on UDC in LSI projects, we sought to determine how and how well LSI projects support UDC.

With regard to current communication structures in LSI projects, the results of the study indicate that **most LSI projects feature no direct communication between developers and users.** The experts described some setups for communication with the users, such as communication between IT consultants and users, but none of these setups focuses on our research target, the design and implementation activity.

The obstacles for implementation and reasons for communication gaps that the experts identified (e.g., lack of motivation on the part of users and/or developers and lack of a common language for business and IT) **are in line with the literature** (Harris & Weistroffer, 2009; Bjarnason et al., 2011). However, the experts stated that there was a clear connection between communication gaps and increased implementation costs and required effort for testing.

We classified the experts' ideas for overcoming the obstacles to communication into **user-centered approaches** (e.g., show users prototypes), **developer-centered approaches** (e.g., have developers mediate between user groups), and **organizational approaches** (e.g., use test data early in the project). Some of the suggestions have also been described in the literature, b ut the detailed descriptions of successful setups in LSI projects and the developer-centered approaches have implications for future work. The experts did not report on any successful, sustainable solutions that would overcome the communication gaps in LSI projects, particularly solutions that would improve UDC in the design and implementation activity.

In order to figure out what needs to be communicated to the users, i.e. the user-relevant decisions; we present a descriptive classification including examples in the next chapter of this thesis.

Chapter 5
A Descriptive Classification of User-Relevant Decisions in Large-Scale IT Projects

"The most difficult thing is the decision to act. The rest is merely tenacity."

Amelia Earhart

5.1. Abstract

Context: As we find out in the expert interviews, LSI projects with traditional development methods remain common in practice. Most of these projects involve the user in the beginning and at the end of the development, but here are also user-relevant decisions in the phases in between.

Objective: The objective is to determine what decisions are made and which are user-relevant. This chapter presents and validates our classification based on the TORE method and collects exemplary user-relevant decisions by experts in LSI projects.

Method: We conducted an interview series with twelve experts.

Results: The interviews confirmed that our classification is comprehensive and helpful in structuring decisions and also offered several amendments. The examples the experts provided led to a comprehensive list of user-relevant decisions and our descriptive classification.

5.2. Introduction

This chapter investigates the details of user-relevant decisions. Many user-relevant decisions are made in the design and implementation phases of projects that use traditional software development methods, so communication between users and IT personnel should be enhanced in those phases.

We argue that a user-relevant decision is a trigger point from which to start communication, so we use the term *trigger point* for user-relevant decisions in this chapter. To the best of our knowledge, no other research has addressed what user-relevant decisions are made during the design and implementation phases or when it is useful to trigger communication with users. Therefore, we developed a classification for trigger points based on the Task-Oriented Requirement Engineering (TORE) method (Paech & Kohler, 2004). We presented this approach and validate the classification with experts in this chapter.

The chapter is structured as follows. Chapter 5.3 outlines the research questions. Chapter 5.4 presents the initially developed classification. Chapter 5.5. presents the enhanced classification, while chapter 5.6. reports on the results of the expert interviews. We conclude with a summary in chapter 5.7. This chapter is based on the author's peer-reviewed publication (Abelein & Paech, 2013a), which is not referenced in the chapter to enhance readability.

5.3. Research Questions for the Descriptive Classification

Many user-relevant decisions are made in the design and implementation phases. In seeking how to ensure helpful communication between users and IT personnel in these phases, we answer the following research questions:

RQ 4 - What are user-relevant decisions in the design and implementation phases?
- RQ 4.1 – How useful is the suggested classification of user-relevant decisions?
- RQ 4.2 – What decisions made by IT project members are relevant to users?

In order to answer the two research questions (RQ 4.1 and RQ 4.2), we conducted semi-structured interviews with twelve experts in LSI projects with various backgrounds. The interviews showed the general usefulness of the classification, which we adapted throughout the interviews based on feedback from the interviewees. We also collected a list of eighty-one exemplary decisions. The validated classification and the exemplary decisions form the descriptive classification.

5.4. Background

Our classification of user-relevant decisions regarding the translation of user requirements into a technical specification is based on the TORE method (Paech & Kohler, 2004). Using this method, we defined sixteen implicit or explicit decisions regarding the system's behavior. We group the decisions into four abstraction levels: *The task level* consists of decisions about the roles and tasks the system will support. *The domain level* includes decisions about the activities the system will support and the domain data that is relevant for these activities. *The interaction level* refers to decisions about the distribution of activities between humans and computers that are aligned with decisions on the UI structure. Finally, *the system level* concerns decisions about the internals of the application core and the graphical user interface (GUI). The task level requires only one decision about user roles and their task, while the domain level comprises four decisions: determination of the relevant as-is activities, definition of to-be activities, system responsibilities (here we will use the more prominent term, system "feature"), and decisions on the relevant domain data. The interaction level also has four decisions concerning system functions, user-system interaction, interaction data for input and output of the system and structure of the UI. Finally, the system level has two decision clusters, one on the core application (high-level application architecture, internal system actions, and internal system data) and one on the GUI (navigation and support functions, dialog interaction, detailed UI-data, and screen structure). We use the outlined decisions to structure our classification.

5.5. A Classification with Which to Structure User-Relevant Decisions

In a first step, which content is important for the user—the reasonable points at which to start communication, i.e. a *trigger point*—should be identified. Those trigger points can be decisions made in the translation or changes on agreed user requirements. As shown in **Table 12**, the trigger points correspond to a subset of the TORE decisions, so they can be aligned to the TORE levels. As we focus not only on software development but also on project management, we extend the trigger points to the project level (including decisions regarding the project's cost, schedule, and scope). In order to cover all decisions in a project, we also introduce the business process level, which is comprised of decisions about the functionality and features of business processes. The trigger points vary with roles and occasions, so, we use an RACI (R–Responsible, A–Approved, C–Consulted, I–Informed) matrix (Hallows, 2002). A RACI matrix is a tool to analyses and present responsibilities for different roles, thus there is one or many roles that are responsible, needed for approval, needed to be consulted or informed. For our approach of UDC we developed a RACI matrix with the abstraction levels and trigger points and the involved roles. Regarding the roles, we focus on users and their management. Developers take responsibility (R) for all decisions listed in **Table 12** (one exception can be cost allocations, which is explained below), but this is not mentioned explicitly in **Table 12**. We also do not list an "I" for a role if the role is consulted (C) or approved (A), as approval and consultation requires information in advance.

Table 12: RACI Matrix for Responsibilities

Abstraction level	Trigger points regarding	Users' managers	Users	IT personnel
Project level	Cost allocation	(R),A,C	I	R
	Timing (go-live dates)	A	C	R
Business process level	Business processes	A	C	R
Task level	Responsibilities of the users	A	C	R
Domain level	To-be activities	I	A,C	R
	Features	I	A,C	R
	Domain data	I	A,C	R
Interaction level	Workflow	-	A,C	R
	UI (incl. I/O)	-	A,C	R
System level	Technology	(A), C	I	R

As summarized in **Table 12**, changes in cost are relevant to management, as, depending on the project structure (e.g., the. budget for system development is directly paid by the business unit), managers may be directly responsible for costs. Therefore, they should always be consulted and approve changes that affect costs. We suggest also informing users so they understand resulting changes, but as they are not directly involved, there is no need to consult them or get their approval. Management should also approve changes in timelines, business processes, or user responsibilities, but most of the issues require input from the user. Changes on the domain level require domain knowledge in order to ensure that consequences are recognized, so the user should approve them; management should be informed in order to avoid problems, but there is no need to consult managers, as they will not be interested in this level of detail. The same is true on the interaction level, as changes in UI or workflows are not relevant for management; they should be approved by the users, and as these changes should not have other dependencies, there is no need to inform the management. Changes or decisions regarding technology should be discussed with the management, and depending on the governance structure, they might need approval from management. Decisions on the system level can have consequences on other levels, so we suggest informing the users. We assume that GUIs are designed in concert with the users, so they do not need additional communication about these changes. We assume that all other changes in technical details are not relevant to the users or their management.

The granularity level for communication with the user is given through the abstraction levels of TORE. We assume that most discussions will be on the domain level (e.g., changes to features) or on the levels above the task level, such as the task, business process, or project levels. However, for changes in workflows or UI (e.g., UI structure), we have to step down to the interaction level. Furthermore, how the results of the decisions (content) and the changes that result from them can be communicated to the user must be determined. We suggest using the existing documentation to represent the content and highlighting the changes in the documentation.

A list of possible representation models for each level is provided in (Paech & Kohler, 2004).

5.6. Results of the Expert Interview Series

This chapter presents the validation of the classification and its extension with examples from the interviews, which together build the descriptive classification. In the interviews we presented the RACI matrix (**Table 12**), with one example for each trigger point and ask the experts interview questions 9. - 13. (see Appendix II). The research methodology we use, as well as the identification and base data of the interview series, is outlined in chapter 0.The threats to validity are presented in chapter 4.7.**5.6.1. Validation of the Classification (RQ 4.1)**

Nine of the twelve experts (75%) stated that they consider the classification valid and comprehensive. Of the remaining three, one did not comment on the classification; one suggested another structure with business, application, and infrastructure levels; and the third had issues with the trigger points on the project level because this expert's company is organized so decisions on the project level are targeted to another central department that is not connected with the users. Still, a majority of our interviewees validated the classification.

One aspect of the abstraction levels that was discussed in several interviews was whether it is reasonable to combine the business process and task levels into one abstraction level. Four of the twelve interview partners suggested combining them because these two levels are closely connected or may not even be able to be considered independently. However, two experts argued strongly against combining them, reasoning that the business process level regards changes in business concerns and the task level represents the system's perspective. As there was no mutual agreement, we decided to keep the original four levels.

One expert suggested combining the task, domain, and interaction levels in one application level. As none of the other experts made a similar suggestion, we also set this suggestion aside. Another expert commented that some decisions are not strictly confined to one level but produce trigger points on several levels (e.g., which technology is used is important on the system level but also on the project level, as it influences costs and timing, and it could have an influence on the business process level, as it might cause the system to work differently). Even though this observation is correct, it is useful to have separate abstraction levels in order to support users, IT personnel, and project management in LSI projects, so we set this suggestion aside as well (see chapter 7.4. for more details on the use cases).

Finally, one interview partner suggested that decisions on the project level should not be communicated to the user but to a steering committee. This suggestion is addressed by our RACI matrix approach (**Table 12**), which also suggests that the users' managers approve these decisions. The same interview partner also suggested that trigger points on the system level not be communicated, as the tool stack (i.e., which frameworks and platform to build upon) should be fixed, but the interviewee also admitted that this issue is highly specific to his company. In addition, the fact that we identified eight examples of decisions in this category shows that there are decisions that concern the user.

The interviews produced three suggestions regarding the categories of trigger points, which we integrated into the classification. First, the trigger points regarding cost allocation and timing on the project level should cover project not only costs or go-live dates but also cost and timing implications for the operation of the to-be-developed system. Second, two experts suggested including a third category, organization/skills, on the project level. They reported that decisions often influence the organization, such as on testers or skills that are required for the new system's operation. Third, two interview partners suggested including system interfaces on the interaction level. Their experience is that many trigger points that concern related systems can be relevant to the user (i.e. concerning how many systems they need to use in parallel).

5.6.2. List of Examples (RQ 4.2)

To answer RQ 4.2, we collected examples of decisions (i.e., trigger points) from LSI projects in practice. Classifying all examples with respect to their abstraction levels and trigger point category enabled us to create a descriptive classification, which is presented in

Table 13. We collected eighty-one examples from our interviews and formatted them in a schema with context (C) (if the context was named in the interview), decision (D), and Impact (I). This approach helped us to classify the example in the category where the decision had the highest impact. We assigned the letters A-L to our twelve interview partners and assigned each example to interviewee who provided it using the corresponding letter. The number of examples per trigger point category varies from two to twelve. Experts gave an average of between 6 and 7 examples, which is another indicator that the classification is helpful to structure trigger points in LSI projects.

A more detailed look at the examples revealed seven reoccurring topics:
- *License cost:* In the cost allocation category, license cost, including the tradeoff discussion about open source vs. proprietary software, was named three times.
- *Staffing for test:* The newly integrated trigger point category, with implications on organization and skill, revealed that staffing for tests is a common discussion topic in projects.
- *Standard central processes:* On the business process level, the topic of standard processes, which often suggests central handling of process steps, was named four times.
- *Access rights and automation of approvals:* On the task level, four experts named access rights and automation of approvals.

- *Manual vs. automated activities:* On the domain level, manual vs. automated activities is a common topic discussed with users.
- *Infeasible user requirements:* Concerning the category features, four interviewees mentioned that user requirements that are not feasible primarily because of their complexity should be discussed with users.
- *Support of user devices*: On the system level, the topic of supported user devices was named three times.

As described in the research method chapter 4.5., we answered the interview questions twelve and thirteen indirectly based on whether an expert was able to name an example (Appendix II). A summary of the number of examples is given in

Table 13. On the project level, nine experts used cost allocation, and ten experts used timing. Only four experts gave examples for the organization and skills category, perhaps because it is a new category. On the business process and task levels, nine experts named an example. For the domain level, twelve experts used the feature category, so it seems to be the most important category to be discussed with the users. The other two categories (to-be activities and domain data) seem to be less important than features, as only six and four experts, respectively, named examples. On the interaction level, decisions on workflows seem to be common, as the experts named five examples. The UI category received only four examples, and only two experts had examples for the other new category, system interfaces. Finally, seven experts named an example for the technology level.

Table 13: Descriptive Classification of User-Relevant Decisions

Abstr. level	Project level		
Trigger points	Cost allocation (project and operations)	Timing (project and operations)	Organization/Skills (suggestion of expert)
Interview examples from experts	• D: new system requires new hardware. I: increase in operating and hardware costs (B) • D: use of new base technology (i.e., use of open source software) I: increase in project cost (especially in case of a time and material contract), but decrease in license cost (C) • D: support of several application server platforms I: increased maintenance and operation cost (C) • C: travel booking system D: when is the right time to access an external vacancy database (e.g. early or only at the end of the order) I: massive influence on operating costs (E) • C: CRM telecommunication contract system D: flexibility of promotions for contracts (i.e., adaptable from the business team or	• C: customized HR of a standard system D: prolongation of project plans (often foreseen by project team) kept hidden until the last moment before telling users I: System could not be tested before planned to go live (B) • C: large projects with waves of implementation D: IT project teams change orders of features or cut down features I: features are available at times other than the user expected (D) • D: no implementation of temporary access rights for proxies in case of vacation and illness, because of complexity I: leads to a delay of one year (D) • D: no detailed data checks (e.g., compulsory date	• D: change of implementation order of features x and y I: changes in test schedule, so changes for testers (i.e., users) (C)) • D: changes in timing with effect on testing

	need to change system configuration) I: large implementation cost implications (F) • D: no need for proprietary software (e.g., use of open source enterprise service bus) I: reduced license cost (H) • C: management information system D: fix a serious performance issue in underlying systems that is due to a missing definition of non-functional requirements I: required complete new infrastructure and, therefore, large investments (L) • D: use of proprietary components (e.g.. data bases or servers instead of open source) I: changes in licenses and tools cost and cost of internal IT (J) • D: strategic decision from IT to use a two-vendor strategy to prevent dependence on one vendor I: additional cost but no implication for the user (K)	field could have been empty in the old system) I: leads to serious project delays (D) • C: telecommunication systems with critical time-to-market business opportunities D: decide on an interim "quick and dirty" solution I: reduced quality of features and need to allocate resources for next phase (F) • D: support for old systems ends I: prologues project, as system needs to be replaced (G) • D: software from third parties delayed I: system delays are due to waiting time on third-party system (H) • C: ERP system D: adaptations of original template for some business units I: changes in roll-out alter the whole project plan (J) • D: architectural changes (e.g., refactoring, improvement in maintainability) I: leads to delays of 3-4 months and is difficult to discuss with users (K) • D: refactoring phase after	and marketing I: require different business expertise skills for project and operations (E) • C: insurance industry (with seasonal business) D: changes in project schedule I: requires early communication to all stakeho

		first go-live I: delays in roadmap (L)	lder (G) • D: delay in testing I: influences the need for business employees (L)
Count	9	10	4

Abstraction level	Business process level	Task level
Trigger points	Business processes	Responsibility of the users
Interview examples from experts	• C: standard ERP system D: use efficient standard central dunning process I: change to central instead of local dunning process (B) • D: integrate a content management system (CMS) function within a larger system I: changed business process, as user needed to use only one system instead of two (C) • D: use standard incoming payments process (including one chart of accounts) for all	• D: centralized invoice process I: took responsibility for printing and mailing invoices from branch employees (B) • D: automatic validation checks from a legacy health care system cannot be implemented in the new system I: users now need to implement a new process to check the validity of input (e.g., double entry) (D) • D: use own user management instead of single-sign-on solution

subsidiaries of a company I: subsidiaries with differing payment process need to change them (E) • C: CRM system in telecommunication that combines landline and mobile contracts D: missing definition of IT architecture I: business processes need to be altered to enable the possibility to see both contracts from one customer (F) • C: information system in insurance industry D: use standard business processes (e.g., what is a lead for an insurance sale) I: process steps change after an object is a lead (G) • D: use a standard process I: two or three departments required to adapt process (H) • D: use different IT architectures in different business units I: prevention of harmonization of companywide business processes (J) • C: processes-efficient industries (e.g., banking) D: have two more clicks in the process through introduction of SEPA I: users denied change, as	I: business side needs to maintain 120,000 new users (D) • D: decide that shipping order can be changed after initial entry only by manager roles I: control of shipping order is no longer with the standard user (E) • C: information system in the insurance industry that is accessed by self-employed salespeople D: all users have access rights to additional customer data I: self-employed salespeople need to share their additional knowledge (G) • D: decide to no longer have the possibility to change documents before printing I: user can no longer do final corrections (I) • D: implement new mandatory check in the system if material is really available I: blue-collar workers in production need to check in new system (J) • D: define roles that have rights to insert changes in the FAQs I: not all users can access FAQs later (K) • C: Information system in the insurance industry D: implement automated approval of risk assessment I: user no longer has responsibility for the check (L)

	this summed up to two additional employees in efforts (K) • C: insurance industry D: introduction of PostIdent I: leads to changes in business processes, as users need to include manual steps (L)	
Count	9	9

Abstraction level	Domain level		
Trigger points	To-be activities	Features	Domain data
Interview examples from experts	• D: no testing and communication of performance requirements (not defined in requirements phase) I: printing took two minutes instead of milliseconds before (B) • D: new data security regulations prohibited sending passwords via email I: new manual steps from the business side was required (C) • C: CRM system in the call center D: automatic assignment of queues I: employees no longer get to choose (even though it's a limited choice that is relevant to them and their motivation) (G) • D: which steps are covered by the system vs. remaining manual (e.g., calculations for tax evaluations) I: algorithm calculations can have	• D: no implementation of features for specific user groups (e.g., deal calculation for researchers) I: researcher cannot calculate deals (A) • C: ERP system in the retail industry D: implement auto-disposition of orders to improve sales condition instead of possibility to complete orders every day I: employees in shops were trained to order on specific days, while the old feature needed to be implemented additionally (B) • C: ERP system in the retail industry D: gift baskets could not be charged by commission • I: gift baskets can be paid only directly at a cashier (B) • D: support of all possible browsers is not realizable I: use only by supported browsers (C) • D: no implementation of transferability to other system (e.g., contact in Microsoft Outlook and Apple iPad) I: user has to maintain multiple contacts (E) • D: implementation of only one	• D: SAP standard system did not allow 20-digit account numbers • I: dismissal of SAP for accounting system (E) • D: extend order form with more data (e.g., price or conditions of contract) I: more details availabl

	incorrect output and require manual correction, which may take longer than the initial manual input (H) • D: no implementation of automatic email distribution for the mailing list I: activity no longer available for user (K) • D: include manual, as dependencies of backbone systems can lead to a system that IT cannot maintain I: user needs to perform manual steps, such as printing (K)	payment option for additional mobile packages abroad I: user can use only one payment option (F) • C: online web system for sales in insurance • D: no implementation of offline functionality I: system is not usable, as sales employees sometimes have no internet access (G) • D: have direct data base input and no UI for workflow with only ten cases p.a. I: difficult user experience (H) • D: no support of multiple languages or no currency support I: all users need to work in one language and currency (I) • C: user requirement requested to know who was at an ATM when it failed D: not possible in system failure I: feature neglected (K) • D: build feature only for online version I: features not available for internal clerk (L) • D: support only one bank account in the system I: users could change only their main bank accounts instead of individual bank accounts per contract (L)	e for user (F) • D: input for system parameters (e.g., "Sterbetafel" in insurance systems) can only be filled with SQL statements I: changes in user experience (H) • C: new products for insurance system D: new data structure and input fields required I: user needs to input more

Count		6	12		4 data (L)
Abstraction level	Interaction level				System level
Trigger points	Workflow		Technology	System Interface (suggested by expert)	Technology
	• C: System in the public sector, where users have been trained on new workflows • D: roll-out without real workflow and use direct entries in the data base, as implementation time was too short I: users' workflows differ (B) • D: Change to workflow of standard SAP solution I: Required two		• D: use user devices for services employees with GPS tracking I: no communication of that feature leads to worker council's request to turn out function (B) • D: no support of iPads because of use of standard calendar package I: user cannot use iPads (C) • D: Upgrade ORACLE systems I: fulfillment of	• D: all decisions that influence other systems in the IT landscape • I: have implications for the business side (E) C: Call center D: decide how many systems are used in parallel I: call center employees need to know how many systems (L)	• D: use user devices for services employees with GPS tracking I: no communication of that feature leads to workers council's request to turn out function (B) • D: no support of iPads because of use of standard calendar package

	clicks instead of one, which influenced resource demand if 100,000 service employees do the process 10 times a day (D) • C: travel booking system D: decide on order of transactions (e.g., flight, hotel, rental car) I: significant influence on rollback effort (E) • D: invoices of the contract were included in online portal (instead of PDF attachment in emails) I: user can see all contract data, etc. (F) • D: Implement a workflow for German power users with an efficient way to do data entry I: not usable in the US, where users need a lot of drop-down	users' service level agreements (F) • D: use specific front-end technology (e.g., HTML5) I: performance might significantly drop in cases of slow internet connection (G) • D: implement data security requirement for tablet PCs I: use of tablet PCs is possible (H) • D: use of a light or a fat client as user device I: different user experience (J) • D: support of OSs and/or user devices (e.g., tablets or switch from Blackberry to android devices) I: determines which devices users can use (L)		I: user cannot use iPads (C) • D: upgrade ORACLE systems I: fulfillment of users' SLAs (F) • D: use specific front-end technology (e.g., HTML5) I: performance might significantly drop in cases of slow internet connection (G) • D: implement data security requirement for tablet PCs I: use of tablet PC is possible (H)

	menus (J)			
Count	5	4	2	7

5.7. Summary of the Descriptive Classification

This chapter reported on the descriptive classification of trigger points. We proposed a classification based on TORE and conducted an interview series with twelve experts to determine what decisions in LSI projects are user-relevant and to extend our classification to a descriptive classification. The expert interviews provided eighty-one examples of trigger points. From these examples we derived seven common discussion topics with users: license cost, staffing for test, standard central processes, access rights and automation of approvals, manual vs. automated activities, infeasible user requirements, and support of user devices.

Eight of twelve experts considered the suggested classification to be valid, while the remaining four did not have strong arguments against it but suggested changes. The analysis showed that the experts use most of the trigger points, as they were able to name examples.

After understanding the state of the art and the state of practice, as well as user-relevant decisions, we present next the thereof derived requirements of the UDC-LSI methods.

PART III
TREATMENT DESIGN

Chapter 6
Requirement for the UDC-LSI Method

"How wonderful it is that nobody needs to wait a single moment before starting to improve the world."

Anne Frank

6.1. Abstract

Context: As we find out in the expert interviews, LSI projects with traditional development methods remain common in practice. Furthermore there are user-relevant decisions that are trigger points to start communication with users.

Objective: The objective is to define requirements for the newly designed UDC-LSI method.

Method: We build a conceptual framework and define requirements for the method based on the guidelines of Wieringa (2012).

Results: We defined a conceptual framework, based on UDC, software activity, project context, and system success. Furthermore, we identified three requirements (LSI Project, customer-specific software development, low level of UDC) for the UDC-LSI method. Finally, we describe the transfer from exiting results to the design of the UDC-LSI method.

6.2. Introduction

This chapter describes the requirements and the design process of the UDC-LSI method. We first present a conceptual framework, including the population and affected stakeholders (Wieringa, 2012a). Finally, we describe how we transferred the findings from existing solutions and interview to the parts and tasks of the UDC-LSI method.

As confirmed in the expert interviews, LSI projects often still use traditional software development methods (Alleman, 2002). LSI projects that use traditional software development methods seek to benefit from the advantages of these methods, such as high stability and clear agreements on price, timeline, and scope (see chapter 1.).

The interviews revealed consequences of communication gaps, such as misunderstanding of requirements, ad-hoc changes required because of unclear requirements, increased implementation costs, and increased testing effort because of reworks. Clearly, there is a need to improve communication between developers and users. To avoid these consequences, our approach addresses the lack of communication between developers and users (i.e., the communication gap).

The chapter is structured as follows. Chapter 6.3 presents the conceptual framework of the method. Chapter 6.4. describes requirements for the UDC-LSI method and chapter 6.5. presents the transfer from the findings of the systematic mapping study and expert interviews to the UDC-LSI method. We conclude with a summary in chapter 6.6.

6.3. Conceptual Framework of the UDC-LSI method

Here we define a conceptual model based on the guidelines of (Wieringa, 2012a). A conceptual model is a collection of concepts and their relations (Wieringa, 2012a). We build upon our findings from the meta-analysis (**Figure 9**) to define the desired effects of the UDC-LSI method. Increasing UDC will increase system success.

To model and measure communication, we build on the model of Mohr and Nevin (1990) (see chapter 2.1.). The hypothesis from Mohr and Nevin (1990) states that, "in mutually supportive and trusting climates (in comparison with unsupportive, distrustful climates) communication has: higher frequency, more bidirectional flows, more informal modes, more indirect content." Therefore, we assume that increased frequency, bidirectional flows, informal nodes, and indirect content increase the climate of support and trust in the project. To model system success, we build upon the aspects of system success we defined in chapter 3.6.1. Finally to describe the context factors for our method, we use software activities, focusing on the design and implementation activity. The project context is described by LSI projects that use traditional methods and develop customer-specific solutions (see **Figure 18**).

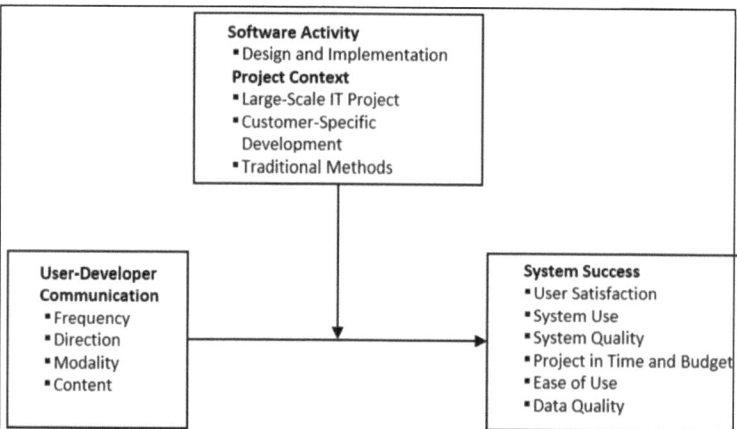

Figure 18: Conceptual Framework of the UDC-LSI Method

Therefore, we can define our **population** as LSI projects that use traditional methods in customer-specific software development with a low level of UPI.

We target three groups of **stakeholders**:

> **Business side**: This group is comprised of all users and their managers from the business organization that will be using the new system.
>
> **IT Personnel:** This group is comprised of all IT project members, such as designers, architects, and developers, including their managers, who are involved in the development project. However, we do not include those who are involved in the maintenance or operations of the system after its rollout, as these phases are not in focus for our method.
>
> **Project management:** This group is comprised of all project members whose main focus is on coordinating, organizing, and managing the LSI project.

6.4. Requirements for the UDC-LSI Method

The UDC-LSI method is defined for LSI projects, and its purpose is to improve system success by increasing UDC in the design and implementation phases. To identify an LSI project with issues in UDC for the evaluation, we defined three requirements:

- **Requirement 1 - LSI Project:** LSI projects are defined as having a large number of users (more than 1000 users), rolling out a system in multiple (minimum of three) countries or business units, having a large budget (1 million EUR), and/or having a project duration of at least one year.
- **Requirement 2 - Customer-specific software development:** We target projects that develop software that is specifically designed and programmed for an individual business organization, including projects that implement a high level of customization of standard software packages. Therefore, we do not target IT projects that develop market-driven software or end-consumer software for a mass market.
- **Requirement 3 - Low level of UDC:** We define UDC as all communication between the users (all users from the business organization who use the new system, including the users' manager) and the developers (all IT project members, including designers, architects, developers, and IT managers involved in the development project). We also include communication that is mediated through project management. Typically, projects that use traditional methods have a lower level of UDC. Traditional project management and software development methods, such as the waterfall model, are characterized by clear phases for the development (specification, design and implementation, validation and verification, rollout, and evolution). The advantages of these traditional methods are high stability and clear agreements, while the drawbacks are waiting periods between the

requirement definition and the system validation on the business side that are due to long development cycles. This waiting period reduces the level of UDC, but it should be possible to instantiate the methods in projects that use other development methods when there is a low level of UDC.

6.5. Findings from Interviews and Existing Methods

Through the interviews with experts (chapter 4.6.3.), we found that the reasons for communication gaps are lack of developers' or users' motivation, lack of a common language between business and IT, and lack of appreciation between business and IT. The expert interviews also revealed that there is no direct communication between developers and users in most LSI projects. Even though some setups for such communication have been described, none of them focuses on the design and implementation activity.

The UDC-LSI method focuses on communication of the reasons behind decisions made when developers refine user requirements into system requirements and/or code. Direct UDC (i.e., between developers and users) after the requirement definition and before verification and validation is an important part of the UDC-LSI method In order to define the UDC-LSI method, we used the some practices in the existing approaches we identified in our systematic mapping study (chapter 3.7.5.). **Table 14** provides an overview of these practices and the derived task and parts of the method (see **Figure 21**).

Several authors have suggested that identifying the right users, using stakeholder analysis, and keeping people informed are all relevant to adequate communication (Amoako-Gyampah & White, 1997; Kujala, 2008; Kamal et al., 2011; Begier, 2010a), so we used these suggestions to define the first part of the UDC-LSI method: "setup of communication structures." Kensing et al., (1998) stated that it is important to develop a vision of the overall change, which we included in the method's second part. Since it is important to use representatives to mediate communication, we defined a format for decision capture and requirements changes.

Table 14: Design of the UDC-LSI Method Based on Existing Solutions

Suggestion from existing solution (see	Tasks from method (see Figure 21)	Part
Identify the right users (Amoako-Gyampah & White, 1997; Kujala, 2008; Kamal et al., 2011).	Define user representatives.	1 – Set up the communication structure.
Perform stakeholder analysis (Kamal et al., 2011).	Map user requirements to representatives.	
Keep people informed and give them timely feedback (Amoako-Gyampah & White, 1997; Begier, 2010a).	Define notification preferences with representatives.	
Develop a vision of the overall change in design and have management and the steering committee, the technical and organizational implementation team, and the users anchor the vision (Kensing et al., 1998).	Develop the change story, including trigger points.	2 – Train developers on capturing decisions or changes.
Use shared representations to mediate communication between professional groups (Pries-Heje & Dittrich, 2009).	Develop a format to capture decisions.	
	Develop a repository that captures decisions.	
	Develop a format to capture changes in requirements.	
Keep people informed and give them timely feedback (Amoako-Gyampah & White, 1997; Begier, 2010a).	Map requirements to decisions and/or code	3 – Set up how decisions will be traced.
	Implement a process for notification (manual or tool).	

Collocate users and developers (Berger, 2011; Kautz, 2000).	Set up agendas for meetings with managers.	4 – Define the means of communication.
Have mid-iteration communication with users (i.e., face-to-face or meetings/video conferences (Korkala et al., 2006).	Set up agendas for workshops with representatives.	
Have weekly feedback meetings with onsite customers during working software presentations (Kautz, 2011).	Ensure notification about smaller decisions that affect representatives/managers.	
Keep people informed and give them timely feedback (Amoako-Gyampah & White, 1997; Begier, 2010a).	Set up a general information platform.	

Based on Amoako-Gyampah and White (1997) and Begier (2010b), the UDC-LSI method seeks to keep people informed and give them timely feedback, so we ensure that decisions can be a traced in the third part of the UDC-LSI method.

Finally, Korkala and colleagues (2006) and Kautz (2011) suggested mid-iteration communication with users, so it is important to define sophisticated means of communication.

We constructed the method based on existing theory and knowledge, but by defining a clear problem context that is not targeted by an existing method, the UDC-LSI method is fulfills the criteria of an innovative solution to a known problem (Hevner et al., 2004).

6.6. Summary of the Requirements for the UDC-LSI Method

In this chapter, we defined a conceptual framework based on the instructions of (Wieringa, 2012a). Therefore we describe a model based on UDC, software activity, project context, and system success.

Furthermore, we define three requirements (LSI Project, customer-specific software development, low level of UDC) for the UDC-LSI method. Finally, we describe the transfer from exiting results to the design of the UDC-LSI method.

Based on those findings, we describe the four parts of the UDC-LSI method in detailed in the following chapter.

Chapter 7
The UDC-LSI Method to Enhance User-Developer Communication in Large-Scale IT Projects

"I've learned that people will forget what you said, people will forget what you did, but people will never forget how you made them feel."

Maya Anglou

7.1. Abstract

Context: Based on the defined requirements: LSI Project, customer-specific software development, low level of UDC, as well as the findings from the interviews, we see a need for a method to enhance UDC in LSI projects.

Objective: The step in software development when developers translate (and interpret) user requirements into a technical specification (i.e., system requirements, architecture and models) is a critical one for user participation, as many decisions are made in this step, some of which should be communicated to the users. Therefore, we seek to document these decisions in order to increase UDC in the design and implementation phase of LSI projects.

Method: Based on the results on the proposed practices of exiting methods for UPI and the findings from the expert interviews, we created the UDC-LSI method to enhance communication between users and developers in the design and implementation phase of an LSI project and increase system success.

Results: We identified four parts—setup of communication structures, training of developers on capturing decisions or changes, setup of the traceability of decisions, and definition of the means of communication—that must be instantiated in order to implement the method.

7.2. Introduction

As described in chapter 2., we build this thesis on the TAR approach, which is based on design science. Design science "seeks to extend the boundaries of human and organizational capabilities by creating new and innovative artifacts" (Hevner et al., 2004). This process starts with an organizational problem to be solved and then designs an artifact to solve this problem. Wieringa and Moralı (2012) defined such an artifact as a method that interacts with a problem context. Therefore, a useful way to present a method is to describe the problem context, the conceptual framework (including concerned stakeholders), and the design process based on existing knowledge. This type of design uses an iterative build-and-evaluate loop (Hevner et al., 2004).

The results of our systematic mapping study help us to define the problem context. In particular, the meta-analysis showed that UPI has a positive effect on system success and is important to UDC. Therefore, we conclude that there is also a positive relationship between UDC and system success (chapter 3.6.6.). The analysis of current methods also showed a focus on UDC and that there is no particular method for increasing UDC in LSI projects. The expert interviews revealed no direct UDC in LSI projects. In addition, there is a clear connection from communication gaps to increased cost and effort, that is, to the project's being on time and on budget as criteria for system success.

This chapter presents the UDC in LSI projects (UDC-LSI) method to enhance communication in projects that use traditional methods in customer-specific software development. Furthermore, based on the results of the interviews, we developed use cases for three stakeholder groups (users, IT personnel, and project management) for the descriptive classification.

The chapter is structured as follows. Chapter 7.3. presents the general idea, as well as the four parts of the UDC-LSI method. Chapter 7.4. describes use cases of the descriptive classification, and chapter 7.5. concludes with a summary.

7.3. The UDC-LSI Method

As described in the chapter 5.4., the UDC-LSI method is designed for LSI projects, which use customer-specific software development, and have a low level of UDC.

The general idea of the UDC-LSI method is to improve the UDC in the design and implementation phase of a large-scale IT project through the two areas: documentation of user-relevant decisions, including IT personnel's decision rationales and structural communication of these decisions from IT personnel to users.

Therefore, a template for documentation of user-relevant decisions is required, an example of which is presented in **Figure 19**. Such a template should include general information about the project and the reporter; context information, such as the abstraction level and implications, based on the descriptive classification (chapter 5.5.); and a description of the decision.

Exemplary Template

General Information

ID:	0010	System:	XXX	Project:	XXX
Employee	M. Smith			Date:	06/30/2013

Context

User/System Requirement:	
Affected Business Area:	If known
Abstraction Level:	[Project, Process, Task...]
Implication:	[Cost, Responsibility, ...]

Decisions Description

Question:	
Description (incl. Alternatives):	
Assumption:	
Rationale:	
Implication:	

Figure 19: Exemplary Template for Documentation of Decisions

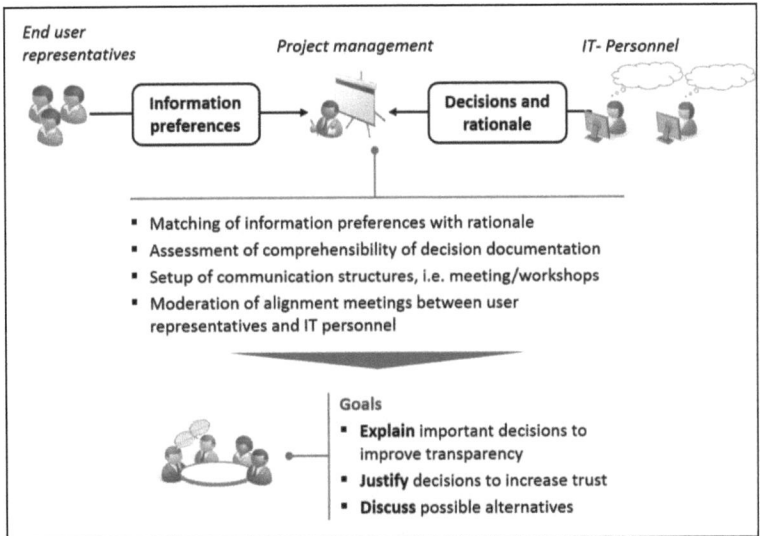

Figure 20: Conceptual Communication Process between User Representatives and IT Personnel

A communication process between user representatives and IT personnel should also be set up. A conceptual design of that communication process is presented in **Figure 20**. The main goal of the process is to ensure that decisions are explained and justified decisions and alternatives are discussed. The process should be guided by the project management, who is in charge of matching the notification preferences with rationales, assessing the comprehensiveness of the decision documentation, and setting up and moderating the meetings or workshops with user representatives and IT personnel.

However, the UDC-LSI method has four parts: 1 – set up communication structures, 2 – train developers on capturing decisions or changes, 3 – set up the decision traceability, and 4 – define the means of communication.

Each part has several tasks. We explain these parts and their tasks in detail in the following subsection.

An overview of the UDC-LSI method can be found in **Figure 21**

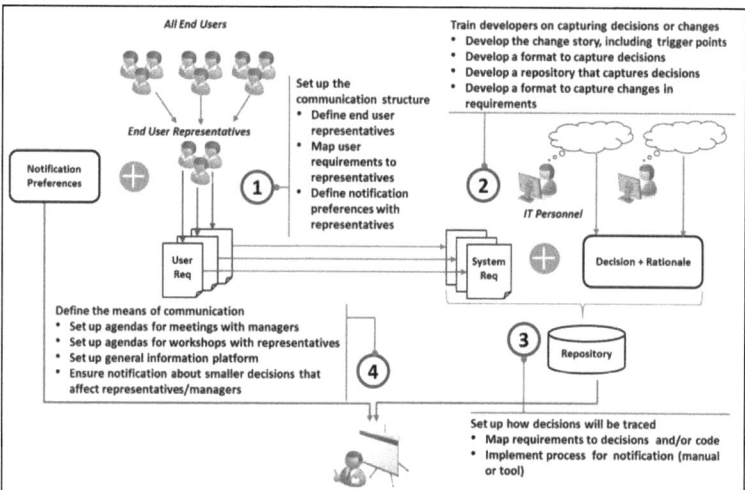

Figure 21: The Four Parts of the UDC-LSI method for User-Developer Communication

7.3.1. Part 1 – Set up the Communication Structure

As a first step in the first part, a project should define representatives for each 'class' of users, such as Ms. Smith for finance and Mr. Jones for marketing, because there are so many users in LSI projects that it is impossible to involve them all (Amoako-Gyampah & White, 1997; Kujala, 2008; Kamal et al., 2011). A helpful method can be a stakeholder analysis, which first step is to identify stakeholders that are involved in the project (Kamal et al., 2011). Then, the next step of stakeholder analysis is to map the user requirements to one or more end-user representatives in order to make clear who is concerned with changes or decisions (Kamal et al., 2011). Finally, the project defines notification preferences of information about user-relevant decisions with the user representatives to determine the desired level of abstraction and the frequency and type of communication. This is also suggested by (Amoako-Gyampah & White, 1997; Begier, 2010b).

7.3.2. Part 2 – Train Developers on Capturing Decisions or Changes

To develop a vision of the overall change is suggested by (Kensing et al., 1998). Thus, a project should develop a change story that explains the method's benefits to the developers (Aladwani, 2001) in order to motivate them to undertake the additional effort needed to capture the user-relevant decisions. The developers must also be trained to be aware of which of the decisions they make are relevant to the users. Therefore, it is helpful to explain typical decisions and examples, which will also help increase thinking "outside the developer's box." (See the descriptive classification use cases in chapter 7.4.)

Depending on the organization and the project setup, a project must develop a format for capturing decisions, such as the use of the Question Option Criteria Method (QOC) (MacLean et al., 1991), which phrases a decision as a question, defines options for solutions, rates them according to established criteria, and states reasons for the solution. In addition, a project must define a format for changes in requirements, for example by using different colors in use case diagrams, using "track changes" for documents, and/or showing differences in the prototype. Finally, a repository for decisions must be built. This repository can be a lightweight solution like a shared Excel file or Access database or a sophisticated tool. An example for implementing these tasks is given in our case study (see chapter 9.5.).

7.3.3. Part 3 – Set up How Decisions Will Be Traced

In order to be able to inform users about each decision and change should be mapped to a requirement such that the link from user representatives to user requirements is extended to system requirements and the user-relevant decisions. Thus, a project ensures that each user requirement is linked to all implementing system requirements and that the user requirements are updated throughout the project. A process that links each user-relevant decision to one or more system requirements is also required. According to our expert interviews, this is provided by most LSI projects (see chapter 8.4).

When decisions are traceable, the project can implement the notification process for users by means of either be a manual process to remind developers when communication is needed (e.g., project manager/controller checks decisions and notification preferences and sends a reminder to the developer) or a tool-supported process with automatic reminders. An example notification process can be seen in chapter 8.4.

7.3.4. Part 4 – Define the Means of Communication

Finally, the means of communication must be specified. According to the media richness theory (MRT), an activity that requires communication must be matched to the medium's ability to convey information (Dennis et al., 2008). Dennis and colleagues (2008) distinguished between uncertain communication and equivocal communication. Equivocal tasks should be managed by rich communication channels, whereas standard data can be handled by leaner channels. Based on the MRT, face-to-face communication is the richest channel. Videoconferencing is a bit leaner, but it restricts some visual cues. The telephone cannot transmit visual cues, but instant feedback is possible. Email has the lowest richness, so it is a good fit for communicating well-understood issues (Dennis et al., 2008).

Therefore, based on the MRT, in-person meetings with users or users' managers should be held whenever possible (Dennis et al., 2008), preferably using a fixed agenda. In these meetings the most important decisions made since the last meeting, along with any impact on the project's timing and budget, should be explained. Users who do not attend the meetings should be informed about its outcomes.

We also suggest that projects conduct workshops with the user representatives to answer questions related to the status of the project, decisions made, and why they were made. Managers should be notified of these workshops.

Finally, the documented decisions and changes should be used to enhance the project's transparency, so we suggest setting up a general information platform, such as a Wiki or a shared document that contains all decisions of a project. Users who are not user representatives can use this information platform to get information about the project or after the project is finished to find out why decisions were made.

7.3.5. Operationalization

During the process of finding a case company to instantiate the UDC-LSI method in a real-world project, we communicated the method in several proposals. During this process we realized that the structure of the four parts is difficult for practitioners to understand, but the parts and related tasks are required for an operationalization of the UDC-LSI method.

Table 15: Approach to Operationalizing the UDC-LSI Method

Area	Question	Criteria	Part of Method
Documentation of user-relevant decisions	Which decisions should be documented?	User-relevant decisions	-
	How will decisions be captured?	Format	Part 2
	Where will decisions be captured?	Tool	Part 2

	How can traceability of decisions be ensured?	Traceability	Part 3
Structural communication with users	Which users will be integrated in the project?	User representatives	Part 1
	When will users be integrated in the project?	Trigger	Part 3
	What will the meetings with users look like?	Means of communication	Part 4

Based on these two areas and the four parts with their tasks, we define questions that are easier for the practitioners to understand. These questions should be answered and the criteria should be used in implementing the UDC-LSI method. An overview of the questions and criteria is presented in **Table 15**.

7.4. Use Cases for the Descriptive Classification

Based on the results of the interviews, we developed use cases for three stakeholder groups (users, IT personnel, and project management) for the descriptive classification (RQ 4.3).

In order to show the relevance of the descriptive classification to practice, we developed seven use cases for three actors for our descriptive classification, which can be seen in an adapted use case diagram in Figure 22. From our descriptive classification, we propose deriving the artifacts *customized descriptive classification, classification structure,* and *checklist,* which can be used in various use cases.

The decision examples help users understand what decisions are being made during the design and implementation phase. Therefore, a customized descriptive classification should be identified by selecting the two to three examples from our collection that are most appropriate for the project or the industry. With our classification of abstraction levels, the user gets an overview of typical implications of the decisions. In addition, the examples will help users understand the abstraction levels and the trigger point categories. Successful UDC also requires that the user explicitly defines the decisions about which he or she wants to be informed (notification preferences).

The classification structure (without examples), including the abstraction levels and trigger points, can be used for this purpose. For example, a user can define that he or she wants to be informed about project-level decisions immediately and decisions regarding UI, but only once a month.

It can also be useful for IT personnel to understand the effect their decisions can have on their users. To that end, we suggest using a customized descriptive classification (depending on the project and the organization, the selected examples can differ from those used for users). This approach can help developers, architects, and designers understand typical issues in LSI projects and raise their awareness of topics that should be communicated to the users. IT personnel who understand the consequences for the users (i.e., the business side) in detail can help to ensure the users are well integrated into the development process, which will help the IT personnel develop high-quality software (Harris & Weistroffer, 2009; McGill & Klobas, 2008). IT personnel can also use the classification structure to record decisions and their implications. For example, a database or a project management tool can store all of the decisions made in an IT project and offer the abstraction levels and/or trigger points to classify the decisions.

The descriptive classification can be useful for the project management of LSI projects, as the abstraction levels and trigger point categories can be used as a checklist to determine what user-relevant important decisions were made during a certain time during the software development project. (One of our interviewees suggested this use case.) For this purpose, the abstraction levels and trigger points can be formulated as questions like "Did any decision influence project costs?" or "Were there any changes in the UI in the last week?" As described in the use case for users, the classification structure can also be useful in tracking the notification needs of users. In addition, the classification structure might be useful in meetings with the users or the users' managers (i.e., the business side).

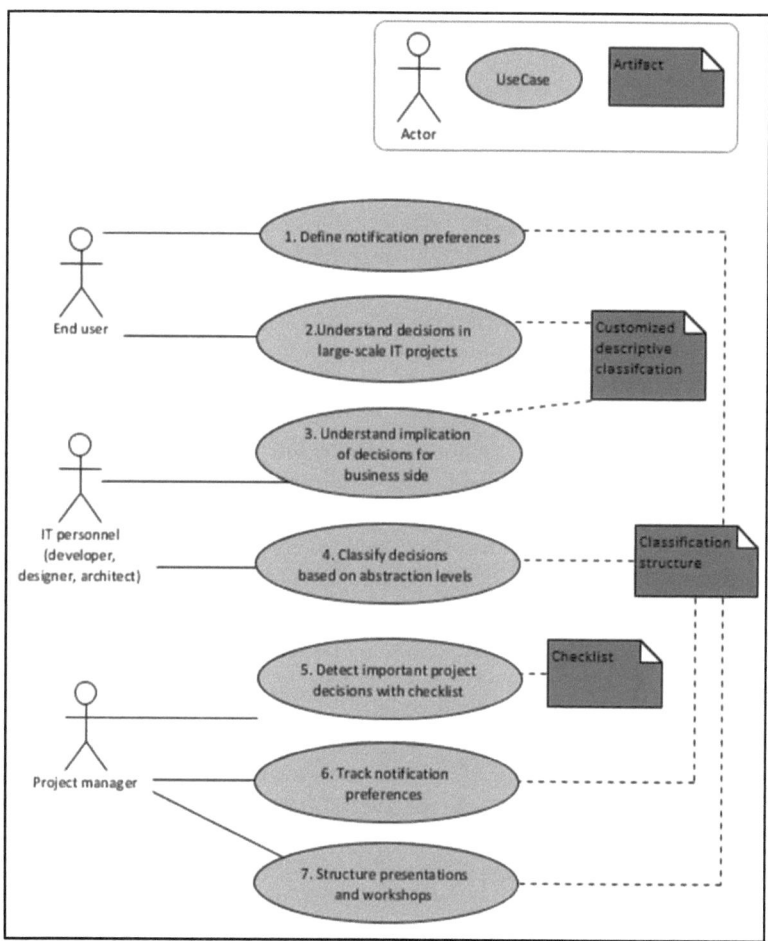

Figure 22: Use Cases for the Descriptive Classification

7.5. Summary of the UDC-LSI Method

This chapter presented the UDC-LSI method to enhance user-developer communication in LSI using traditional methods to develop customer specific software systems.

The UDC-LSI method has four parts, each with several subtasks (see **Figure 21**). Since two central areas—documentation of user-relevant decisions, and structural communication with users—are the focus, the user-relevant decisions, format, tool, traceability, user representatives, trigger, and means of communication should be defined.

We also developed use cases for the descriptive classification, so we propose deriving the artifacts *customized descriptive classification, classification structure,* and *checklist,* which can be used in seven use cases. The decision examples could be useful sin defining notification preferences and in helping users understand what decisions are being made during the design and implementation phases. It can also be useful for IT personnel to understand the effect their decisions can have on their users, and the descriptive classification can be useful for the project management. The abstraction levels and trigger point categories can be used as a checklist to determine what user-relevant decisions were made during a certain period in the software development project. Finally, the classification structure can be useful in tracking the notification needs of users and might be useful in meetings with the users or the users' managers (i.e., business side).

In order to improve the concept of the UDC-LSI method, we present the design validation of the UDC-LSI method in the next chapter. We therefore asked twelve expert of the opinion in interviews.

PART IV
DESIGN VALIDATION AND IMPLEMENTATION EVALUATION

Chapter 8
Expert Assessment of the UDC-LSI Method

"An unexamined life is not worth living."

Socrates

8.1. Abstract

Context: The systematic mapping study and the expert interviews helped to design the UDC-LSI method to enhance UDC in LSI projects. However, based on the TAR approach such a design need to be validated.

Objectives: We seek to evaluate the potential of the UDC-LSI method with regard to its usefulness, benefits, and obstacles to implementation.

Methods: We conduct a series of semi-structured interviews with twelve experts who work in the coordination of business and IT to collect their experiences with LSI projects. We transcribed, coded, and analyzed the interviews.

Results: The experts made an overall positive assessment of the UDC-LSI method but also named obstacles to implementation and possible extensions of the method. The experts described improved preparation of the business organization and an increase in transparency as benefits of the UDC-LSI method. The analysis of the obstacles to its implementation helped us to identify further work that should be done on the UDC-LSI method.

8.2. Introduction

The research methodology used in this thesis is the TAR approach, which is based on design science (see chapter 2.). As Hevner and colleagues (2004) stated, the TAR approach is a process that requires iteration to find effective solutions. Therefore, we evaluated our concept of the UDC-LSI method with experts in order to improve the design and to determine whether we can expect positive effects. We presented the UDC-LSI method (chapter 7.3.) to experts in LSI projects and evaluated the potential of our method concept in interviews. Most of our interview partners deemed it feasible to implement this method concept in LSI projects and recognized its usefulness and benefits. The interviewees also identified obstacles to its implementation and possible extensions for it. We analyzed the obstacles and include some of the suggested extensions in this paper. This assessment is valuable for our own research and helps other researchers to understand some of the practical implications of new methods.

This chapter is structured as follows. In chapter 8.3., we motivate our research questions. We present the results on the potential of the UDC-LSI method in chapter 8.4. and discuss them in chapter 8.5. Chapter 8.6 concludes the chapter with a summary.

8.3. Research Questions for Design Validation

This chapter validates the UDC-LSI method with experts. The research methodology of the expert interview series is discussed in chapter 4.5., and the threats to validity are discussed in chapter 4.7. The interview question 14 to 20 can be found in Appendix II. In particular, this chapter answers the following research questions:

RQ 5 - What is the potential of the UDC-LSI to use UDC in LSI projects to improve system success?
- RQ 5.1. How do experts assess the UDC-LSI method?
- RQ 5.2. Is the UDC-LSI method feasible to implement, and what are possible obstacles to implementation in LSI projects?
- RQ 5.3. How can the UDC-LSI method be extended to improve its benefits and feasibility or to overcome the obstacles to its implementation?

8.4. Potential of the UDC-LSI

This chapter describes the experts' assessment of the potential of our UDC-LSI method. Asking the experts to assess our UDC-LSI method in terms of its general structure, major parts, and the benefits resulted in positive comments. However, the experts also mentioned examples of obstacles to implementation and possible extensions to add to its benefits and feasibility or eliminate obstacles to its implementation in LSI projects.

8.4.1. Assessment of the UDC-LSI Method (RQ 5.1)

Ten out of the twelve experts we interviewed considered the UDC-LSI method to be useful. However, the discussion with the other two experts led in other directions, so they were not explicitly asked for their assessment of its usefulness. Six of the experts opined that all four parts of the UDC-LSI method are required in order to get a comprehensive method to enhance UDC in LSI projects, while one expert commented that the UDC-LSI method is necessary but not sufficient, as more agile approaches are needed.

In order to learn what parts of the UDC-LSI method the experts consider important, useful, or possible, we asked for their views on the parts of the UDC-LSI method (**Table 16**). Regarding the first part, setting up communication structures, eight experts stated that it is important to select user representatives, as not all users can be consulted because of their large numbers. However, they also stated that the process should be actively managed so the user representatives are known to all project members and have a clear responsibility.

As for the second part, training developers on capture decisions, four experts stated that it is important to have a tool-supported repository for the decisions and to train the developers to capture decisions, while three experts opined that developing a decision format is also required.

For the third part, setting up decision traceability, eight experts viewed setting up traceability from users to user requirements to system requirements to decisions as possible and important. Five experts viewed the process of notifying the users as essential, but believed it should be implemented manually. The experts argued for the need for human judgment to prevent too much communication with the users.

With regard to the fourth part, defining the means of communication, five experts agreed that meetings with the users should be conducted in person.

Table 16: Comments of Experts on the UDC-LSI Method

Part	Comment	Count
1	It is important to get user representatives.	8
2	It is important to build a tool-supported repository.	4
2	Developers can be trained to capture decisions.	4
2	It is important to develop a decision format.	3
3	Traceability between requirements and decisions is possible.	8
3	The notification process should be manual.	5
4	In-person meetings are required for good communication.	5

We identified eight benefits of the UDC-LSI method (**Table 17**). Overall benefits were discussed in nine interviews but not in the other three interviews. The benefits named most often (each named by four experts) were better preparation for the business organization and increased transparency in the project. Increased transparency is achieved primarily by building a tool-supported repository. Most of the experts thought that developers can be trained to capture decisions and that it is possible to link requirements and decisions, which would ensure consistent documentation and, thus, the traceability of decisions. As a consequence of the continuous communication and the resulting integration of users, the experts suggested, it is possible to reduce project costs and increase the chances of staying on schedule.

Another benefit of the method that was mentioned was strengthening the relationship between business and IT, which is in line with the comment that it is important to get user representatives. One expert reported that his experience was that projects that had no early communication with the users switched to an escalation mode shortly before their deployment, where users were not willing to find compromises but insist on every detail with regard to functionality. One benefit of our UDC-LSI method is to prevent those conflicts through early communication.

Another benefit mentioned was that developers get to know a business context, which helps them to overcome the lack of common language between business and IT. Finally, one expert mentioned that the method will help to improve system quality.

Table 17: Benefits of the UDC-LSI Method

Benefit	Count
Better preparation of new IT system for the business organization	4
Increased transparency of decisions in the project	4
Reduction in project costs	3
Better chance to stay on schedule	2
Strengthened relationship between users and IT	2
Conflicts in projects avoided through early communication	1
Developers prepared for business contexts	1
Higher system quality	1

8.4.2. Extensions of the UDC-LSI Method (RQ 5.3)

The expert interviews identified six possible extensions of our UDC-LSI method (**Table 18**).

One extension, named by three experts, was to install a skilled project management office (PMO) to conduct the manual notification process of the users. This suggestion refers to the third part of our UDC-LSI method. The PMO would also serve as a quality gate to ensure the correctness and clarity of the documentation of the decisions and prevent there being too many meetings for the users. Such a quality gate could also help to overcome the obstacles regarding the discipline and motivation of the developers.

A similar idea, named by two experts, was to use the representative concept also for the IT personnel, so not all developers would capture decisions and explain them to the users, but only certain representatives selected to take this responsibility. As these skilled representatives would have more experience, it would be easier for them to be aware of decisions and to decide which ones were relevant to the users.

Another suggestion was to extend the documentation of the rationale for the decisions to include alternative solutions. This extension would help the users understand the documentation of the decisions and give them a chance to decide on alternatives, rather than only being informed about them.

Two suggestions for extensions referred to the user representatives. One expert suggested using user representatives as multipliers for user training on the system; because they would be closely involved in the project, they should be able to explain the system to other users and to share their enthusiasm for the system. The other suggestion was to strengthen the multiplier effect by exchange the user representatives regularly in order to involve as many users in the project as possible.

Table 18: Extensions of the UDC-LSI Method

Extension	Count
Use of a skilled PMO leads to channel communication and select decisions.	3
Have IT personnel representatives also.	2
Include options for alternatives to the decision, not only rationale.	2
Use representatives for training as multipliers throughout the project.	1
Exchange user representatives regularly.	1
Document decisions made in meetings.	1

Finally, one expert pointed out that the outcome and the discussions in the meetings with the users should also be documented, especially if the discussions lead to more changes in the requirements.

8.4.3. Implementation Feasibility and Obstacles to the Implementation of the UDC-LSI Method (RQ 5.2)

Eight experts stated that it is feasible to implement the UDC-LSI method in LSI, while two suggested the need for a more agile development approach (i.e., have weekly meetings with the users without documenting the decisions or implementing a formal process for communication), and two did not address the question of feasibility explicitly.

All twelve experts mentioned at least one possible obstacle to its implementation (**Table 19**).

Two obstacles the experts mentioned are that the method can be implemented only in very LSI projects (budgets more than 200 million Euro) that are conducted by mature IT organizations. The experts argued that immature IT organizations are not aware of the need to integrate users, so they would fail to implement the UDC-LSI method, and the effort to implement the method would be too great for smaller projects.

Four obstacles were identified that are related to the first part of the UDC-LSI method. First, two experts argued that the users want to decide on changes, rather than just be informed about them. An open decision meeting in the design and implementation activity would lead to unstable user and system requirements and, thus, to "scope creep". Second, one expert mentioned that, especially in large-scale ERP implementation, users use and know about only a small part of the system, so too many representatives would be required. The expert suggested using managers instead of user representatives, as managers usually have broader knowledge of the system. Third, one expert's view was that it is difficult to get clear notification preferences of the users and suggested using existing relationships with users and the knowledge of the IT personnel about their preferences instead of asking the users for their preferences up front. Fourth, one expert said that it is difficult to set up the communication structure with the users, as the requirements are never stable enough to build notification preferences on them.

Table 19: Obstacles to the Implementation of the Method

Part	Obstacle	Count
General	Not for immature IT organizations	2
	Not for small-scale projects (<200 million EUR)	1
1	Users want to decide, not only to be informed	2
	Users are too diverse, so too many representatives would be required	1
	Difficult to get clear notification preferences from users	1
	Difficult to have stable requirements	1
2	Difficult to motivate developers to document decisions	6
	Developers are not aware of decisions	4
	Difficult to keep the discipline required for documentation throughout the project	4
	Developers cannot decide which decisions are relevant	3
	No realistic tool to capture requirements is available	2
	Many developers are external, so training is difficult	1
3	Mapping between requirements and users is difficult	4
4	Users do not understand documentation of decisions	1
	Email should not be used for communication	1

The highest number of obstacles were named for the second part of the UDC-LSI method, training developers to capture decisions, especially motivating the developers to document their decisions. The experts stated that the developers are not even aware of their decisions, that it will be difficult for developers to keep up the discipline to document decisions throughout the whole project, and that it is difficult for developers to decide which decisions are relevant for users. Two experts also mentioned that there is no appropriate tool to capture the requirements linked with decisions, and one expert mentioned that many developers are external employees (e.g., consultants), so it is difficult to oblige them to be trained.

Even though eight experts thought it is possible to set up the traceability of decisions, the third part, four saw it as an obstacle because of the complexity of the relationship between users and system requirements (often a many-to-many, or n-to-m, relationship) and the need to keep user requirements updated throughout the design and implementation activity.

Regarding the fourth part, defining the means of communication, one expert mentioned that users will not be able to understand the documentation of the decisions because most developers will argue in technical terms instead of in terms of business impact. Finally, one expert commented that email should not be used for communication with the users, as it is complicated to reconstruct information trails in an LSI project. Overall, the design validation shows that there are obstacles; however most of them can be overcome (see **Table 43**).

8.5. Discussion of the Design Validation

This chapter reports on the results of our efforts to assess the potential of the UDC-LSI method (RQ 5). We relate these results to our previous results and the state of the art, which we collected in our systematic mapping study (chapter 3). We also analyze the obstacles to and reasons for communication gaps in order to establish the current status of our UDC-LSI method (chapter 8.4.) and discuss the study's threats to validity.

Even though our analysis of existing methods for UPI in the systematic mapping study indicated that all methods affect all activities in software development, in practice most of the communication is done either in the early or the late activities of software development (i.e., in the specification phase or the acceptance phase). The resulting lack of communication, combined with the large number of decisions that are relevant to users from the descriptive classification, shows that there are decisions in the design and implementation activity that are relevant to users. Although the experts described some setups for communicating with users, none of these setups explicitly captures the decisions made in the design and implementation activity.

The reasons for communication gaps (lack of motivation among developers and/or users, lack of a common language between business and IT, and lack of appreciation between business and IT) and the consequences of these gaps (misunderstanding of requirements, ad-hoc changes required because of unclear requirements, increased implementation costs, increased test effort because of reworks) are in line with current literature, where the benefits of UPI include improved quality resulting from more precise requirements, avoidance of unnecessarily expensive features, and a more positive attitude among the users about the resulting system.

The experts' presented several ideas for overcoming the organizational obstacles to and reasons for communication gaps and mentioned ideas from the literature as well, such as presenting prototypes to users (Dean et al., 1998; Humayoun et al., 2011; Cohen et al., 2010) or doing house tours with running software in various business units (Kautz, 2000; Martin, 2010). However, the experts did not mention a successful, sustainable solution to overcome the communication gaps in LSI. Therefore, we see the need for a method that enhances UDC in LSI projects.

Most of the experts agreed that the UDC-LSI method could be useful and named potential benefits of the solution. The benefits "better preparation of the business organization" and "increased transparency in the project" will help to increase the users' acceptance rate (Cavaye, 1995; Harris & Weistroffer, 2009), and based on the results of the correlations in our systematic mapping study, will increase use of the resulting system

(Igbaria & Guimaraes, 1994; Rouibah et al., 2008). These benefits, together with the benefit of reduced project cost, will increase the value created by the software system.

We analyzed the organizational obstacles, the reasons for communication gaps, and the obstacles to implementing the UDC-LSI method in order to determine the work that is still to be done on our UDC-LSI method (**ss** and IT

Table 20). The organizational obstacles "different opinions between user groups," "get the right user representatives for large-scale projects," and "no access to users/users unknown" are covered by the first part of the UDC-LSI method, where we suggest to doing a stakeholder analysis and ensuring that the user representatives' responsibilities are clear. The obstacle "missing local mediators" will be overcome when we include the experts' suggested extension to use a skilled PMO. The PMO will mediate between IT and business, so in addition to regular project management skills, the PMO will need knowledge of both the IT and the business side.

The issue with motivation of developers or users will be mitigated by the second part, where we suggest that projects develop a change story for developers. The well-known issue of the lack of a common language between business and IT should be improved by the customized descriptive classification, which uses examples that will help users understand decisions and their implication. The explanation of rationale will also help users understand decisions and raise the level of appreciation between business and IT

Table 20: Analysis of Obstacles to and Reasons for Future Work on our UDC-LSI Method

	Obstacles/Factor	Covered in UDC-LSI method by:	Extension of descriptive classification from experts/ Use Cases
Organizational Obstacles	User groups' opinions differ.	Part 1 – Have designated user representatives and notification preferences.	n/a
	It is difficult to get the right user representatives for large-scale projects.	Part 1 – Do a stakeholder analysis to identify the right users.	n/a
	There is no access to users or users are unknown.		n/a
	Local mediators are lacking.	n/a	Use of skilled PMO leads to channel communication select relevant decisions
Reasons for Communication Gaps	Motivation among developers or users is lacking.	Part 2 – Develop a change story for developers.	n/a
	A common language for business and IT is lacking	n/a	Support users and developers by customized descriptive classification.
	Appreciation of business and IT is lacking.	Explanation of rationale will help users understand decisions.	n/a

Obstacles to implementation of UDC-LSI method	The method is not appropriate for immature IT organizations.	The method targets LSI projects. (Adhere to this requirement for the case study.)	n/a
	Not for small-scale projects (<200 mill. EUR)		
	Users want to decide, not only to be informed.	n/a	Include options for alternatives to the decision, not only the rationale.
	Users are too diverse, so too many representatives would be required.	Part 1 – Do a stakeholder analysis to identify the right users (8 experts think it is possible.)	n/a
Obstacles to implementation of UDC-LSI method	It is difficult to get clear notification preferences from users.	n/a	Support users through descriptive classification.
	It is difficult to have stable requirements.	n/a	n/a
	It is difficult to motivate developers to document decisions.	Part 2 – Develop a change story to motivate developers.	n/a
	Developers are not aware of decisions.	n/a	Support developers through customized descriptive classification.
	Developers cannot decide which decisions are relevant.	n/a	Support developers by customized descriptive classification.
	It is difficult to keep discipline for documentation throughout the project.	n/a	Support project management by checklist of possible decisions.
	No realistic tool for requirements capture is available.	n/a	n/a

	Many developers are external, so they are difficult to train.	n/a	n/a
	Mapping between requirements and users is difficult.	Part 3 – Set up traceability of decisions (8 experts think it is possible.)	n/a
	Users do not understand documentation of decisions.	n/a	Support users by customized descriptive classification.
	Email should not be used for communication.	Part 4 – Define means of communication (email only for information, not as main communication channel).	n/a

The obstacles to implementing the UDC-LSI method that suggest it is not for immature IT organizations or small-scale projects (<200 million EUR)' are addressed by the UDC-LSI method's intention to target LSI projects. In order to overcome the obstacle that users want to decide, not only to be informed, we will include options for alternative decisions. Users should appreciate this step, and it should enhance the users' discussions in the meetings with developers. In response to the obstacle that users are too diverse in large-scale ERP projects to identify user representatives, we suggest doing a stakeholder analysis to identify the right users.

As described in the use cases of the descriptive classification (chapter 3.2), the classification structure will help users to define their notification preferences. We do not have a clear mitigation approach to ensure stable requirements in LSI projects, but as this is not the focus of our research, we refer to the many approaches in the RE field (e.g. Humayoun et al., 2011; Takats & Brewer, 2005). The developers' motivation can be improved if a change story clearly explains the benefits of the UDC-LSI method (e.g., greater appreciation by the business side). In addition, the customized descriptive classification will increase developers' awareness of decisions and help them decide which decisions are relevant to the users.

In order to ensure the required discipline for documentation is maintained throughout the project, we suggest that the project management use the checklist of possible decisions. The obstacle that there is no realistic tool for requirements capture available could be overcome by an analysis of available tools, such as the SAP solution manager or IBM Doors. However, as the choice of such a tool depends on the individual project, we do not plan to integrate this choice into our UDC-LSI method. We also have no answer for how projects can overcome the obstacle that many developers are external so they are difficult to train, but we will look into the issue when we implement the UDC-LSI method in a LSI project. As eight experts thought it would be possible to set up the traceability of decisions, we overcome the obstacle "mapping between requirements and users is difficult" in the third part of the UDC-LSI method. With the help of the customized descriptive classification, it will be easier for users to understand the documentation of decisions. Based on the MRT (Dennis & Valacich, 1999), we suggest in the fourth part of our UDC-LSI method that email is not suitable as the main communication channel.

Most of our interview partners thought it was feasible to implement the UDC-LSI method in a large-scale IT project, but these are only the opinions of twelve experts and are not based on experience with an implementation of the UDC-LSI method. Therefore, we evaluate the method's feasibility through a case study in which we implement the method in an LSI project.

8.6. Summary of the Expert Assessment

This chapter presented the experts' validation of the UDC-LSI method. We conducted twelve semi-structured interviews and collected data from about eighteen hours of interview time. For our analysis we transcribed the interviews and coded them with descriptive codes based on our research questions. Our experts were involved in sixty-nine LSI projects, so their experience was widespread.

Overall, the experts see potential for our UDC-LSI method. They saw the four parts (1 – setting up communication structures, 2 – training developers on capturing decisions or changes, 3 – setting up the traceability of decisions, and 4 – defining the means of communication) as useful. In particular, they thought it is important to get user representatives and that it is possible to get traceability between system requirements and decisions. Among the method's benefits, the experts named improved preparation of the business organization and increased transparency of the projects most often. Our interviews showed that we should implement the UDC-LSI method only in a mature IT organization. Many of the experts believed that it will be difficult to make developers aware of the decisions and to motivate them to document decisions and to keep the discipline required for documentation throughout the project.

To overcome the obstacles to implementing the UDC-LSI method, we developed use cases for the descriptive classification (chapter 7.4.), which we expect to help in several ways, including in motivating the developers and raising their awareness of decisions. To ensure the discipline for documentation, we plan to follow an extension suggested by the experts by installing a PMO that ensures the documentation's clarity and quality.

To further ensure the value and purpose of the UDC-LSI method, we will present the implementation evaluation, i.e. instatiation of the UDC-LSI method in a real-life case study, in the next chapter.

Chapter 9
Evaluation of the UDC-LSI Method:
the iPeople Case Study

"I have been impressed with the urgency of doing. Knowing is not enough, we must apply. Being willing is not enough, we must do."

Leonard da Vinci

9.1. Abstract

Context: We defined the UDC-LSI method and evaluated its potential with experts. The experts see potential for our method concept and named benefits such as "improved preparation of the business organization" and "increased transparency in the projects." However, it is important, especially for newly designed methods, to evaluate them in a real-world context.

Objective: We study the utility and usability of the UDC-LSI method by validating the method retrospectively in a real-world, practical context. We analyze the as-is status of the iPeople project. Based on that, we simulated an instantiation of the UDC-LSI method for the iPeople project and evaluated this instantiation with project participants with regard to utility (i.e., feasibility, effectiveness, and efficiency) and usability, (i.e., acceptance).

Method: We conducted a case study of a software company's LSI project based on Runeson's guidance. We studied the case company's currently used processes and tools by conducting several formal and informal interviews, participating in meetings and workshops, and reviewing existing project documentation. To evaluate the project participants, we conducted nine fully structured interviews with open and closed questions.

Results: The as-is analysis revealed the need for the project to enhance UDC. The assessment of the current status of system success indicated potential for improvement. The adaptation of the UDC-LSI method in the iPeople project showed that it is possible to instantiate the method for the project under study. The evaluation showed a positive effect of the UDC-LSI method on system success (effectiveness), and the project participants confirmed the feasibility of the method, showed a high level of acceptance of the method, and confirmed a positive effort-benefit ratio (efficiency).

9.2. Introduction

According to Hevner and colleagues (2004), a method "must be evaluated with respect to the utility provided for the class of problems addressed."

This chapter reports on a case study that seeks to define the utility and usability of the UDC-LSI method by validating the method retrospectively in a real-world, practical context. With this case study, we seek to determine the effects of a concrete instantiation of the method in a real-world LSI project.

The case study concerns the iPeople project. We analyzed the as-is status of the project with regard to the current development process and established communication structures, revolving issues, and decisions relevant to users. Building on that analysis, we simulated an instantiation of the UDC-LSI method for the iPeople project based on detailed process descriptions and practical examples. We also evaluated this instantiation with project participants in terms of its utility (i.e., feasibility, effectiveness, and efficiency) and usability, (i.e., acceptance).

The main results suggest the need to enhance UDC, especially in the design and implementation phases of the project. The assessment of the current status of system success also indicated potential for improvement. The simulated use of the UDC-LSI method in the iPeople project showed that it is possible to instantiate the method for the project under study and revealed the importance of a project-specific application of the method. The evaluation showed that the UDC-LSI method could have a positive on system success (effectiveness). Furthermore, the project's participants confirmed the feasibility of the method, showed a high level of acceptance of the method, and confirmed a positive effort-benefit ratio (efficiency).

This chapter is structured as follows. We first present the case study design, along with the research questions, case selection, and the general research method in chapter 9.3. Then we describe the results of the as-is analysis in chapter **9.4.** and the simulated instantiation in chapter 9.5. The results and discussion of the evaluation are provided in chapter 9.6. We discuss the threats to validity in chapter **9.7.** and conclude with a summary in chapter 9.8.

9.3. Case Study Design

In this chapter we introduce the case study design in terms of its defined goals, research questions and hypotheses, case selection process, the case itself, and the research method. The specific data collection procedures differ for the as-is study, the instantiation, and the evaluation of project participants through interviews. Therefore the detailed research designs and data collection procedures are presented in subchapters 9.4.1., 9.5.1., and 9.6.1.

We designed and conducted the case study according to instructions from Runeson et al. (2012). A case study is defined as an empirical method that aims at "investigating contemporary phenomena in their context" (Runeson et al., 2012) or that is "an empirical investigation of an instance of a phenomenon in its natural context" (Wieringa, 2012b).

The case study we conducted can be categorized as a single case study with one unit of analysis. The iPeople project is a customer-specific implementation of a mobile business application for a large European retailer. The "object of study" is defined as an IT artifact interacting with a context (i.e., the unit of analysis) (Hevner et al., 2004; Wieringa, 2012b), so the object of study in this case study is the UDC-LSI method.

This research should be categorized as action case research, as we propose to change the development process with regard to UDC, which can be categorized as software process improvement (Runeson et al., 2012).

However, since this type of research is closely related to case studies, Runeson's guidelines still apply (Runeson & Höst, 2008).

One possible research method in pursuit of our objectives is to instantiate and apply the method directly in a large-scale project. However, it is difficult, if not impossible, to convince managers of LSI projects, which tend to have high-risk profile, to apply the method directly without proof of consent. According to Wieringa (2012) it may take years to gain a company's trust to implement a newly proposed method.

However, the instantiation is an important part of our validation study, as it shows that constructs and methods can be implemented in a working system (Hevner et al., 2004). An instantiation also enables the researcher to learn about the method's utility and usability in a real-world context (Wieringa, 2007). Hevner et al. (2004) stated that the utility, quality, and efficiency of a design artifact must be rigorously demonstrated via well-executed evaluation methods, so it is essential for newly proposed methods to study the utility (i.e., feasibility, effectiveness, and efficiency) and usability (i.e., acceptance by the users) of the method in a real world context. For this reason, we chose another form of evaluation.

We define this method of evaluation as a retrospective validation composed of two steps:
- Based on an as-is analysis, we instantiated the UDC-LSI method by describing its application to the project in detail.
- We evaluate this simulated instantiation with project participants with regard to the feasibility, effectiveness, level of acceptance, and efficiency of the UDC-LSI method.

In order to conduct this form of evaluation, we must understand the as-is status of the project structurally and find detailed examples to describe the instantiation on a level that allows project participants to evaluate the method's instantiation. We executed the retrospective validation of the UDC-LSI method a software company's LSI project that focuses on development of mobile business applications. Further details of the case selection and company are presented in subchapter 9.3.2.

To understand the as-is status of the project, we studied the processes and tools the client company used. Based on that knowledge, we instantiated the UDC-LSI method through a detailed hypothetical description of the new processes, including two hands-on examples. Finally, we evaluated the instantiation with project participants.

9.3.1. Research Questions, Goals, and Hypotheses

According to case study research in software engineering and information systems (Hevner et al., 2004; Runeson et al., 2012; Wieringa, 2007), the goals of a case study must be clearly defined. The objective in this case is to validate the UDC-LSI method with regard to its utility and usability in a real-world context. The goals can be formulated as:
- Goal 1: Assess the AS-IS status of the unit of analysis (iPeople project).
- Goal 2: Validate the UDC-LSI method in the unit of analysis retrospectively.
  - Goal 2.1 Instantiate the UDC-LSI method in the unit of analysis (iPeople project).
  - Goal 2.2. Evaluate this instantiation of the UDC-LSI method in the unit of analysis (iPeople project) from the perspective of project participants.

The central research question is:
RQ 6 – What effects on the resulting system's usability and utility does the UDC-LSI have on LSI projects?
In order to answer them we developed subsequent RQs in the following.

Understanding the current status of the project (AS-IS study)

The UDC-LSI method presented in chapter 5 has a flexible design. In order to instantiate the UDC-LSI method on a project, we had to understand the as-is status of the project, particularly the processes and tools used, and the established communication structure (e.g., meetings, document-based communication), issues, and decisions in the project that are relevant to users. This analysis is required in order to ensure an efficient implementation of the method and to lower the barriers to using the method for all project stakeholders.

To identify the established communication structures, we built upon the model of Mohr and Nevin (1990), who measured communication based on its frequency, direction, modality, and content (see chapter 2.).

We distinguish between formal and informal communication, such that formal communication structures include established meetings and document-based communication (Stapel & Schneider, 2012) and informal communication structures include ad-hoc meetings, phone call, and emails.

We need to collect revolving issues in order to ensure that we target existing issues related to UDC in the project. The summary of decisions that are relevant to user helped us to design the instantiation since we need to know what kind of decisions are there. Finally, we assessed the as-is status of the iPeople project's system success in order to ensure that there is improvement potential. In particular, we formulated the following research questions:

- RQ 6.1: What is the as-is status of the unit of analysis (the iPeople project)? In particular:
  - RQ 6.1.1. What were the steps in the development process?
  - RQ 6.1.2 What were the established formal and informal communication structures (meetings, document-based

- communication, and ad-hoc communication) in the project?
- RQ 6.1.3 What issues occurred that were due to the established development process and communication structures?
- RQ 6.1.4 What were user-relevant decisions in the project?
- RQ 6.1.5 What is the as-is status of the system's success (ease of use, system quality, system use, project on time and on budget, user satisfaction)?

Apply the UDC-LSI method to practice (Instantiation)

Instantiations show that constructs, models, or methods can be implemented in a working system (Hevner et al., 2004). They demonstrate feasibility and enable concrete assessment of an artifact's suitability to its intended purpose. Therefore, we raise the following research question:
- RQ 6.2. What would an instantiation of the UDC-LSI method in the unit of analysis (iPeople project) look like?

Evaluating this instantiation of the UDC-LSI method in the unit of analysis from the perspective of project participants

Hevner et al. (2004) stated that the utility, quality, and efficiency of a design artifact must be rigorously demonstrated via well-executed evaluation methods. According to Wieringa (2007), usability questions ask whether these effects satisfy usability requirements like understandability, ease of use, and ease of learning. Utility questions define how the method contributes. Therefore, we evaluate the utility (feasibility, effectiveness, and efficiency) and the usability (acceptance) from the perspective of project participants.

Feasibility

Since we use a simulation for our evaluation, we extend the process of the instantiation by means of a concrete assessment of its feasibility through the project participants and define the following research question:

- RQ 6.3. From the perspective of the project's participants, is it feasible to implement the UDC-LSI method in the unit of analysis?

Hypothesis H1: Project participants consider it feasible to implement the UDC-LSI method in the project and see advantages of its implementation.

Effectiveness

To determine the method's effectiveness, we build upon the conceptual framework we defined for the UDC-LSI method (chapter 0 and **Figure 18**). Therefore, we raise three research questions:

- RQ 6.4. Is the UDC-LSI method in the project effective from the perspective of the project participants? In particular:
  - RQ 6.4.1. Does an implementation of the UDC-LSI method increase system success from the perspective of project participants?

Hypothesis H2: Application of the UDC-LSI method has a positive effect on system success.

- RQ 6.4.2. What are other effects of the method from the perspective of the project participants?

Efficiency

To determine whether the effort required to execute the method is worthwhile in terms of its value, we raise three research questions:

- RQ 6.5. To what degree is the method efficient from the perspective of project participants? In particular:
  - RQ 6.5.1. What effort is required in order to execute the method?
  - RQ 6.5.2. Is the effort required to execute the method worthwhile in terms of its value?

Hypothesis H3: The benefits of applying the UDC-LSI method balance the effort required.

Acceptance

To study acceptance of the method, we use the TAM model (see chapter 2.). Therefore, to determine acceptance of the method, we raise five research questions:

- RQ 6.6. From the practitioners' perspective, to what degree is the UDC-LSI method usable? In particular:
  - RQ 6.6.1. What is the perceived ease of use of the UDC-LSI method?

Hypothesis H4: The project participants perceive the UDC-LSI method as easy to use (perceived ease of use).

- RQ 6.6.2. What is the perceived usefulness of the UDC-LSI method?

Hypothesis H5: The project participants consider the UDC-LSI method to be useful (perceived usefulness).

- RQ 6.6.3. What is the project participants' attitude toward using the UDC-LSI method?

Hypothesis H6: The project participants have a positive attitude toward using the UDC-LSI method (attitude toward using).

- RQ 6.6.4. What is the project participants' behavioral intention toward future use of the UDC-LSI method?

Hypothesis H7: The project participants intend to use the UDC-LSI method in the future (behavioral intention to use).

9.3.2. Case Selection

The UDC-LSI method is defined for LSI projects, and its purpose is to improve system success by increasing UDC in the design and implementation phases. To identify an LSI project with issues in UDC for the evaluation, we defined three requirements: LSI Project, customer-specific software development, low level of UDC (see chapter 6.4.).

The case company: The case company, Sovanta AG, is a rapidly growing firm that currently has about sixty employees. The advantages of choosing this company include that their products, mobile business apps, must be strongly user-centered and the company is open to new concepts and methods in their software development processes.

Next, we describe the context of the method instantiation, that is, the iPeople project.

Historical project characteristics:

- Effort: ~ 750 person days and overview of activities (**Table 21**).
- Number of users: ~4500 (4000 sales managers, 500 senior sales and regional managers)
- Project run time: February 2012 – present (ongoing)
- Many releases

- Rollout in twenty-eight countries

Table 21: Overview of the Activities and Effort Associated with the

Activity	Total working hours [h]	Total working time [person days]	Percent
Design	504	63	8%
Development (front end)	2515	314	42%
Development (back end)	2006	251	33%
Project management	898	112	15%
other (IT admin, travel, sales, consulting)	101	13	2%
Total	6024	753	100%

iPeople Project

Project history: Initially, the iPeople project was an implementation of a standard product with small customer-specific customizations, but extensive customization after August 2013 led to a customer-specific development project. Since August 2013 there has been a continuous design and implementation process (approximately four hotfixes per year, plus new releases). In addition, there has been considerable ad-hoc communication within the project team but no communication between IT personnel (IT project manager, developer, designer) and users.

Politics: A European retail company is the case company's largest customer, so the case company has a high degree of interest in fulfilling this customer's requirements. A project setup that ensures a high level of system success is important for the customer, and the customer's project manager has considerable interest in keeping the project going, as this is the project manager's main responsibility.

Description of the iPeople system: The main purpose of the business application is to support managers in the personnel management, so their managers meets monthly with assigned branch managers to discuss Human Resource (HR) Key Performance Indicators (KPIs). As these sales managers are on the road for most of their work time, the software is distributed on tablets (iPads), but there is also a web version that works on browsers. The main functions of the software are to:

- present the organization structure, including employee master data (e.g., personal information, such as the employee's address; organizational information, such as the employee's position and branch; and work contract details, such as the employee's salary)
- provide HR KPIs up to the individual employee level, such as planned working hours, actual working hours, and remaining vacation days
- provides important events, such as employees' birthdays, end of probation periods, which are imported into the iPads' calendar.

Project stakeholders: The business side is represented primarily by one project manager from the customer side, whose main job is to coordinate requirements and manage development with the case company. Users are currently sales managers, but also branch managers, senior sales managers, and regional managers from twenty-eight countries. Each country has a key user for the iPeople system, but we had access only to the IT personnel, not to the business side. However, since we covered one side of the communication dyad, we are convinced that we are aware of all communication structures. The IT personnel are the project sponsor and project manager, six developers (three front end, three back end), and one UI/UX designer.

The project fulfills the three criteria of our definition of an LSI project (large number of users, rollout in multiple countries, and project duration more than a year). The project is a customer-specific software development project that uses a flexible, agile-like development, so it does not use traditional methods. However, there are issues in the communication with the customer's project manager and key users. Since it is difficult to build trust with a client company and to convince them to use a newly defined, not yet tested method (Wieringa, 2007), we believe that the context is suitable for a case study.

9.3.3. Research Method

We built the case study design based on guidelines from Runeson et al. (2012). The case study can be categorized as an interpretive case study since it "attempts to understand phenomena through the participants' interpretation of their context" (Runeson & Höst, 2008). As suggested, we use a mixed method approach with several data sources, that is, archival data, interviews, and attendance in meetings and workshop sessions. Several data sources are necessary in order to limit the effect of interpreting data from one data source. We triangulate the data and the method by combining qualitative methods (e.g., answers to open questions in interviews) and quantitative methods (e.g., questionnaires rated on Likert scales). We also take into account viewpoints of those in various roles.

Runeson and Höst (2008) defined three levels of data collection techniques: first degree, second degree, and independent methods. We used primarily first-degree methods (i.e. interviews and meeting attendance), and independent methods (i.e. analysis of existing project documentation).

In particular, we used archival data, informal and unstructured interviews, and observations in meetings for the as-is analysis. Formal and fully structured interviews with a closed questionnaire allowed us to get objective and comparable answers for the evaluation of the UDC-LSI method. The qualitative data from open questions are summarized into categories (Runeson & Höst, 2008).

The detailed research design and data collection procedures differ for the three parts of the study, so they are presented separately for the as-is analysis, the simulated instantiation, and the evaluation. We outline the design and data collection procedures in subchapters 9.4.1., 9.5.1., and 9.6.1., where we also present the Goal Question Metric (GQM) table for each of them (Basili et al., 1994).

9.4. Understanding the Current Status of the Project (As-is Study)

As defined in chapter 9.1, we need to understand the as-is status of the project in order to apply the UDC-LSI method retrospectively. This chapter addresses RQ 6.1.1 – RQ 6.1.5.

The first chapter explains the data collection procedures, including the mapping from research questions, data sources, and measurements. Then we discuss the results by presenting the steps of the development process and the established formal and informal communication structures and resolving related issues. Next, we identified decisions relevant to users and assessed the as-is status of the system's level of success. We conclude with a short summary.

9.4.1. Design and Data Collection Procedure

The main source of information for the as-is analysis was our three months of work in the case company to understand its organizational culture, processes, and tools. We conducted two preparation meetings with the IT project's sponsor and project manager before we finalized our selection for the case study project. Then we held a workshop session for a half day to record the as-is development process (RQ 6.1.1) and had a formal, semi-structured interview with the IT project manager to record current communication structures (RQ 6.1.2). We recorded and transcribed the interview. As described in chapter 9.1, we built upon the communication model of Mohr and Nevin (1990), who differentiated among the direction, modality, frequency, and content of communication. Our goal was to determine:

- For meetings:
  - who participates in the meetings (direction)
  - what medium is used (modality)
  - how often the meetings occur (frequency)
  - what is the purpose of the meeting, and where are the results documented (content)
- For document-based communication:
  - who is the sender and receiver (direction)
  - what is the format of the document (modality)
  - what is the trigger that initiates creation of the document (frequency)
  - what is the purpose of the document (content)
- For ad-hoc communication:
  - who are the senders and receivers (direction)
  - what is the medium (modality),
  - how often does it occur (frequency),
  - what is the purpose of the communication, and where are the results documented (content)

Therefore, the interview question were:
1) What are the fixed meetings (purpose, participants, frequency, occurrence, medium, and result-documentation)?
2) What kind of document-based communications (document, sender, receiver, trigger, purpose) are used?
3) Where does ad-hoc communication (trigger, sender, receiver, frequency, medium, and result-documentation) occur?

To answer RQ 6.1.3, we held seven informal, unstructured interviews with project participants. This informal method is suggested and commonly used in case studies (Runeson & Höst, 2008).

To identify the decisions that are relevant to users, we analyzed email communication, recordings in tickets for developing tasks, meeting minutes, and other project documentation (RQ 6.1.4). In addition, we had one open question in the evaluation interviews (chapter 6.1) to reveal examples of decisions that are relevant to users (RQ 6.1.4).

Finally, we used two closed questions in fully structured interviews, measured with a 5-item Likert scale, to reveal the importance of the as-is status for system success criteria (RQ 6.1.5).

A GQM table (Basili et al., 1994) in **Table 22** provides an overview of the RQs, data sources, and metrics.

Table 22: Research Questions, Data Sources, and Metrics of the As-is Analysis

Research Question	Data Source	Metric
1. What is the as-is status of the project?		
1.1. What are the steps in the current development process?	• Half-day workshop with developer and designer, validation with project manager	Notes by researcher
1.2. What are the established formal and informal communication structures (meetings, document-based communication, and ad-hoc communication) in the	• Interview with project manager	Notes by researcher

		project?	
	1.3.	What are issues that occur because of the established development process and communication structures?	• 7 informal interviews with project participants	Notes by researcher
	1.4.	What were user-relevant decisions in the project?	• Analysis of meeting minutes, comments in tickets, and email communications • Open question in 9 evaluation interviews	Notes by researcher
	1.5.	What is the as-is status of system success (ease of use, system quality, system use, project on time and on budget, user satisfaction) in the project?	• Closed questionnaire in 9 evaluation interviews	5-point Likert Scale

9.4.2. Results

This chapter presents the answers we derived to RQ 6.1.1 – RQ 6.1.5. First we present the current development process. Then we explain the currently used formal and informal communication structures. Next, we identify the decisions that are relevant to the users and analyze the current status of the iPeople project's system success. We conclude with a summary of the as-is status.

Steps of the current development process (RQ 6.1.1)

To facilitate a simulated instantiation of the UDC-LSI method in the iPeople project, we had to understand the steps in the current development process. To answer RQ 6.1.1 we held a half-day workshop with a developer and a designer and then validated the results with the project manager. We structured the tasks along the roles of users, the customer project manager, and the IT personnel with the IT project manager, developers, and designer. For the notation we build upon the Business Process Modeling Notation (BPMN) (OMG, 2009). The current development process is presented in **Figure 23**.

Current development process of the iPeople project. The first sub-process, customer requests for requirements, which elicits the requirements, is not transparent to the IT personnel. However, the designer, the developer, and the project manager indicated that several stakeholders are involved: The users are the customer's sales organization (business side). Each country the system serves has at least one key user in the sales organization who is responsible for the iPeople solution, and each region has a regional manager. Users request requirements for new features from their key users, who collect the requirements for their countries. The regional manager then collects all requirements from the key users in his or her region and selects the most relevant requirements from his or her perspective.

The next step is the collection of all requirements by the customer's project manager. After the requirements are collected, the project manager writes a first version of a specification document for each requirement (Spec 1.0). The specification documents are then discussed on a high level with the IT personnel (IT project manager, front-end and back-end developers). Next, the IT personnel assess the specification and determine whether there are open questions, in which case another discussion with the customer PM is initiated. When there are no more open questions, the customer's project manager creates another version of the specification document (Spec 2.0). The effort required for design, front-end development, and back-end development is estimated based on that document, and the release planning (i.e., which features can be implemented with the available resources for the release) is done. After release planning, the customer gets an offer. In addition to the release planning, the estimation of effort required is also used to define work packages, and based on the offer and the work packages, tickets for each feature are created.

Then a process for each feature starts. The designer creates wireframes or mockups if there are larger UI changes, and the developer starts to implement the feature. When he or she is finished with the development, the tickets are finalized and a demo is created. Then the customer's project manager tests the feature and either accepts the feature or reports it as a bug or a wrong implementation in the test document. If the feature is a bug, the developer continues the development of the feature until the bug is fixed, and if the feature is classified as a wrong implementation, the IT project manager determines whether it is a bug or a change request. If it is a bug, the developer continues the development of the feature until the bug is fixed, and if it is a change request, the request is usually included in the collection of requirements for the next release.

If the customer's project manager accepts all of the features, the country-specific test starts. If the test reveals a bug, the developers fix it, and when there are no more bugs, the new release is rolled out to the countries that use the iPeople system.

During our three months working in the case company, we also learned about other projects' processes.

An overview of the standard development process of the Sovanta AG, presented in **Figure 24**, shows the phases: scoping, scribbles, architecture, mockups, development, testing, and release. Part of the development process is workshops with the customer, especially at the beginning, that is, the scoping and scribble phases.

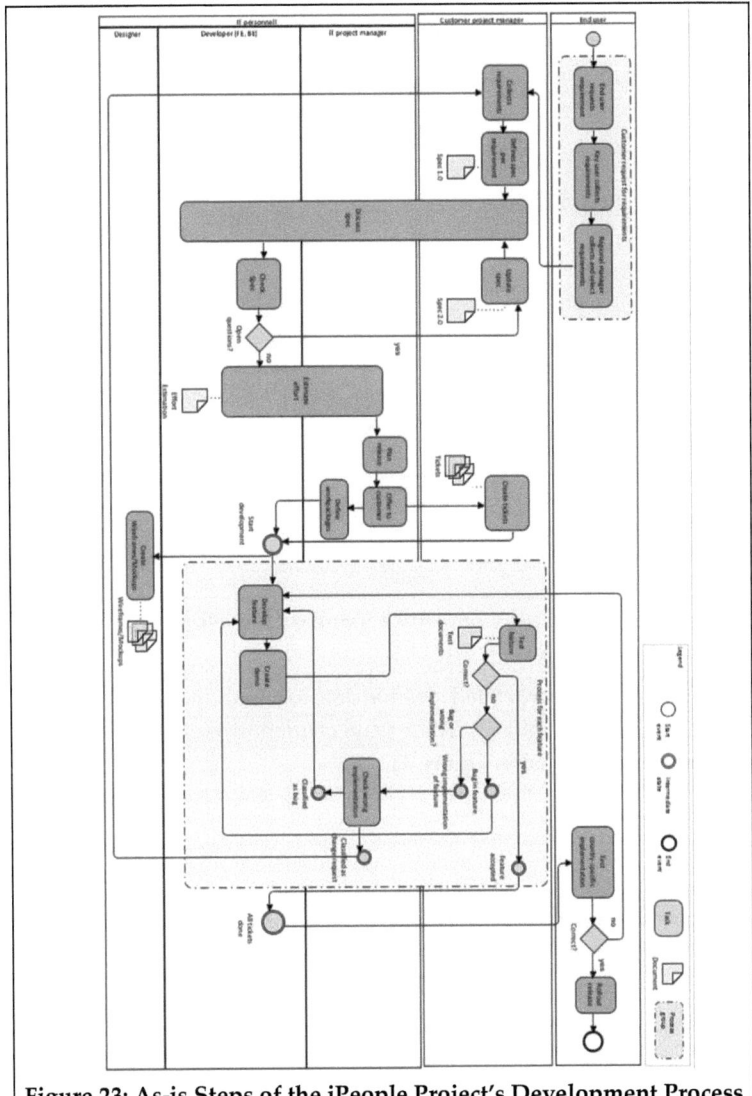

Figure 23: As-is Steps of the iPeople Project's Development Process

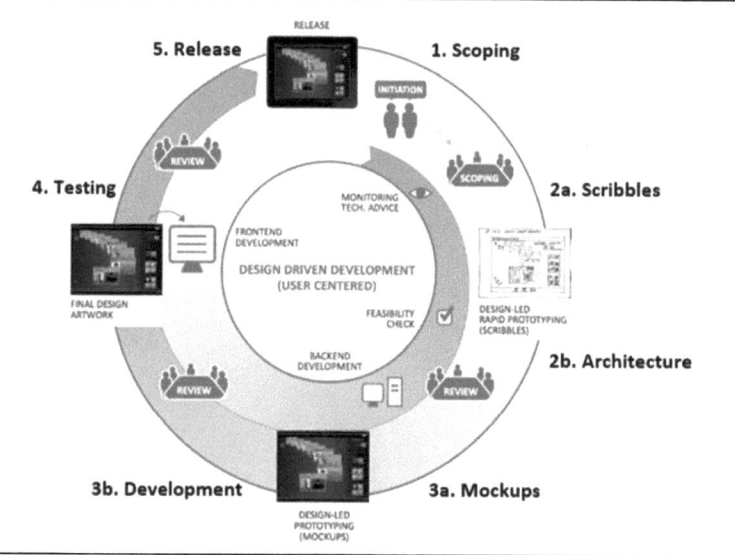

Figure 24: The Case Company's Standard Development Process

Other projects use a tool called scribble doc, to summarize the results of the scoping and scribbles phases. There is no commonly used template yet, but an example is presented in **Figure 25**.

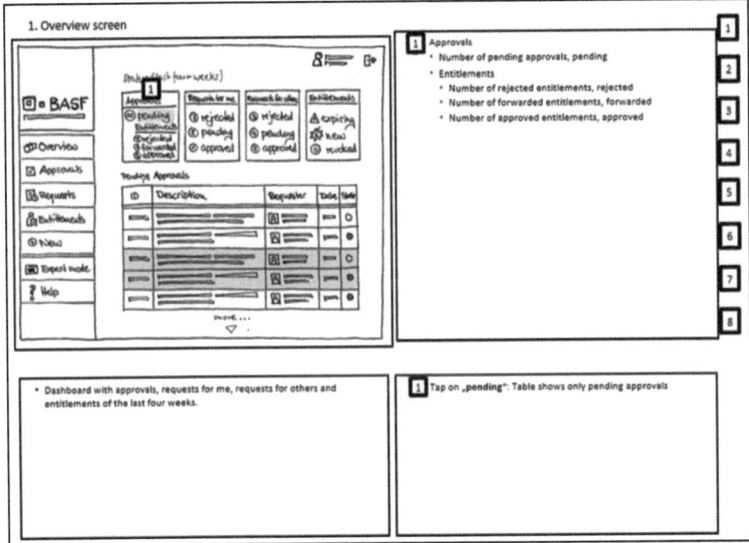

Figure 25: Example of a Scribble Doc Template from Other Projects

The case company also uses JIRA, a central project management tool that uses a ticket-based system (Details on the tool can be found at https://www.atlassian.com/software/jira). The workflow of tickets in the case company is presented in **Figure 26**.

Formal and informal communication structures (RQ 6.1.2)

To answer RQ 6.1.2, we conducted a 45-minute interview with the project manager. We had to understand the status of UDC in order to know where the UDC-LSI method can improve communication. We distinguish between formal and informal communication, where formal communication structures include established meetings and document-based communication (Stapel & Schneider, 2012), and informal communication includes ad-hoc meetings, phone calls, and emails.

Figure 26: Workflow of Tickets using the JIRA Tool

Established meetings

We identified five fixed meetings in the iPeople project, as shown in **Figure 29**. The first meeting is a monthly meeting between all customer managers (i.e., those responsive for the project), the IT company manager, and the IT project sponsor to update the managers with an overview, important results, and next steps for the projects. The status update for the iPeople project, which is prepared by the IT project manager, is recorded in the presentation, but there is no resulting documentation.

Another regular meeting is the project jour fixe, an hourly phone call once per week during the project. Currently, only the customer's project manager and the IT project manager participate to clarify organizational topics and timeline issues, but preparation for the meeting is sometimes done with the developers. The results of the meeting are recorded in meeting minutes.

The third meeting happens only once, at the beginning of a release or hotfix. The purpose of the meeting between the customer's project manager, the IT project manager, one front-end developer, and one back-end developer is to discuss the specification document 1.0. The results are recoded in changes in the specification document, but there is no other documentation of the decisions.

After the discussion of the specification document, the effort estimations are discussed between the customer's project manager and the IT project manager. The purpose of this phone call is to finalize which features will be implemented in the next release or hotfix, based on the available resources. The results are recorded in meeting minutes and the resulting tickets.

The last fixed meeting is an internal meeting of the IT personnel, where all project managers and the IT company manager decide on how to staff the projects. The result of this weekly meeting is represented in the project management tool JIRA. An overview of the formal meetings is presented in **Table 23** and Figure 28.

Table 23: Formal Communication Structures - Meetings

No.	Commun-ication Interaction	Participants	Medium	Frequency	Purpose	Result Documentation
1	Manager meeting	Customer managers (i.e., project managers of all projects), IT company manager, all project sponsors from IT personnel	Personal meeting	Monthly	Update managers on overview of all projects, most important work results of the last 4 weeks, and next steps for projects	Not recorded
2	Project jour fixe	Customer project manager, IT project manager	Phone call	Weekly	Clarification of organizational project topics, timeline issues	Meeting minutes
3	Discussion of specification document	Customer project manager, IT project manager, 1 back-end developer, 1 front-end developer	Personal meeting	One meeting at the beginning of new release/hotfix	Discussion of specification documents	Changes included in the specification document
4	Meeting to estimate effort	Customer project manager, IT project manager	Phone call	One meeting after discussion of specifications	Finalize the scope of the release/hotfix based on available resources	Meeting minutes and tickets
5	Jour fixe for projects and staffing	All IT project managers, IT company manager	Personal meeting	Weekly	Define resources for all projects	Update resource allocation in JIRA

Established document-based communication

We identified six document classes that are used for communication. All documents are also included in the overview of the development process (**Figure 23**). The first document is specification document 1.0, which is written by the customer's project manager after requirements from the user are collected and sent to the IT personnel. The purpose of this document is to determine which requirements will be implemented in the next release or hotfix.

The second document, specification document 2.0, is an update of specification 1.0. It is also written by the customer's project manager after the developers' technical assessment. Its purpose is to record the detailed specifications of the requirements.

The third document is the effort estimation, which is written by the IT project manager with input from the developers. Its purpose is to specify the effort required for the agreed project scope, and it is updated for every change request from the customer's project manager during the development.

The fourth document is wireframes or mockups created by the project designer. Wireframes are computer-drawn sketches of the application (**Figure 27**) that contain the design decisions but do not show details like pictures, colors, or icons. Mockups are computer-drawn UI screens that show how the screen will look in the application (**Figure 28**) in order to give the customer's project manager the "look and feel" of the new implementation. They are also produced when there are large UI changes after the specification is finished.

The fifth document is the tickets for each new feature, which are created by the customer's project manager and sent to the IT project manager, who assigns them to the developers. These tickets describe the defined work packages for the next release or hotfix.

The last category of documents is test documents that the customer's project manager creates during the test phase and sends to the IT project manager and the developers. They describe bugs that the developers are supposed to fix. An overview of the document-based communication is presented in **Table 24**.

Table 24: Formal Communication Structures – Document-Bases Communication

Document	Sender	Receiver	Trigger	Purpose
Specification document 1.0	Customer's project manager	IT project manager, designer, front-end and back-end developers	After collection of requirements by customer's project manager	Analyze scope of next release or hotfix
Specification documents 2.0	Customer's project manager	IT project manager, designer, front-end and back-end developers	After technical assessment from front-end and back-end developers	Document required changes that are due to technical analysis of specification from development
Effort estimation	IT project manager (input from developers)	Customer's project manager	- Initially based on specification 2.0 - Change requests during development from customer's project manager	Specify effort for agreed scope

Wireframes/mockups	Designer	Customer's project manager	After specification 2.0 is finished	Give customer's project manager the look and feel of the new implementation
Tickets for each new feature	Customer's project manager	IT project manager (assigns to developers)	Wireframes/mockups accepted	Define work packages for next release
Test Documents	Customer's project manager	IT project manager and developers	During test phase	Describe bugs for developers to fix

Ad-hoc communication

We identified three categories of informal communication structures. First, there are ad-hoc internal alignment meetings within the IT personnel, which occur three to five times a week. One type of ad-hoc meeting is that held between the IT project manager and a front-end or a back-end developer, in which they discuss new requirements or changes in the requirements after the jour fixe with the customer's project manager. The other type is that held between developers, in which issues related to features are discussed.

The second category of informal communication is ad-hoc communication between the customer's project manager and the IT project manager or developers. The customer's project manager calls the IT project manager at least once a day and writes four to five emails per day is to request new requirements or report on test results. The results are documented in the tickets and sometimes confirmed with an email to the customer's project manager. The customer's project manager makes about three phone calls and writes four or more emails per week directly to the developers for the same reason, but the results are not documented.

The third category of information communication is the ad-hoc internal status meeting between the IT project manager and the project sponsor, which occur once or twice a week for about five minutes to update the project sponsor about the status of the project. There is usually no documentation of these personal talks.

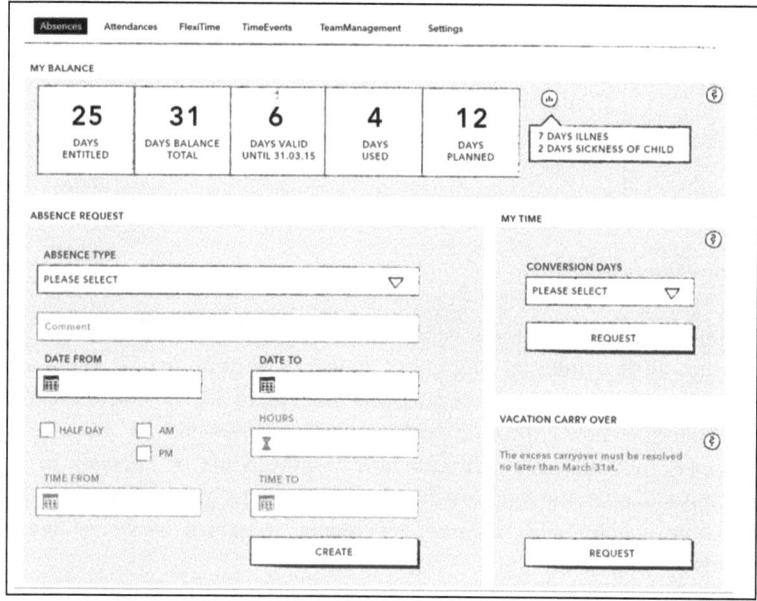

Figure 27: Example of a Wireframe

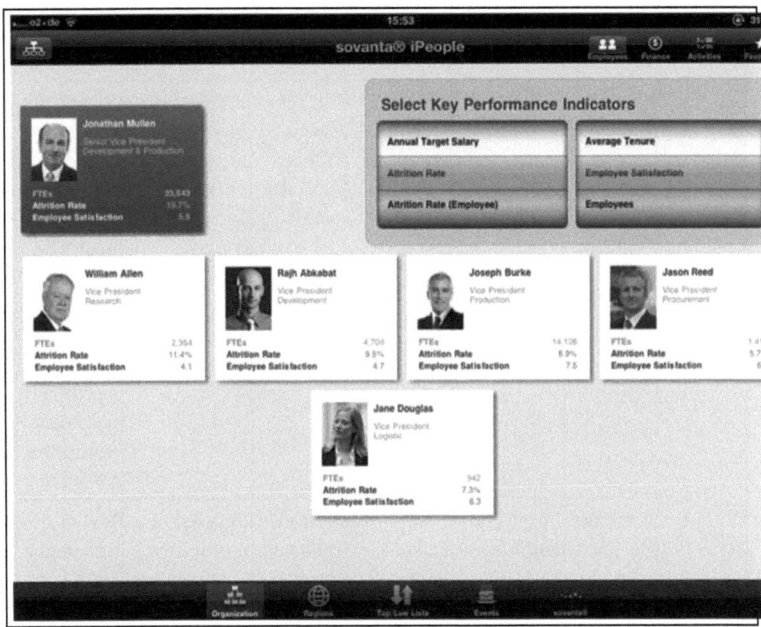

Figure 28: Example of a Mockup

Table 25: Informal Communication Structures – Ad-hoc Communication

Communication Interaction	Sender	Receiver	Medium	Frequency	Purpose	Documentation
Ad-hoc internal alignment meetings	IT project manager	Front-end or back-end developer	Personal meetings	3-5 times per week	Discuss new requirements/ changes in requirements after *jour fixe*	No documentation
	Front-end	Back-end developer	Personal meetings	3 5 times per week	Discuss issues with	No document

	developer				features	ation
Ad-hoc phone calls and emails from customer PM	Customer's project manager	IT project manager	Phone calls, email	> 1 phone call per day, 4-5 emails per day	Request new requirements, report test results, etc.	Tickets (normal request), additional email from IT project manager to customer's project manager (important results)
	Customer's project manager	Front-end and back-end developers	Phone calls, emails	3 phone calls per week, > 4 emails per week	Request new requirements, report test results, etc.	No documentation
Ad-hoc internal status meeting	IT project manager	IT company manager (project sponsor)	Personal talks	1-2 times per week	Update project sponsor on status of project	Usually none, although important decisions, such as new resources, justify email to customer's project manager

We consolidated the communication structures in **Figure 29**, which shows that the communication with users occurs only when mediated through the customer's project manager.

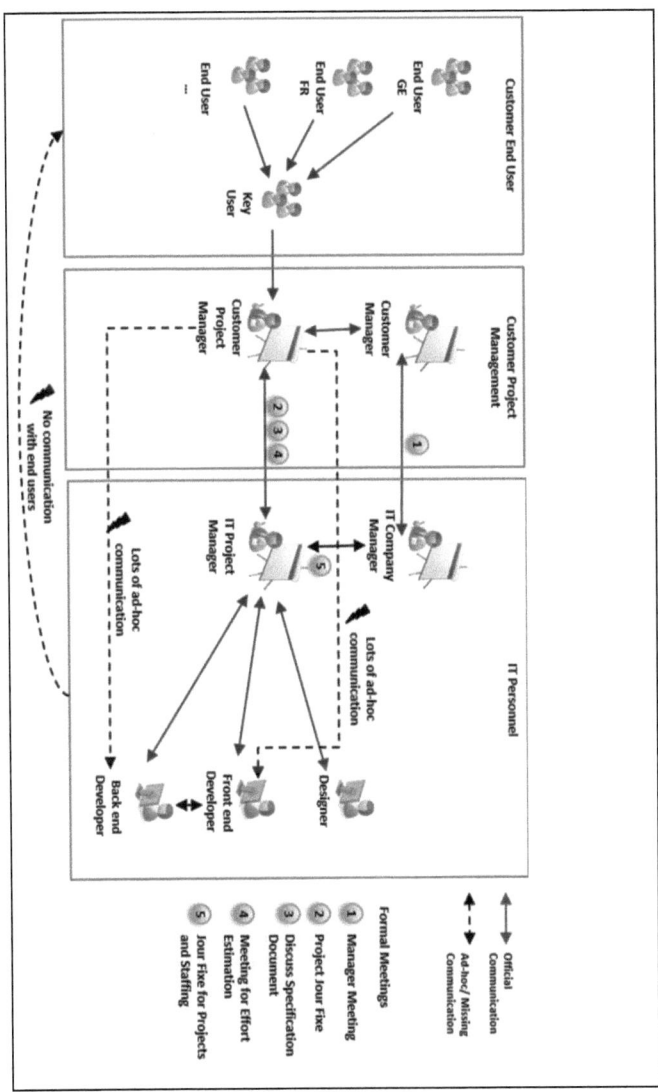

Figure 29: Established Communication Structures in the

iPeople Project

Issues that are due to the current development process and established communication structures (RQ 6.1.3)

To answer RQ 6.1.3, we transcribed and translated the informal interviews and extracted the most important issues. We also identified several issues during our analysis of the current development process and the established communication structures. **Table 26** presents the issues and related evidential quotes from the interviews.

Table 26: Issues of the iPeople Project

Evidential quotes from interviews	Issue
"The project did not build a real template for the application, and now we just ask each country what they want." "Requirements are not questioned or challenged."	Requirement elicitation process is not transparent to IT personnel.
"I do not even know what the information is needed for. How should I create a cohesive design?" "The interaction design is not clear during development, but I need to have this information to program the features."	Designers are not involved in the discussion of specifications or other meetings.
"The timeframe was fixed before the specification was discussed." "Effort estimations are required in two days, without clear specifications."	Design phase to create a software concept is very short: the time between the presentation of the specification to IT personnel and when implementation efforts have to be estimated.

Evidential quotes from interviews	Issue
"The commission of a new release is not a clear milestone, but it starts when the tickets are in the ticket system."	There is no official sign-off on the agreed scope.
"There have been six different versions of a specification document for one feature. The last one came two weeks after development close."	There are many changes in specifications during the development phase.
"Lots of countries still use the old version." "The customer's central IT department has to force the countries to upgrade to the most recent version." "Meeting with one user revealed that only one feature of the new release is of value, and one feature (planning functionality) is missing."	Unneeded features are implemented / Needed features are not implemented.
"Phone calls and emails from the customer's project manager distract me from development and cost a lot of time." "There is a lot of ad-hoc communication from the customer's project manager to developers to clarify requirements."	There is no clear communication structure to clarify requirements/features between users and IT personnel.
"The system needs complete redesign." "The system is even too complex to understand as a developer."	No information from users about how and for what they use the system leads to high complexity of the system.

User-relevant decisions in the iPeople project (RQ 6.1.4)

We used several data sources to identify decisions that are relevant to users and answer RQ 6.1.4. We studied existing project documentation (iPeople product description, meeting minutes, tickets, and emails) and asked the project participants in the fully structured interviews for examples. We identified eighteen such decisions and classified the implications based on our descriptive classification (chapter 6). Eight decisions had more than one implication.

We identified six implications at the project level, among which five had cost implications and one had timing implications. We did not identify an implication on the business process level since the influence of business processes on the app is limited. There are three implications on the task level, that is, implications that are related to changes in the users' responsibilities. There are seven implications on the domain level, one each for changes in to-be activities and features and five that have implications on the domain data. We also identified seven implications on the interaction level, where five affected the system's workflow and two the UI. Finally, there are two implications on the system level, both regarding changes in technology. An overview of the decisions that are relevant to users, the decisions' abstraction level, the area in which changes/decisions occur, and the decisions' implication(s) is presented in **Table 27**.

Table 27: User-relevant Decisions in the iPeople Project

User-relevant Decision	Abstraction Level	Area Affected by Change/ Decision	Implication
Implement time-picker functionality, where users can see historical KPI data of the last twelve months.	Project level	Cost allocation	High effort, as different data privacy laws for each country require implementing customizable solutions in each country in the back-end system

User-relevant Decision	Abstraction Level	Area Affected by Change/ Decision	Implication
	Task level	Users' responsibilities	Privacy concerns, as if there are quick promotions or changes in organizational units, it is possible to see sensitive data, such as salary, of former bosses or peers
	System level	Technology	Effort required implementing a work-around of the tested SAP back-end authorization system.
Add list view in the app that enables users to see KPI data structured by employee criteria.	Project level	Cost allocation	Different filling of back-up structure was needed, which was expensive to implement.
	Domain Level	Domain data	Have different sums; for example, the manager is excluded from the calculation in the organizational view and included in the list view
	Interaction Level	System's workflow	Change in the logical structure of the app by having two views of the same information
Countries like Belgium and Switzerland can use multiple languages that are non-ISO conforming.	Project level	Cost allocation	High effort in testing, as standard functionality is not used
	System level	Technology	Need to implement an add-on that loads language, not loaded from the iPad, but from the back end.
KPIs will be grouped according to four HR	Interaction Level	System's workflow	Users have trouble finding KPIs, as they do not know which KPIs are grouped in

User-relevant Decision	Abstraction Level	Area Affected by Change/ Decision	Implication
processes.			which process.
New features to define users' own KPI sets (favorites) are implemented without the possibility to change the order of KPIs.	Project level	Cost allocation	The KPI sets view has been implemented twice, as it was confusing for users (additional effort of about 40%).
Users' own KPI sets (favorites) are stored in an app cache and are not synchronized with the back end.	Domain Level	Domain data	KPI sets are deleted if user uninstalls app or gets a new iPad.
Define inactive employees as people on long-term vacations, long-term sick leave, or maturity leave, but do not include laid-off persons.	Project level	Timing	Need to include laid-off persons after the end of development, as the information is relevant if there are outstanding costs related to those employees. (For additional details, see chapter 9.5.3.)
Include year of birth in events.	Project level	Cost allocation	Needed to be removed after users complained
Adopt from the backup SAP system the requirement that users have to change their passwords every ninety days.	Task level	Users' responsibilities	Users have to change their passwords on their iPads every ninety days too.

User-relevant Decision	Abstraction Level	Area Affected by Change/ Decision	Implication
Adopt a new authorization concept where users can see specific organizational units and KPIs depending on their roles and organizational units.	Task level	Users' responsibilities	Users feel restricted by this new requirement.
Users must adherence to rules for data privacy protection.	Domain level	To-be activities	Pictures of laid-off employees are automatically deleted; in case of re-entry, a new picture has to be taken.
	Domain level	Domain data	Pictures of employees are shown only if the employee agreed to sign the data privacy form.
Load detailed information asynchronously from the back end.	Interaction Level	System's workflow	User has to wait for details for a few seconds but can use the app while waiting.
	Interaction Level	UI (including I/O)	Need to include activity indicator in UI.
The app works only in online mode, as data is filled in real time from the back end.	Domain level	Features	Users cannot use the app if they have no internet access.
Display training details in personal employee information.	Domain level	Domain data	Users might not find or expect personal employee information.

User-relevant Decision	Abstraction Level	Area Affected by Change/ Decision	Implication
Turn off caching to protect data privacy.	Domain level	Domain data	Users no longer see data of previous users.
	Interaction Level	System's workflow	Users have to wait for the system to load data.
Only iOS7 will be supported.	Interaction Level	UI (including I/O)	User gets a new UI.
Implement different sorting (hierarchy, branch number, alphabetical) of employees per organizational level.	Interaction Level	System's workflow	Users are confused by different sorting logics.
Show 0 percent if there is a breach in the work-time report.	Interaction Level	UI (including I/O)	Users are confused, as the value is actually below 25 percent. (For additional details, see chapter 9.5.3.)

AS-IS status of system success (RQ 6.1.5)

In the course of a pre-assessment, we asked the project participants (i.e., project manager, project sponsor, designer, and developers) about their opinion of the current success of the iPeople system (RQ 6.1.5). We also asked them about the importance of the criteria for the iPeople project and about other possible criteria. We build upon our system success criteria defined in chapter 2.4 and used a 6-point Likert scale. We analyzed the answers for each system success criterion (**Table 28** and **Table 29**). **User satisfaction:** The majority of participants had a medium level of satisfaction with the iPeople system, while four project participants considered their satisfaction level as good. It is clear that user satisfaction is an important factor.

Ease of use: The opinions about ease of use are relatively widespread, but most people viewed the ease of use as low. Two participants thought the ease of use was at a medium level, two considered it as good, and one saw it as very good. We considered whether the opinions depended on the respondent's role in the organization, but there was no clear pattern. (Project management: 1 low, 1 good; front-end developer: 2 low, 1 medium; back-end developer: 1 medium, 1 good, 1 very good; designer: 1 low). The "very good" response was from a back-end developer who did not have much experience in UI and may have compared the UI to other back-end solutions that are more complex to use. These results show that ease of use is a highly subjective concept, but the project participants agreed that it is an important factor for the iPeople project.

Table 28: Aspects of System Success of the iPeople Project

Aspects of system success	1: very low	2: low	3: medium	4: good	5: very good	Average
User Satisfaction	0	0	5	4	0	3.4
Ease of Use	0	4	2	2	1	3.0
System Use	0	0	5	4	0	3.4
Project on Time and on Budget	1	3	2	3	0	2.8
System Quality	0	1	3	5	0	3.4
Data Quality	0	0	4	4	1	3.7
Total	1	8	21	22	2	
Percent	2%	15%	39%	41%	4%	

Table 29: Importance of Aspects of the iPeople Project's System Success

Aspects of system success	1: not important	2: somewhat unimportant	3: important	4: rather important	5: very important	Average
User Satisfaction	0	0	0	2	7	4.8
Ease of Use	0	0	0	3	6	4.7
System Use	0	3	4	1	1	3.0
Project on Time and Budget	0	3	2	3	1	3.2
System Quality	0	0	1	2	6	4.6
Data Quality	0	0	0	1	8	4.9
Total	0	6	7	12	29	
Percent	0%	11%	13%	22%	54%	

System Use: the majority believed it is medium and four interviewees considered it good. The answers are grouped closely. However, the opinions about its importance vary widely, as three people believed it is rather unimportant because the app is not a system that is used every day. However, the majority considered system use as important, and two project participants even considered it to be rather or very important. We also checked for dependencies on the participants' roles but identified no pattern.

Project on time and on budget: This aspect of the iPeople system saw the widest spread in ratings of the system, as well as in its importance. The majority of participants believed the project's timeliness and ability to meet budget were low or very low (44% = 4 participants), while 22 percent believed they were medium, and a third thought they were good. The spread continues terms of the importance of being on time and on budget, as a third believed it was rather unimportant, as the customer has a fixed contract with the software company and the resources per release are fixed in advance. The other six believed it was at least important. **System Quality:** The majority believed the system quality was good, a third considered is as medium, and the designer believed it was low. However, the designer probably did not have many insights about the system's code or stability. As for the importance of system quality, all project participants believed it is at least important, and the majority considered it as a very important aspect of the iPeople project. **Data quality:** The majority of project participants considered the system's data quality to be good or even very good, and the rest considered the data quality to be medium. All project participants saw data quality as the most important aspect of system success, as the purpose of the iPeople system is to present KPI and employee-specific data.

We also asked the project participants whether there are other important criteria for the iPeople solution. While most participants said that the aspects of system success about which they had been asked covered everything, others named four additional criteria: The designer mentioned joy of use but commented that this is not so important for business application. A back end developers suggested separating ease of use between customizing users and users. Another back-end developer referred to SAP's sixteen product standards (e.g., data security, only certified shareware). Finally, one project participant said that customer communication is an important criterion.

9.4.3. Summary of the As-is

Our analysis shows that there are issues in the development process and in the current communication structures with the user, so improvement in the UDC process would be useful for the iPeople project. (The iPeople project is the "oldest" project in the company, so it does not use successful processes developed later in the company.) However, not all processes and communication structures should be replaced; only specific parts and a smooth, efficient integration of improvements in the UDC process are targeted, so a project-specific adaptation of the UDC-LSI method is required. We also identified eighteen decisions that are relevant to users and that should be discussed with them.

We asked participants who play various roles and who have differing experience levels to assess the system's success, and the average assessment of "medium" for all aspects of system success indicates there is room for improvement in many respects.

9.5. Applying the UDC-LSI Method in Practice (Simulated Instantiation)

We instantiated the UDC-LSI method using two detailed process descriptions and a corresponding practical example of the iPeople project.

9.5.1. Design and Data Collection Procedure

Based on the results of the as-is study, we instantiated the UDC-LSI method for the iPeople project to answer RQ 6.2. We identified eighteen user-relevant decisions for discussion with the users: design decisions that are based on the users' requirements and have to be discussed in the design phase and decisions to be discussed with the users in the implementation phase. These two types of decisions differ in terms of their documentation and communication needs, so we present the adaptation process in two parts, one for the design phase of the project and another for the implementation phase. We build upon our proposed UDC-LSI method, introduced in chapter 7, but we also consider the extensions suggested during the validation with experts in chapter 8 (the expert suggestions are presented in chapter 8.4.)

9.5.2. Adaptation Process

In the following we motivate the instantiation of the four parts of the UDC-LSI method (chapter 7) in the iPeople project. We evaluate each subtask for opera rationalization, including the extension ideas from the experts, as well as existing processes and tools that are already used in the company. Then we present the simulated instantiation solution for the design and implementation phase.

Part 1 – Setting up Communication Structures with User Representatives

The first part is comprised of three subtasks: define representatives for each class of users, map user requirements to one or more user representatives, and define notification preferences with the user representatives.

A stakeholder analysis is used in the first subtask, defining representatives for each class of users. There are four user classes in the twenty-eight countries in which the iPeople system is used, which mean that, ideally, user representatives would be required for each role and country. However, we mapped the usage profiles of all features by role, based on the iPeople product description, and found that most features differ only a little between roles. Therefore, we decided that the already existing key users in each country are suitable user representatives. One of the experts' suggestions was to exchange user representatives regularly, but as the key users of the iPeople project already have the role of multiplying the iPeople solution throughout their countries, we believe we should not exchange them.

The second subtask is to map user requirements to one or more user representatives in order to ensure requirements/features are discussed with the right user representative. Since we do not differentiate among users' roles, mapping the user requirements to the different user representatives is not required. However, there is implicit mapping as the key users request the requirements.

The last subtask of the first part is to define notification preferences with the user representatives. Since we did not have direct access to the users, we were not able to ask them about their notification preferences, but we define explicit triggers where input is needed. We believe that the key users, with their role of spreading the iPeople solution in their countries, are interested in all of the project's user-relevant decisions. An overview of the instantiation of the first part is presented in **Table 30**.

Table 30: Instantiation of Part 1 of the UDC-LSI Method

Criteria	Design Phase	Implementation Phase
User	Use 28 key users, one from each country	4 to 5 key users with a good availability who are interested in development progress and willing to clarify issues that come up during development

Part 2 – Training Developers on Capturing Decisions and Changes

The second part is comprised of four subtasks: develop a change story, including trigger points; develop a format to capture decisions; define a format to capture changes in requirements; and build a repository that captures decisions.

Developing a change story, including trigger points requires explaining typical decisions' trigger points and examples. Since we build on existing processes and tools, the developers do not have to be trained in detail. The evaluation showed that the level of acceptance, particularly the developers' perceived ease of use, is high (chapter 9.6.). In an implementation of the UDC-LSI method in the project, a meeting with the project participants to explain the new processes for documentation and communication of user-relevant decisions will be sufficient. Typical user-relevant decisions in the iPeople project are presented in chapter 9.4.2., and two detailed examples are presented in chapter 9.5.3.

The second subtask, to develop a format to capture decisions, required that we study the existing processes throughout the company, especially for the design process, where communicating design decisions via mockups/wireframes is already established. However, in other projects we observed issues with the technical assessment and detailed description of required data. The central project management tool during development is the JIRA tool, which holds all the relevant documents and represents each requirement and feature in a ticket. By including alternatives to and implications of decisions in the communication process between users and IT personnel, we included a suggestion from the experts that the communication include options for alternatives to the decision, not only the rationale for the decision.

In performing the third subtask, defining a format to capture changes in requirements, we observed that changes in requirements occur mainly in the design phase, as more detailed decisions are required in the implementation phase. We suggest as a pragmatic solution the scribble doc, which just highlights changes by formatting the new parts (bold, italics). For the implementation phase, we suggest recording the results in JIRA tickets.

The final subtask of the second part is to build a repository to capture decisions. Since this process differs in the design and implementation phases, we chose two tools: the scribble doc for the design phase and the standard project management tool for the implementation phase, as IT personnel uses JIRA during development anyway. We suggest documenting the results either in an updated version of the scribble doc or in JIRA. It is also possible to do a report in JIRA and send that around as meeting minutes. An overview of the instantiation of the second part is presented in **Table 31**.

Part 3 – Setting up the Traceability of Decisions

The third part has only two subtasks: map requirements to decisions and implement the notification process for users.

The first subtask differs for the design and implementation phases. In the design phase mapping is done by guiding the user through wireframes—that is, through the conceptualization of a requirement—so mapping from requirement to feature is done implicitly, where each feature gets an ID in the scribble doc (see chapter 9.5.2.) and a wireframe/mockup and the data definition describes the feature. In the implementation phase, we reuse the scribble doc ID to enable a communication with the users based on visual representations.

As for the second subtask, implementing the notification process for users, there is currently no communication about design decisions with users in the design and implementation phases. For the design phase, we use two workshops to discuss and align the concept with users. For the implementation phase we replace the ad-hoc communication with the customer's project manager with a two-level process. For both phases we defined a trigger and included a suggestion from the experts that we use a skilled PMO for channel communication and to select a decision. We use the existing project management structures in the IT personnel and the customer to support communication and documentation. An overview of the instantiation of the third part is presented in **Table 32.Table 32Table 31: Instantiation of Part 2 of the UDC-LSI Method**

Criteria	Design Phase	Implementation Phase
User-relevant	Design decisions on how	Decisions based on a new

decision	to implement requirements	requirement, unclear specification, or technical issue
Format for decision capture and requirement changes	Wireframes + data definition Update changes through formatting, such as bolding, italics	Structured field (question, alternative, implication) in a JIRA tool that can be filled per ticket Update chosen alternative in the ticket
Tool/repository	Scribble doc, where each wireframe is one page where content and data description are specified	Existing project management tool JIRA

Table 32: Instantiation of Part 3 of the UDC-LSI Method

Criteria	Design Phase	Implementation Phase
Traceability of decisions relevant to users	Requirement –> feature > wireframe/mockup + data definition → scribble doc ID	Scribble doc ID
Notification process/trigger	Completion of first concept in scribble doc 1.0	1. level: in each weekly jour fixe 2. level: at least five open decisions for clarification with users

Part 4 – Defining the Means of Communication

The fourth part has four subtasks: set up agendas for meetings with managers and workshops with the user representatives, set up a general information platform, and ensure notification about smaller decisions that affect representatives / managers.

The first subtask is to set up a fixed agenda for meetings with managers. Currently, there is one monthly manager meeting (chapter 9.4.2.), but when we analyzed typical user-relevant decisions in the iPeople project, most did not need that escalation level. Therefore, we do not suggest manager meetings for the iPeople project unless a particular decision requires that level of escalation.

The second subtask is to have workshops with the user representatives. There is no communication with users from IT personnel, but IT personnel are interested in getting feedback from users. In addition, the as-is analysis showed a clear need to increase communication between users and developers. Based on a suggestion from the experts, we use IT representatives for each role: one designer, one front-end developer, and one back-end developer. Since the workshop concept is already used, we suggest reusing that concept (i.e. Design - workshop series with 28 user representatives; participation of 1 designer. 1 front end and 1 back end developer, and Implementation – 2 level process with customer PM/selected user representatives). Currently these workshops are moderated only by designers. However, we believe that is important to include all roles, i.e. include developers and IT PM from IT personnel.

The third and last subtask of the fourth part is to set up a general information platform. , and ensure notification about smaller decisions that affect representatives/managers. We did not implement these subtasks in the iPeople project, but both suggested repositories (scribble doc and the JIRA tool) can be used to circulate among all users.

An overview of the instantiation of the fourth part is presented in **Table 33**

Table 33: Instantiation of the Fourth Part of the UDC-LSI Method

Criteria	Design Phase	Implementation Phase
Means of	Workshop series with 28 key	1. level: existing telephone

	communication	users with one designer, one front-end developer, and one back-end developer	conference with one designer, one front-end developer, and one back-end developer

9.5.3. Results

Overview of the instantiation (RQ 6.2)

To give a complete overview of the instantiation, we combined all adaptation decisions in **Table 34**.

Table 34: Instantiation of the UDC-LSI Method in the iPeople Project

Area	Criteria	Design phase	Implementation phase
Documentation	User-relevant decision	Design decisions on how to implement requirements	Decisions based on new requirements, unclear specifications, or technical issues
	Format	Wireframes/mockups and data definitions	New field in JIRA tickets (structured with question, alternatives, implications)
	Tool	Scribble doc	JIRA (existing project management tool)
	Traceability	Requirement –> feature > wireframe/mockup + data definition → scribble doc ID	Scribble doc ID
Communication	User representatives	28 existing key users, one per country	1. level: customer project manager 2. level: 4-5 selected key users
	Trigger	Completion of first concept in scribble doc 1.0	1. level: In each weekly jour fixe 2. level: at least five open decisions for clarification with users
	Means of	Workshop series with 28	1. level: existing telephone

Area	Criteria	Design phase	Implementation phase
	communication	key users; participation by one designer, one front-end developer, and one back-end developer	conference with participation by one designer, one front-end developer, and one back-end developer 2. level: Workshop with 4-5 selected key users and participation by one designer, one front-end developer, and one back-end developer

New Processes for Design and Implementation Phase with the UDC-LSI Method

Methods define processes, and the processes provide guidance on how to solve problems (Hevner et al., 2004). Here, the textual descriptions of "best practice" approaches are described for the design and implementation phases (**Figure 30**).

Design phase. The new process at the beginning of the design phase starts when the IT personnel receive the requirements list from the customer's project manager.

The first step (D1a) is to create a UI concept, that is, to design how the new requirement will be included in the existing application. For completely new requirements, these decisions are captured in wireframes (**Figure 23**), and features that are part of existing UIs are captured in mockups (**Figure 28**).

In step D1b, which occurs parallel to step D1a, the developers assess the feature's technical implementation by determining which data are available in the back-end systems and how they can be retrieved to include in the iPeople system. The results of the assessment are captured in data definitions.

Next, step D2 combines the wireframes or mockups with a content and data description in the scribble doc (**Figure 33**).

Step D3 is a workshop discussion of the first version of the scribble doc with the twenty-eight key users. In this first workshop all requirements/features are presented by the IT personnel through wireframes/mockups, including the content description and the data definition. The discussion occurs among the IT personnel (IT project manager, designer, front-end developer, and back-end developer) and the users in order to ensure each knows the rationale and use cases for each feature.

In step D4 the scribble doc is updated with the new information gained in the workshop. The result is scribble doc 2.0.

Finally, a second workshop with the twenty-eight key users is held to agree on the concept and sign off on the scope of the release or hotfix (D5). After the sign-off, the estimate for the development effort is fixed.

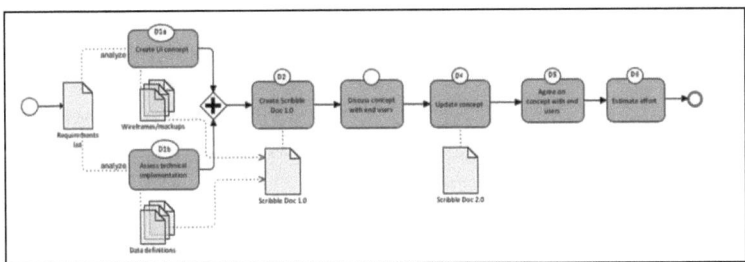

Figure 30: New Process with UDC-LSI Method in the Design Phase

Implementation phase

Three kinds of change events can occur during development: a new customer request from the customer's project manager is formulated, an unclear specification issue requires a decision, and a technical issue requires information from the customer (**Figure 31**). If one of these three events happens, step I1 is to document the request in the new field, "customer-relevant decision," in a JIRA ticket. The structure of the documentation is questions, alternatives, and implications of the alternatives.

Step I2 is to prepare each weekly jour fixe with the customer's project manager. The IT project manager creates a report of all entries in the field of customer-relevant decisions in the iPeople project.

In step I3 all requests from the report are discussed in the jour fixe with the customer's project manager and classified with the IT project manager, the designer, and the developers. The discussion determines whether the customer's project manager can clarify the request or it should be discussed with the user. Requests that the customer's project manager can clarify will be directly updated in JIRA, and user-relevant decisions are collected.

If there are several (e.g., 5) user-relevant decisions or a defined period of time (e.g., four weeks), a workshop with four or five selected key users takes place (step I4). The IT personnel present the required decisions in the format of questions, alternatives, and implications and include a visual indication (either from the scribble doc or a screenshot from the current development prototype). A decision about an alternative is made in a joint discussion between the IT personnel and the user.

Step I5 is to update the field "customer-relevant decision" in JIRA with the decision.

The last step, step I6, is to continue the development of the feature.

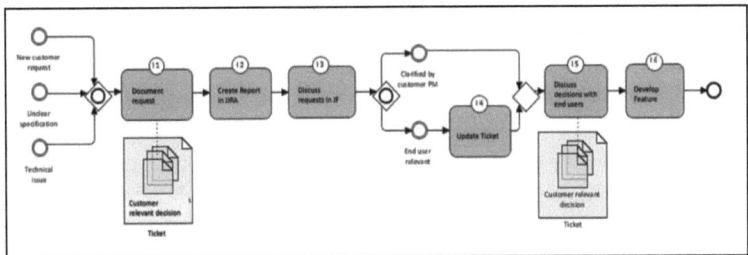

Figure 31: New Process with UDC-LSI Method in the Implementation Phase

In order to describe the instantiation in as detailed a way as possible, we extracted an example of each process.

Example Design Phase – Inactive employees

In the current iPeople solution, only active employees are displayed in the organizational tiles. The example refers to the extension to display inactive employees as well as those on long-term leave. The initial requirement from the first document is presented in **Figure 32**. It is clear that this description is specific, as a source (data base table IT9006) is given, but there is no indication of the reason that this information is needed, which makes it difficult for designers or developers to include the feature in the application.

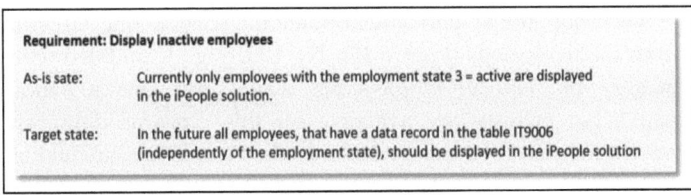

Figure 32: Initial Requirement Related to Inactive Employees

Based on this initial requirement, two steps occur in parallel. The designer creates the UI concept, which is displayed in the screenshot in **Figure 33**. The designer decides to include a banderole to indicate whether an employee is inactive ("abwesend") and describes the content on the screen as active and inactive employees. In parallel, the developers create the data description. As there is no information in the initial requirement, the developer analyzes the data table IT9006 and creates the data description: "Inactive employees are employees who are permanent workers but do not affect company performance, that is, those on maturity leave or long-term sick leave or who are temporarily laid off."

This initial scribble doc 1.0 is then discussed with the twenty-eight key users in an in-person workshop, where the IT personnel (IT project manager, designer, one front-end and one back-end developer) present the UI concept and the data description to the user. An exemplary course of action is presented in **Figure 34**. The IT personnel ask for what purpose the users need to display inactive employees, and the user explains that they need this feature in order to replace a paper-based list (cost center list). To ensure they can abolish that list, they need to get an overview of all outstanding payables to the inactive employees. The direct discussion reveals that, not only inactive employees but also employees who have been laid off could still have outstanding bonuses to be paid or travel expenses to be reimbursed. Therefore, a third category of employees must be displayed.

After the workshop, the IT personnel update the scribble doc 2.0 with the results from the workshops (**Figure 35**). The UI design is updated with the third category of "laid-off employees," which also gets a banderole ("entlassen"). No pictures are available for this class, as data privacy protection requires that pictures be deleted when employees are laid off. In addition, the data description is adapted and the changes are made clearly recognizable (here, using bolding and italics). This new version of the scribble doc is presented to the twenty-eight key users in a second workshop. When the users agree on the concept, the design decisions are final and the effort required for implementation can be estimated.

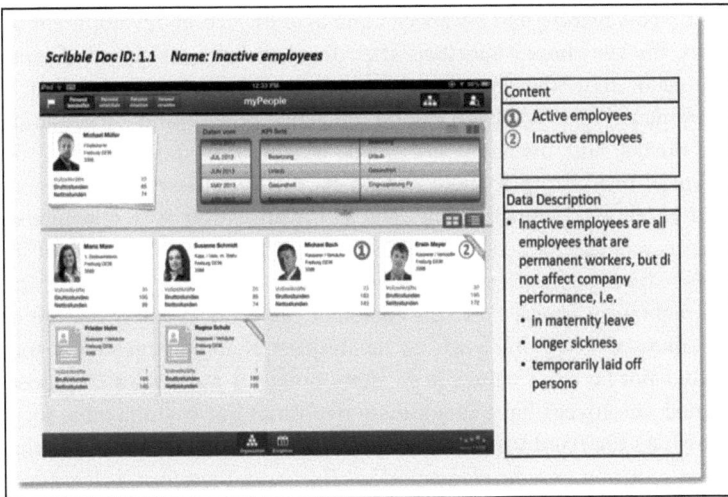

Figure 33: Scribble Doc 1.0 of Inactive Employees

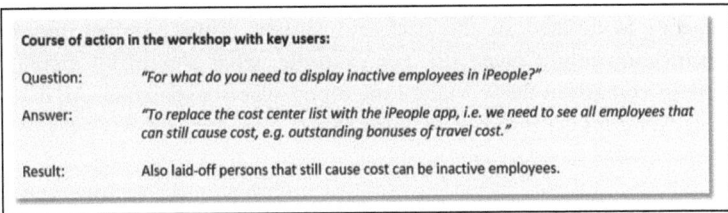

Figure 34: Course of Action in the First Workshop that Addresses the Requirement Related to Inactive Employees

Example Implementation Phase – Working time report

The example for the implementation phase is the feature "working time report." This feature had six specifications in the actual development of the project, the last change specified after development was closed. Therefore, it is clear that the specification was not sufficiently detailed. The requirement is to include KPIs for breaches of working time standards (e.g., breaks and overtime not used, etc.) in the detailed view of an employee. For example, there should be a KPI to describe deviations in actual vs. allowed working time. The KPI is presented as an absolute value and in percentage of actual vs. allowed working time. As described in the process description, three kinds of events can cause decisions in the implementation phase: First, the customer can request a new feature or an adaptation of a feature, such as the request that the thresholds for the breaches not be fixed values (e.g., show breach if more than 25 percent of assigned employees have illegitimate overtime) but customizable for each country. As the fixed values were specified in the requirement, this change request required new implementation effort and, therefore, a decision. The second kind of decision in the implementation phase occurs when a technical issue occurs during development. For example, it was not clear to the back-end developer where the mapping of actual breaches to possible breaches is defined in the back-end system. Third, ambiguities in the specification might come up. For example, what should be displayed if there is a breach in the working time report was not specified. An overview of all examples is presented in **Figure 36**.

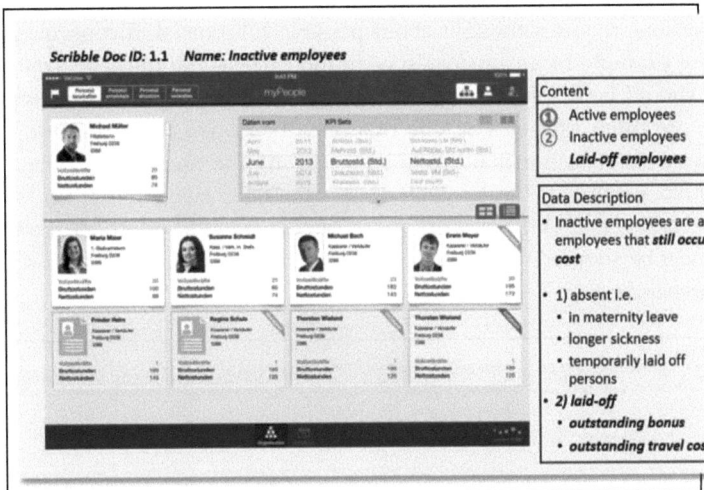

Figure 35: Updated Scribble Doc 2.0 of Inactive Employees

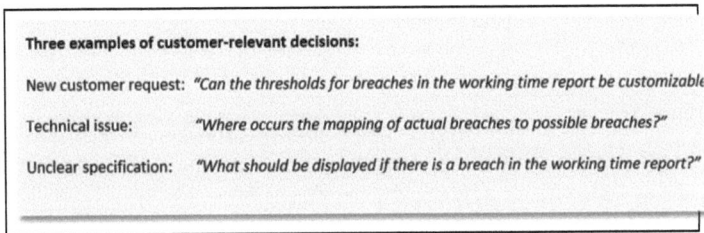

Figure 36: Example of Three Types of Decisions Relevant to Customers

The first step (I1) when any of these three events occur is to document the request in the new field in the affected feature's JIRA ticket. As shown in **Figure 37**, we suggested documenting the request in the format: question, alternatives, and implications. The documentation in the ticket has two advantages: the IT personnel who receive the request must put it into context (i.e., the feature), and the documentation with alternatives and implications requires thought about possible solutions and consequences. For the example of an unclear specification event, the question concerns what should be displayed if there is a breach in the working time report. There are three alternatives: The first one, the easiest to implement, is to display 0 percent, but that might be confusing for users, as the standard threshold is actually "under 25 percent." The other two alternatives, show "-" or show "n/a," both require more implementation effort, as the front end must be adapted, but these alternatives might be easier for the users to comprehend.

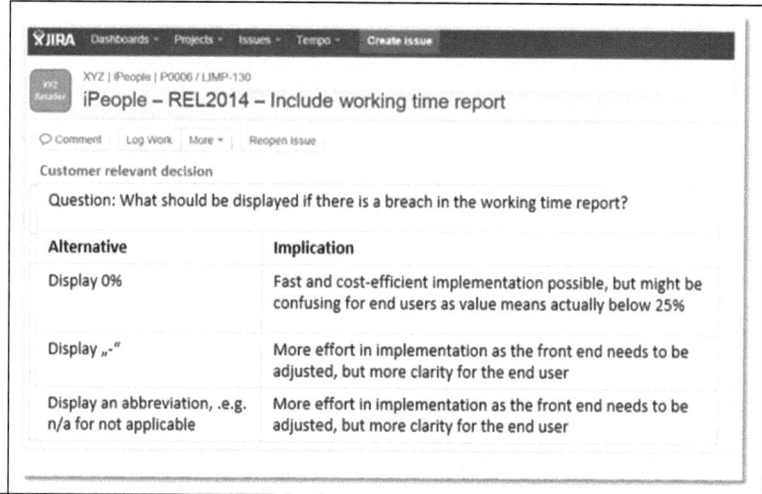

Figure 37: Example JIRA Ticket for a Customer-Relevant Decision

The next step (I2) is to build a report in JIRA that lists all customer-relevant decisions from the last week (**Figure 38**). The advantage of using a separate field in tickets is that it is possible to filter against that field.

The three customer-relevant decisions are discussed with the customer's project manager in the jour fixe (step I 3). The discussion of the new customer request reveals that it is a change request, but as it requires minimal effort, it can be implemented within the current release. The discussion about the technical issue showed that the customer's project manager must ask the customer's IT department where the mapping is available in the back-end system, so these two decisions are classified in "clarified by customer's project manager." However, the last decision about the unclear specification, that is, how the breaches in the working time report should be displayed, requires the users' input. An overview of a possible course of action in the jour fixe is presented in **Figure 39**.

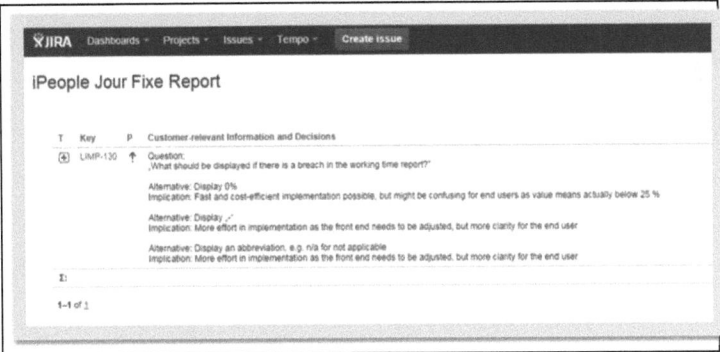

Figure 38: Exemplary JIRA Report for Jour Fixe

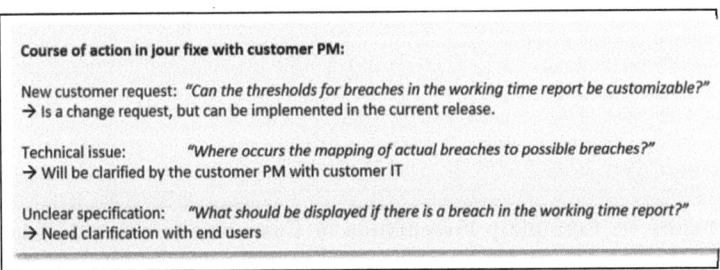

Figure 39: Exemplary Course of Action in Jour Fixe

The next step, I4, is to discuss with four or five key users the decisions that are relevant to the users. In the workshop the IT personnel (IT project manager, designer, and front-end/back-end developers) explain the open question and the alternatives and implications. In order to ensure that the key users know where to place the question, the scribble doc ID and a visual mockup or screenshot are shown. The discussion with the users leads to the decision to use alternative 2, but the users must also understand the consequences of this alternative's higher implementation cost. **Figure 40** shows exemplary presentation format.

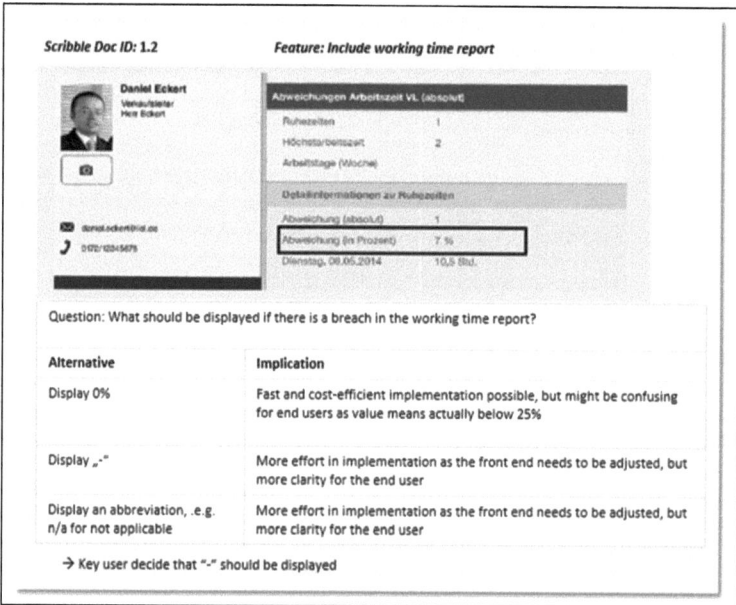

Figure 40: Exemplary Presentation of Customer-Relevant Decision in Workshop with Users

After the decisions are made, the JIRA tickets are updated to ensure the traceability of the decision (step I5). When the result of the decision process is documented, the feature can be implemented.

9.5.4. Summary of the Simulated Instantiation

The simulated instantiation of the UDC-LSI method in the iPeople project defined new processes to document and communicate user-relevant decisions with key users. The new process steps affect all project participants: the designer with the creation of the UI concept and the presentation of those ideas to the users; the developers with the data descriptions, the documentation in JIRA, and the participation in the discussions with the customer PM and the key users; the project management with the coordination and insurance of the right documentation and communication; and the business side mainly with provision of key users for discussions. Some parts have been left out, which is in line with Wieringa and Moralı (2012), who stated that "some parts of the technique may have turned out to be unusable or useless."

However, we still have no information concerning whether this instantiation is actually feasible to implement, whether there are positive effects on system success, and whether the effort is worth the effort and is usable, that is, accepted by the project participants. Therefore, we evaluated this instantiation of the UDC-LSI method with the project participants.

9.6. Evaluation of the Application of the UDC-LSI Method

The general goal is to evaluate this instantiation of the UDC-LSI method in the unit of analysis (iPeople project) from the perspective of project participants. In particular, we wanted to understand the feasibility, effectiveness, efficiency, and acceptance of the instantiation of the UDC-LSI method.

9.6.1. Design and Data Collection Procedure

For the evaluation we conducted nine fully structured interviews with project participants. In a fully structured interview all questions are planned in advance and are asked in the same order. As Runeson and Höst (2008) suggested, we included participants from a variety of roles: a project sponsor, a project manager, a designer, and six developers (three front-end, three back-end). All are project participants from IT personnel who worked on the iPeople project. Their experience level differs; for example, the project sponsor had long experience in sales organizations, one back-end developer had more than twenty years of software development experience, and the project manager was newly trained. As Runeson and Höst (2008) suggested, we mixed open and closed questions in the interview plan.

The nine interviews were done in person, with eight interviews conducted in German and one in English. The interview agenda had three parts: a pre-assessment, the presentation and assessment of the UDC-LSI instantiation, and a post-assessment. In the pre-assessment, we asked the project participants about the as-is status of system success (chapter 9.4.2.), where we introduced the definitions of the aspects of system success (chapter 1) to ensure a common understanding of terminology. In the second part of the interviews, we provided a brief description of the UDC-LSI method in general and then presented the newly designed processes with the detailed examples for each phase (design and implementation) (chapter 9.5.3). Next, we assessed the project participants' opinions using primarily closed questionnaires with a Likert scale to ensure objectivity and comparability in the analysis of the results. To ensure that we interpreted the participants' answers correctly, we also included requests for rationales and open questions. The post-assessment reviewed the effects on system success and other effects that would occur if the proposed

UDC-LSI instantiation were completely implemented. We also asked for additional user-relevant decisions (chapter 9.5.3.). The interview questionnaire in German is presented in its entirety in the Appendix.

For the data analysis we recorded all interviews and transcribed the open questions. We translated the answers to the open questions into English and summarized them by counting similar answers, as suggested by Runeson and Höst (2008).

We recorded 737 min of interview time, with the average interview time of 82 minutes and a range of 64 to 104 minutes. **Table 35** provides an overview of the interviews and the corresponding roles and interview duration. **Table 33** shows the GQM table for the assessment (Basili et al., 1994)

Table 35: Overview of Interview Duration and Interviewees' Roles

No	Role	Interview time [min.]
1	Project manager	71
2	Designer	104
3	Developer (front end)	87
4	Project sponsor	64
5	Developer (back-end)	71
6	Developer (front-end)	86
7	Developer (back-end)	84
8	Developer (front-end)	96
9	Developer (back-end)	74
	Total	737
	Average	82
	Minimum	64
	Maximum	104

Table 36: GQM Table of the Assessment of the UDC-LSI Method

Goal	RQ		Data Source	Measurement
Determine the feasibility of the method	3.1.	Is it feasible to implement the method from the perspective of the project participants?	Closed questionnaire and rationale; open questions in nine evaluation interviews	4-item Likert Scale + notes by the researcher
Determine the effectiveness of the method	3.2.	How effective is the method in the project from the perspective of the project participants?		
		3.2.1. Does an implementation of the UDC-LSI method increase the level of system success from the perspective of the project participants?	Closed questionnaire and rationale	5-item Likert Scale + notes by the researcher
		3.2.2. What are the other effects of the method from the perspective of the project participants?	Open question	Notes by the researcher

Goal	RQ	Data Source	Measurement
Determine the efficiency of the method	3.3. How efficient is the method from the perspective of the project participants?		
	3.3.1. How much effort is required to execute the method?	Estimation by the project manager and project sponsor	Person days
	3.3.2. Does the effort required to execute the method equal its value?	Closed questionnaire and rationale	6-item Likert Scale + notes by the researcher
Determine the level of acceptance of the method	3.4. How usable is the method from the perspective of the practitioners?		TAM
	3.4.1. What is the project participants' perception of the method's ease of use?	Closed questionnaire and rationale	7-item Likert Scale + notes by the researcher
	3.4.2. What is the project participants' perception of the method's usefulness?	Closed questionnaire and rationale	7-item Likert Scale + notes by the researcher
	3.4.3. What is the project participants' attitude about using the	Closed questionnaire and rationale	7-item Likert Scale + notes by the

Goal	RQ	Data Source	Measurement
	method?		researcher
	3.4.4. What is the project participants' behavioral intention regarding future use of the method?	Closed questionnaire and rationale	7-item Likert Scale + notes by the researcher

In order to achieve a differentiated view of the project participants, we separated the method instantiation into four parts for our assessment (**Table 37**).

Table 37: Parts of the UDC-LSI Method Instantiation

Area	Design phase	Implementation phase
Documentation	Part 1. Documentation of design decisions in the scribble doc	Part 3. Documentation of requests in JIRA tickets
Communication	Part 2. Alignment of design decisions in workshops with key users	Part 4. Alignment of request first in the *jour fixe* and then with selected key users

9.6.2. Results

This chapter answers RQs 6.3.1 – 6.3.4. We report on the method's feasibility by means of project participants' assessments and present advantages, barriers to implementation, and improvement ideas. Then we report on the method's effectiveness and efficiency and, with the help of the TAM, show the method's level of acceptance.

Feasibility (RQ 6.3.1)

To answer RQ 6.3.1., we analyzed the method's feasibility in three dimensions:
- The internal development process
- For this system
- With this customer

All participants stated that the method is feasible to implement, but some thought that, especially communication in the design phase could be done only with significant effort. The project participants considered the steps in the process that concern the documentation to be easier than the steps that concern communication. The process suggested for the implementation phase can be implemented with less effort than the process for design phase can because the JIRA tool already exists. However, there are three medium-effort ratings since the new process requires a lot of writing. Overall, the participants estimated that the method would require low to medium effort since mockups already exist and the process has been proven in other projects. However, the project participants rated communication with twenty-eight key users are requiring a high level of effort because of their availability (and unavailability). **Table 38** presents an overview of the results of the feasibility study from the development process perspective.

Table 38: Feasibility with Regard to Development Process

Area	Phase	Is feasible to implement in the iPeople development process with...				Rationale
		Low effort	Medium effort	High effort	No effort	
Documentation	Design	3	6	0	0	Mockup usually exists, so extension to scribble doc is small (5). Two back-end developers think technical description of corner cases can be complex (2). Proven method in other projects (2)
	Implementation	6	3	0	0	JIRA tool already exists (3). Easy to use and administer (5) 3 back-end developers think it requires a lot of writing (3).
Communication	Design	1	4	4	0	Availability and organization of 28 key user from different countries is complex (7). Agreement between key users might be a problem (1).
	Implementation	4	4	1	0	Internal JF is not a problem (3). Availability and organization of 5 key

						users is medium complex (3).
	total	14	17	5	0	
	percent	39%	47%	14%	0%	

The participants also considered instantiation of the UDC-LSI method to be feasible from a system perspective, and most of the participants (69%) even think it would be good to implement. The only doubts lie in the communication part of design phase. The results also show that the process is more difficult to implement in the design phase than in the implementation phase. The results show higher ratings from the system perspective than from the process perspective because the system itself does not have significant influence on the UDC-LSI method. **Table 39** provides an overview of the feasibility from the system perspective.

Table 39: Feasibility from the System Perspective

Area	Phase	Is feasible to implement in the iPeople system				Rationale
		Good	Medium	Poor	Not at all	
Documentation	Design	5	4	0	0	Works in other projects (4) Initial effort to describe technical details (3)
	Implementation	8	1	0	0	No problems as an internal process (8) Little more effort than current process (1)

Area	Phase	Good	Medium	Poor	Not at all	Rationale
Communication	Design	6	0	3	0	No restriction from the system (4) Rollout in several countries with several key users (1)
Communication	Implementation	6	3	0	0	User-centered product (1) Complex to organize workshops (2)
	total	25	8	3	0	
	percent	69%	22%	8%	0%	

Table 40: The Customer's View of Feasibility

		The method is feasible to implement with this customer				
Area	Phase	Good	Medium	Poor	Not at all	Rationale
Documentation	Design	5	2	2	0	Internal process (2) Customer works dynamically with deadlines (3). Customer rejects paying for design work (1). Work with other projects (3)
Documentation	Implementation	8	1	0	0	Internal documentation, so no restriction for customer (4)
Com	Design	1	2	5	1	High effort required to get key users from 28

m u ni ca ti o n						countries (5). Customer's project manager will not give up authority to key users (3).
	Implementation	3	3	3	0	Jour fixe is easy, but workshops are hard to organize (6). Customer's project manager want to keep the mediator role between key users and IT (3).
	total	17	8	10	1	
	percent	47%	22%	28%	3%	

The third category, which concerns whether it is feasible to implement the UDC-LSI method with this customer, had the lowest rating regarding feasibility, but 47% considered it good to implement. Even so, the discussions with the twenty-eight key users showed that the majority believed the method would be difficult to implement with this customer. Again, the project participants considered the documentation part easier to implement than the communication part and the process of the implementation phase more feasible than the process of the design phase.

It was also clear that the customer's project manager did not want to give up the mediator role, making it difficult to implement the method with that particular customer. Only the IT project manager saw implementing the method as not at all feasible because her job would be to convince the customer's project manager. **Table 40** presents an overview of the method's feasibility from the customer perspective.

In addition to the closed questionnaires, we also used open questions to collect advantages, barriers to implementation, and improvement ideas. The advantages are presented in **Table 41**, the barriers to implementation in **Table 42**, and the improvement ideas in **Table 43**.

The results of the feasibility study show that all but one participant considered it feasible to implement the UDC-LSI method, and even if a high level of effort or a low level of ability to implement it was stated, the participant still named advantages. Therefore, Hypothesis H1, the project participants consider it feasible to implement the UDC-LSI method in the project and see advantages of its implementation, is confirmed.

The barriers to implementation can be categorized into three themes. First, there are four timing concerns: time estimation for concept creation is too short in projects; project timelines are too tight for a long communication phase; customer mentality currently requires quick response, such as estimates within two days; and urgent requests might not be able to be postponed until the next jour fixe. Second, there are two tool-related concerns: scribble doc is not yet commonly recognized as a tool, so there is no external JIRA access via VPN yet, and some new customer requests might require a new JIRA ticket. Third, there are three scope-related concerns: managers might want to have a more detailed specification than scribble doc, developers need experience in customer communication for workshops, and there is a danger of scope creep when key users are involved.

Table 41: Advantages of the UDC-LSI Method

Area	Phase	Advantages (count)
Documentation	Design	Increased transparency because of documentation in central document (7)
		Common understanding of requirements (4)
		Security of scope because of sign-off

		(7) Easier communication with the users (4) Helps developers understand the scope (3)
	Implementation	Clear traceability of decision about a feature/ticket (8) Documentation of decision ensures clarity for later questions (8) Faster communication than current tool (2)
Communication	Design	Direct discussion with user enables early adaptation of specifications (9) Increased understanding of rationale behind user requirements (3 Mutual understanding between IT and business teams (1) User is integrated into the process (1)
	Implementation	Less wrong / unneeded development (5) Clearer goal for development (5) Users understand decisions (3) Less ad hoc communication because of organized jour fixe process (2) Increased user acceptance (2)

However, since none of the mentioned concerns questions the general feasibility of the UDC-LSI method, the general concept is considered feasible. Even so, to get ideas for future improvements, we asked project participants for ideas that would enhance this instantiation. The most frequently mentioned improvement idea, to describe the content of a screen in more detail, including corner cases, should be implemented when that process is used. We wanted to keep the description as simple as possible for the user, but from a developers' perspective a detailed description is important and the information and discussion about corner cases can only be done with experts, that is, users. For the same reasons, a field to describe the possible interactions on the screen should be included.

Other ideas concern a stricter process for the result documentation and approval. The use of labels to improve how the customer-relevant decisions are organized in JIRA is a good suggestion from the JIRA expert of the case company, as is an official sign-off after the design phase and the circulation of the result of the *jour fixe*.

The last category of improvement ideas concerns the number of users and what means of communication to use. Five interviewees believed that the workshops should be held with fewer users, but no one had an idea about how to select the users and how to decide which country's key users should not be included. Some suggested including all users by conducting the workshops as online meeting, but other interviewees commented that this approach would also be difficult and that it is important to have these workshops as face-to-face meetings. Another suggestion was to ask all key users separately for their opinion in personal meetings and then discuss their responses in an online workshop. This approach would be more convenient for the business side, but the developer who came up with this suggestion also commented that this approach would be expensive for the IT side.

Table 42: Barriers to Implementation of the UDC-LSI Method

Area	Phase	Barriers to implementation (all named only once)
Documentation	Design	Time estimation for concept creation is too short in projects. Manager might want to have more detailed specification than scribble doc.

		Scribble doc is not yet commonly recognized as a tool.
	Implementation	No external JIRA access via VPN yet. Some new customer requests might require a new JIRA ticket.
Communication	Design	Different opinions of key users can lead to long discussion. Developers need experience in customer communication for workshops. Customer's project manager might use a "short cut" without direct user - developer communication. Project timelines are too tight for a long communication phase.
	Implementation	Customer mentality currently requires quick response, such as estimates within two days. Urgent requests might not be able to be postponed until the next jour fixe. Danger of scope creep when key users are involved.

Table 43: Improvement Ideas for this Instantiation of the UDC-LSI Method

Area	Phase	Improvement ideas for implementation (count)
Documentation	Design	Provide more detailed content description for each field/KPI including corner cases (6). Include interaction field in scribble doc (5).
	Implementation	Use labels in JIRA to organize open and closed decisions (1).
Communication	Design	Use fewer key users because of issues with access and to have a more productive workshop (5); however, there is no selection criteria. Do workshops as an online meeting (3). Ask key users separately and then have an online meeting, but this comes at a high cost for IT (1). Circulate scribble doc with all key users, and then meet only with key users with significant feedback (1). Use designer as moderator, as technical persons do not have the trust of key users (1). Have an official sign-off of scribble doc (1).
	Implementation	Use an online meeting instead of a face-to-face workshop for small changes (4). Send the results of *jour fixe* to customer's project manager, such as via JIRA report as PDF, or customer's project manager needs JIRA access (1).

Effectiveness (RQ 6.3.2)

To determine the method's effectiveness, we focus on aspects of system success. We asked the project participants whether they believed a particular aspect of system success would improve, be unaffected, or decrease with implementation of the UDC-LSI method in the iPeople project. The results, based on a 5-point Likert scale, are presented in **Table 44**.

The results show that most answers indicate that the method improves system success, while a few participants said that system success is unaffected and only one indicated that system success is negatively affected.

All participants believes that user satisfaction, an important aspect of system success, would increase if the UDC-LSI method is implemented.

Most of the project participants we interviewed believed that ease of use will improve with the UDC-LSI method, but three believed it would be unaffected, as ease of use is the designer's job independent of measurements concerning UDC. Most also believed that system use would increase, but a significant number thought system use would be unaffected, as use of the business app is mandatory.

Table 44: Effects of the UDC-LSI Method on System Success

System success criteria	Strong decrease	Low decrease	Unaffected	Low increase	Strong increase	Rationale (count)
User Satisfaction	0	0	0	3	6	More understanding and feeling of integration from users (6) Better satisfaction of users' needs (5) Increased understanding of complex scenarios mean fewer unexpected bugs (2).
Ease of Use	0	0	3	4	2	Enablement of small but relevant UI changes (4) No changes as ease of use

System success criteria	Strong decrease	Low decrease	Unaffected	Low increase	Strong increase	Rationale (count)
System Use	0	0	4	3	2	depends only on the designer (3) Simpler solution because of fewer unneeded features (2) Use is mandatory, so system use is unaffected (4). Increased satisfaction leads to higher usage (3). Better system knowledge leads to high usage (2).
Project on Time and Budget	0	1	0	3	5	Clearer scope leads to better planning and fewer delays (6). Fewer adaptations after go-live (1) Effort required for workshops affects timing (1).
System Quality	0	0	4	1	4	Better comprehension of requirements increases quality (3). More time for right implementation (2) System quality is already high; improvements come only though refactoring (4).
Data Quality	0	0	5	2	2	Data quality is constant, as data backbone does not change (5). Better understanding of scope increases usage of data (3).
Total	0	1	16	16	21	

System success criteria	Strong decrease	Low decrease	Unaffected	Low increase	Strong increase	Rationale (count)
Percent	0%	1%	30%	30%	39%	
Category Total		1		16	37	
Category percent		1%		30%	69%	

Almost all of the project participants we interviewed said that the likelihood that a project will be on time and on budget will increase because of the measurement factors in the UDC-LSI method, as the clearer scope will lead to better planning. However, one participant suggested that the level of effort required from a timing perspective is so high because of the workshops that the project is less likely to be on time and on budget.

More than half of the participants believed system quality would improve with the use of the method, but almost half said that system quality is already high and cannot be influenced by the method—only through refactoring the code.

A slight majority of the participants thought that the final aspect of system success, data quality, would be unaffected by using the method. Their rationale was that the iPeople system reads data from an existing backbone, so changes in the iPeople project would not affect the data. Nevertheless, almost half of the participants said the method could improve data quality, as improved understanding of the project scope will improve data usage.

Almost all of the participants thought the method would have positive effects of system success, while only one answer indicated a negative effect. For some aspects of system success, the opinions were spread between not having an effected and improving system success, but most participants expected an improvement in five out of six aspects of system success. Hypothesis H3 is confirmed because the UDC-LSI method saw a high level of acceptance and the potential for a high level of system use.

In addition to the closed questions regarding the aspects of system success, we asked the project participants open questions about other effects of the implementation of the UDC-LSI method, and the results answered RQ 6.3.2. Seven out of nine interviewees stated that project satisfaction would increase as communication between the customer's IT personnel would increase, and in particular because the customer's project manager would be more satisfied if she gets user feedback. Furthermore, three interviewees believed that transparency would increase because of improved documentation. Finally, an increase in the ease of development and a decrease in complexity because of fewer unnecessary features were mentioned as benefits. The summarized results are presented in **Table 45**.

Efficiency (RQ 6.3.3)

In order to answer RQ 6.3.3, we estimated the additional effort required to implement the UDC-LSI method in the iPeople project with the help of the project manager and the project sponsor. We used the process description (chapter 9.5.3.) to estimate the effort for the IT personnel and the business side for one release (about 12 weeks of development). The results are presented in the **Table 46** and **Table 47**..

The total effort for the design phase is about seventy-five person days, with fifty-eight of these person days on the business side, as the attendance of the twenty-eight key users and the customer's project manager at two full-day workshops is required. On the IT side, the effort is about seventeen person days.

The effort required in the implementation phase, at about twenty person days, is much lower than that in the design phase. There is still a slightly larger commitment required on the business side, at eleven person days.

To answer RQ 6.5.2 we asked the project participants for their opinion on the effort-benefit ratio of the four parts of the instantiation of the UDC-LSI method. Most agreed or strongly agreed that the benefits of executing the instantiation of the UDC-LSI method compensate for the required effort. The level of agreement with the positive effort-to-benefit ratio was a bit higher for the documentation parts than the communication parts, while the high level of agreement was about equal for the design phase and the implementation phase. Only the project manager believed that the effort to get key users involved was too high and did not compensate for the effort.

Since the vast majority agreed that the benefits of all parts of the UDC-LSI method outbalance the effort required, hypothesis H3 is confirmed.

Table 45: Other Effects of the UDC-LSI Method

Additional effect	Count
Increased project satisfaction (users, customer's project manager, project management, designer and developers)	7
Increase transparency because of documentation	3
Greater ease of development	1
Decreased complexity of solution because of fewer unrequired features	1

Table 46: Additional Effort Estimation for the Design Phase

| Step | Task | Description | Effort [person days] | | |
			IT personnel	Business side	Total
D1a	Create UI concept	Initial effort (5 person days) + Administration	7.5	0.0	7.5

Step	Task	Description	Effort [person days]		
			IT personnel	Business side	Total
D1b	Assess technical implementation	(2.5 person days)			
D2	Create scribble doc 1.0				
D3	Discuss concept with users	Preparation (1.5 person days), + Execution (1 IT project manager + 1 designer + 2 developers + 1 customer's project manager + 28 key users for one day = 35 person days)	5.5	29.0	34.5
D4	Update concept	Post-processing of workshop (0.5 person days)	0.5	0.0	0.5
D5	Agree on concept with users	Execution (1 IT project manager + 1 designer + 2 developers + 1 customer's project manager + 28 key users for one day = 35 person days)	4.0	29.0	33.0
D6	Estimate effort	no additional effort	0.0	0.0	0.0
		Total	17.5	58.0	75.5
		Percent of effort	23%	77%	

Table 47: Additional Effort Estimation for the Implementation Phase

Step	Task	Description	Effort [person days]		
			IT personnel	Business side	Total
I1	Document customer-relevant decisions	Initial effort to include field in JIRA (0.5 person days) + Administration (4 requests × 12 weeks × 10 min. = 1 person day)	1.5	0.0	1.5
I2	Build report for jour fixe	1 IT project manager × 12 weeks × 5 min. = 0.1 person days	0.1	0.0	0.1
I3	1. level discuss decisions in jour fixe	Execution (1 designer + 2 developers for 1 day = 3 person days). IT project manager and customer's project manager already have jour fixe.	3.0	5.0	8.0
I4	2. level discuss decisions with users	Execution (1 IT project manager + 1 designer + 2 developers + 1 customer's project manager + 5 key users for 2 half-day workshops = 10 person days)	4.0	6.0	10.0
I5	Update ticket with result of decision	1 IT project manager × 12 weeks × 5 min. = 0.1 person days	0.1	0.0	0.1
I6	Develop feature	no additional effort	0.0	0.0	0.0
		Total	8.7	11.0	19.7
		Percent of effort	44%	56%	

Table 48: Effort-Benefit Ratio of the UDC-LSI Method

Area	Phase	Strongly disagree	Disagree	Somewhat disagree	Somewhat agree	Agree	Strongly agree	Rationale: Benefits	Rationale: Effort
Documentation	Design	0	0	0	1	3	5	Central documentation helps to spot where requirements aren't clear (2) Early avoidance of mistakes/ misunderstandings saves effort later in the process (5) → 10% of project time is worth it.	Admiration only a little additional effort (2). Only initial effort is high (1). Effort for designer is high (1).
	Implementation	0	0	1	0	2	6	Saves development time (2) Developers think about rationale (1) Change request more clearly defined (2)	Low effort since tickets have to be updated anyway (4). Effort for documentation of every decision is high (2).
	Total	0	0	1	1	5	11		
	Percent	0%	0%	6%	6%	28%	60%		
Communication	Design	0	1	0	1	3	4	Avoidance of later misunderstandings (3) 4-hour workshop can save 4 days of development.	High level of effort to organize meetings (3)

Area	Phase	Strongly disagree	Disagree	Somewhat disagree	Somewhat agree	Agree	Strongly agree	Rationale: Benefits	Rationale: Effort
	Implementation	0	0	0	3	3	3	Stay on time because of better planning (1) Saves expensive misunderstandings (2) User can identify with the app (1)	Online meeting would require less effort (1)
	Total	0	1	0	4	6	7		
	Percent	0%	6%	0%	22%	33%	39%		
	Grand total	0	1	1	5	11	18		
	Total percent	0%	3%	3%	14%	30%	50%		

Acceptance (RQ 6.3.4)

To measure acceptance of the method, we build upon the TAM. Therefore, we determined perceived ease of use, perceived usefulness, attitude toward using, and behavioral intention to use. According to TAM, these forecast actual system use and the level of acceptance.

Almost all of the project participants agreed that all parts of the UDC-LSI method are easy to understand and easy to use, so Hypothesis H4 is confirmed.

The only two negative answers regarding the communication part of the design and the implementation phases came from the customer's project

Table 49: Perceived Ease of Use of the UDC-LSI Method

Area	Phase	The instantiation of the USC-LSI method is...	Strongly disagree	Disagree	Somewhat disagree	Neutral	Somewhat agree	Agree	Strongly agree
Documentation	Design	...easy to understand.	0	0	0	0	0	2	7
		...easy to use in practice.	0	0	0	0	1	3	5
	Implementation	...easy to understand.	0	0	0	0	0	3	6
		...easy to use in practice.	0	0	0	0	0	2	7
Communication	Design	...easy to understand.	0	0	0	0	0	3	6
		...easy to use in practice.	0	1	0	0	1	3	4
	Implementation	...easy to understand.	0	0	0	0	0	3	6
		...easy to use in practice.	0	0	1	0	1	1	6
		Total	0	1	1	0	3	20	47
		Percent	0%	1%	1%	0%	4%	28%	66%
		Category total	2			0	70		
		Category percent	3%			0%	97%		

manager, who thought that persuading the customer's project manager to have discussions only in the *jour fixe* and then with users would not be possible in practice. An overview of the results is presented in **Table 49**.

Again, almost all project participants agreed that all parts of the UDC-LSI method are useful, so Hypothesis H5 is confirmed. The only negative answer came from a back-end developer who thought that a more detailed description than the scribble doc would be required to explain user requirements. An overview of the results is presented in **Table 50**.

Almost all project participants agreed that all parts of the UDC-LSI method are useful, so Hypothesis H7 is confirmed. The only two negative answers were, again, from the project manager, who did not believe that the involvement of key users in the design or implementation phase is possible. An overview of the results is presented in **Table 49**. Since the project participants perceived the method as easy to use, had a positive attitude toward using the method, and a behavioral intention to use it, the acceptance and usability of the UDC-LSI method are confirmed. Since all project participants had a positive attitude toward using all parts of the UDC-LSI method, Hypothesis H6 is confirmed. An overview of the results is presented in **Table 51**.

Table 50: Perceived Usefulness of the UDC-LSI Method

Area	Phase	The instantiation of the USC-LSI method…	Strongly disagree	Disagree	Somewhat disagree	Neutral	Somewhat agree	Agree	Strongly agree
Documentation	Design	…is important for my work in the project.	0	0	0	0	0	2	7
		…helps to explain implementation of the user requirements in UI design and concept.	0	0	1	0	0	2	6
		…strengthens the common understanding of UI design and concept among project participants.	0	0	0	0	0	0	9
	Implementation	…is important for my work in the project.	0	0	0	0	1	2	6
		…supports customer	0	0	0	0	3	2	4

Area	Phase	The instantiation of the USC-LSI method…	Strongly disagree	Disagree	Somewhat	Neutral	Somewhat agree	Agree	Strongly agree
		communication.							
		…increases traceability of decisions.	0	0	0	0	0	2	7
Communication	Design	…is important for my work in the project.	0	0	0	2	1	0	6
		…helps me to understand user requirements.	0	0	0	0	1	0	8
	Implementation	…is important for my work in the project.	0	0	0	1	1	3	4
		…avoids corrections in the test phase.	0	0	0	0	2	0	7
		Total	0	0	1	3	9	13	64
		Percent	0%	0%	1%	3%	10%	14%	71%
		Category total	1			3	86		
		Category percent	1%			3%	96%		

Table 51: Attitude Toward Using the UDC-LSI Method

Area	Phase	For this instantiation of the UDC-LSI method, I think…	Strongly disagree	Disagree	Somewhat disagree	Neutral	Somewhat agree	Agree	Strongly agree
Documentation	Design	…it is a good idea to use it.	0	0	0	0	0	1	8
Documentation	Implementation	…it is a good idea to use it.	0	0	0	0	0	3	6
Communication	Design	…it is a good idea to use it.	0	0	0	0	1	1	7
Communication	Implementation	…it is a good idea to use it.	0	0	0	0	0	4	5
	Total		0	0	0	0	1	9	26
	Percent		0%	0%	0%	0%	3%	25%	72%
	Category total		0			0	36		
	Category percent		0%			0%	100%		

Table 52: Behavioral Intention to Use the UDC-LSI Method

Area	Phase	For this instantiation of the UDC-LSI method, I would…	Strongly disagree	Disagree	Somewhat disagree	Neutral	Somewhat agree	Agree	Strongly agree
Documentation	Design	…use it in future projects.	0	0	0	0	0	2	7
Documentation	Design	…advise others to use it.	0	0	0	0	0	2	7

Area	Phase	For this instantiation of the UDC-LSI method, I would...	Strongly disagree	Disagree	Somewhat disagree	Neutral	Somewhat agree	Agree	Strongly agree
	Implementation	...use it in future projects.	0	0	0	0	0	3	6
		...advise others to use it.	0	0	0	0	0	3	6
Communication	Design	...use it in future projects.	0	0	0	1	1	1	6
		...advise others to use it.	0	0	0	2	0	0	7
	Implementation	...use it in future projects.	0	0	1	0	2	1	5
		...advise others to use it.	0	0	1	1	0	1	6
		Total	0	0	2	4	3	13	50
		Percent	0%	0%	3%	6%	4%	18%	69%
		Category total	2			4	66		
		Category percent	3%			6%	91%		

9.6.3. Discussion

The results showed that the project participants had a clear positive assessment of the UDC-LSI method's utility (i.e., feasibility, effectiveness, and efficiency) and usability (i.e., acceptance by the future users). They considered that the feasibility of the documentation part of the method was greater than that of the communication part of the method and rated the process for implementation as easier to implement than the design, mainly because of the involvement of fewer user representatives. This result is in line with the experts' concern that users are too diverse, so too many representatives would be required.

The majority of project participants felt that the method was effective, although about a third believed the method would not affect the system's success factors. Still, the majority thought that the method's benefits outbalance the effort required, a possible indication that there are other positive effects not related to aspects of system success.

Another important result is the finding that the UDC-LSI method must be adapted to the project context, especially in the design and implementation phases' processes. We linked these processes through the scribble doc ID, but they are structurally different in terms of their documented decisions, tools, formats, and so on. This view is in line with Hevner et al.'s (2004) statement that an "evaluation includes the integration of the artifact within the technical infrastructure of the business environment."

We also studied the other obstacles to implementation that the experts named with regard to the case study. The experts' comment that it is difficult to ensure a stable requirement also came up in the scope concern that the project participants named among the barriers to implementation. The experts expected that it would be difficult to motivate developers to document decisions, but they accepted the method and said that they intended to use it in the future, so we set this concern aside along with the concern that "developers are not aware of the decisions" since we were able to identify user-relevant decisions that were named primarily by developers among the project participants. The study setup did not allow us to determine whether it would be difficult keep up the discipline required for consistent documentation throughout the project, but the case company indicated that it plans to implement most of the suggested processes in the future. In our suggested process, we mitigated the obstacle "developers cannot decide which decisions are relevant" by suggesting discussion in the *jour fixe*. The concern about the tool ("no realistic tool for capturing requirements is available") was not a problem in this case since we used the scribble doc and JIRA, which already exist. The same is true for the obstacle "many developers are external, so training is difficult." One developer in the case project was an external freelancer, but he has been integrated into the development process and would be available for a meeting, which is considered sufficient for training. We addressed the suggestion that "email should not be used for communication" by documenting using the scribble doc and the JIRA tool, but meeting minutes were still sent via email, which seemed to be the most practical approach. The obstacles of "mapping between requirements and users is hard to realize" and "users do not understand documentation of decisions" were not at issue in the case project, so solutions could not be tested. Doing so is a suggestion for future work.

We also did not match notification preferences from user representatives with user-relevant decisions in part because we did not have access to user representatives. However, the case study revealed that all user-relevant decisions that occur during design and implementation should be discussed with users, so investigating the need for such match is a topic for future work.

We found that decisions have more than one implication when we studied user-relevant decisions. This finding has implications for our descriptive classification, which can still be used to describe the implications, although not to classify the decisions.

The study also showed that the UDC-LSI method works for other than traditional development methods if there are issues in UDC. Therefore, we concluded that projects with issues in UDC can be improved in the process of improving system success, but we cannot yet explain the influence of the development process.

The improvement ideas and answers to open questions showed that a detailed description of decisions, especially in the design phase, is required, as is finding efficient means of communicating with users.

Questions regarding "not too many people" vs. "all opinions are important" and ideas exchanged through online meetings or individual discussions remain, so there is a clear need for further study on these issues.

9.7. Threats to Validity

Here we consider possible threats to validity based on Runeson et al. (2012): construct validity, internal validity, external validity, and reliability.

9.7.1. Construct Validity

Construct validity reflects the extent to which the operational measures represent what is investigated, based on the research questions.

The case study design included a plan concerning how the data from the various sources are used to answer the research questions. This approach helps to mitigate the concern that the feedback from project participants does not reflect their true opinion (Wieringa, 2007). The researcher who conducted the case study worked in the company for more than three months in order to develop a trusting relationship between the researcher and project participants. This prolonged involvement also helped the researcher understand how project participants interpreted terms and used vocabulary (Runeson & Höst, 2008).

In particular, we ensured construct validity through data source triangulation by using first-degree methods (open interviews, workshops, and closed questionnaires) and second-degree or indirect methods (review of existing project documentation). We also obtained data from participants in various roles with various levels of experience in the project (developers, project managers, project sponsor, and designers) to ensure a holistic view.

We independently applied the method to ensure correct and complete instantiation. Not all parts of the method were instantiated, but by providing the rationale for that decision, we have a clear line of evidence. In addition, other researchers checked the defined processes and examples for understandability.

There is a threat that interview questions could be interpreted differently by researcher and interviewee, but we presented definitions, and the format of personal interviews enabled the interviewees to ask questions if they didn't understand a term or a question. In addition, several researchers checked the questionnaire and the presentation for understandability.

The as-is assessment of the system's success factors was presented as a pre-assessment before any advantages of the method were named to ensure a neutral opinion of the interviewees. In addition, the project participants reviewed the results of the assessment and confirmed that the results reflect their opinions correctly, as suggested by Runeson and Höst (2008).

One interview was conducted in English, as the interviewee understood written German better than spoken German. If the interviewee had questions about a question, we translated it during the interview. All interviews were recorded with the consent of the interviewees so we could transcribe responses to open questions.

Finally, we avoided insufficient operationalization of the variables used in the TAM questionnaire by building on similar measurement instruments used in other evaluations (Heinrich, 2014).

9.7.2. Internal Validity

Internal validity is concerned with causal relationships, particularly whether there are other influencing factors of which the researcher is not aware. A potential threat to internal validity is that the project participants were biased toward acceptance of the method, as they were presented with only a hypothetical instantiation. They could also have been biased because they knew that the researcher was the author of the method. Therefore, we emphasized in the interviews that they should assess the method objectively and kept our involvement during the administration of closed questionnaires to a minimum.

9.7.3. External Validity

External validity is concerned with the extent to which it is possible to generalize the findings of a case study and to what extend the findings are relevant to other cases.

According to Runeson et al. (2012), in case study research the achievement of deeper understanding and improved realism might be preferred to the representativeness of a case. This concern was especially important, as we had to define a project-specific instantiation of the method, but the results achieved in this case study might not be directly transferable to another LSI project. In any case, the project participants found the method instantiation effective, feasible, acceptable, and efficient in this case study, suggesting that similar results can be achieved in other project-specific instantiations of the method.

Another possible threat in the evaluation part of the method is that we could interview project participants only from the IT team, so we lacked users' perspectives. We mitigated this threat by including participants in roles who had backgrounds similar to those of the potential users (e.g., the project sponsor has considerable experience with sales organizations).

9.7.4. Reliability

Reliability is concerned with the researcher's relationship with the data and analysis. All assessments and interviews were done by one researcher to ensure consistency (Runeson & Höst, 2008), but another researcher could have interpreted the data differently.

The researcher documented every step during design, data collection, and analysis, and each step was peer-reviewed by a second researcher. The research design of case study was also discussed with a second researcher, as Runeson et al. (2012), to increase reliability. Therefore, there is a reproducible chain of evidence for the case study.

One possible threat to reliability in the as-is study is the related to the use of informal, unstructured interviews and workshops (without a fixed set of questions) to identify the steps in the software development process. However, another researcher in software engineering should also be able to record such a development process.

A large majority of the subjects who filled out the questionnaires decided in favor of the UDC-LSI method, and another researcher would interpret these data the same way.

In addition, the results of the open questions were clustered by the researcher in a way that other researchers might have interpreted differently. However, this issue should not affect the main results of the case study since the open questions build upon objective questionnaires.

9.8. Summary of the Case Study

This chapter reported on a case study of the utility and usability of the UDC-LSI method in the real-world iPeople project. We conducted a retrospective validation by analyzing the as-is status of the projects. Based on that information, we instantiated the UDC-LSI method for the iPeople project and described that instantiation with two new processes and hands-on examples for the design and implementation phases. We evaluated this simulated instantiation with the project participants in terms of its feasibility, effectiveness, and efficiency, as well as the level to which they accepted the method.

The case study design, which was based on Runeson's (2012) instructions, can be categorized as a single case study with one unit of analysis: the iPeople project and the object of study in the UDC-LSI method. We used a mixed-method approach with qualitative (open questions in interviews and workshops) and quantitative (questionnaire based on a Likert-type scale) data. Our main source of information was various interviews with the project participants; for the evaluation we conducted nine fully structured interviews.

The as-is analysis revealed that the iPeople project has issues that are due to the current development process and communication structures. Other processes used successfully in other projects of the case company, such as the scribble doc, are not used in the iPeople project. We concluded that there is a need to improve UDC, but not all existing processes should be replaced. We also identified eighteen decisions that are relevant to users, so there is a clear indication that there are topics to discuss with the users. The system success analysis revealed that there is room for improvement with regard to the ease of use and project on time and on budget criteria.

During the simulated instantiation, we analyzed the four parts of the method with their corresponding subtasks. We instantiated almost all of the subtasks and described clear rationales for why we did not instantiate the ones we did not use. One reason for this decision was that we did not have access to users in the case study. Through the as-is analyses, we also realized that the method must be adapted to the project and that as many communication structures and tools must be used as possible. Another result is that we must define two different processes for the design and implementation phase since these phases differ in terms of the nature of their decisions, documentation, and tools. In addition, we realized that all roles (designer, developer, and project management) are affected by the suggested process changes.

The evaluation with project participants showed a clear positive assessment of the UDC-LSI method's utility (i.e., feasibility, effectiveness, and efficiency) and usability (i.e., acceptance by the future users).

The feasibility for all studied perspectives (development process, system, and customer) was higher for the documentation part of the method than the communication part, which makes sense since the documentation part can be one internally in the IT Company, whereas the communication part requires contact with the customer.

For effectiveness, we studied changes in the criteria for system success and found that the majority of the participants believed the method increased effectiveness. However, about a third believed that effectiveness was unaffected, but they still named advantages, an indication that the method might have other effects. The efficiency evaluation, which determined whether the project participants believed that the effort required to execute the method outbalances the benefits, revealed that almost all projects participants believed that it did.

To evaluate the acceptance part of the method, we built upon the TAM and asked participants for their perceptions of the method's ease of use and usefulness and for their attitude about using the method and their behavioral intention to it. The large majority of project participants evaluated all four criteria as positive. Therefore, we concluded that the project participants accept the USC-LSI method and would use it in the future.

The case study showed that **the UDC-LSI method fulfills the criteria of utility and usability, but instantiating it requires considering project-specifics and ensuring detailed documentation, especially for the**

decisions made during the design phase. Another **open issue concerns what communication with user representatives should look like**, especially how many representatives are required and what format (i.e., in-person or online meetings) is best, which the case study could not definitively answer. Since we did not have the chance to discuss this issue with users, it remains up to future work to resolve. Initially, the UDC-LSI was defined for LSI projects that use traditional methods, but the iPeople project used more agile processes. Therefore, the influence of the development process on the application of the UDC-LSI method remains to be studied further.

PART V.
SUMMARY

Chapter 10
Conclusion and Outlook

"There is only one way to avoid criticism: do nothing, say nothing and be nothing."

Aristotle

10.1. Major Findings of this Thesis

We structure the major findings of this thesis according to the three problems defined in chapter 1.2. First, we wanted to *analyze the status of UPI in software development in terms of their effects and existing methods*.

We conducted a meta-analysis to validate the effect of UPI. We extracted the correlation data, variation, and number of participants from eighty-six studies and found that **aspects of the development process and human aspects have a positive effect on system success** and that **most studies with negative correlations were published more than ten years ago**. We also found that **UPI has a positive effect on user satisfaction and system use, but the large variation in correlations illustrates the complexity involved in measuring and studying UPI**. Another important contribution of this thesis is the classification of the aspects of UPI into development process, human aspects, system attributes, organizational factors, and system success. The analysis revealed that **UPI is an important research topic**, as it has been researched in a broad manner by those in various fields of research (RQ 6.1.1 and 6.1.4).

Furthermore, we analyzed the thirty-six methods papers' targeted issues, validation contexts, and proposed solutions. An important finding was that **all software development activities** (planning and project management, software specification and requirements engineering, software design and implementation, software verification and validation, and software evolution) **are affected by methods**, but only a few methods focus on the design and implementation activities. An important contribution of this thesis is the structured overview of practices with examples of the method in practice. The overview shows that **practices derived from the solutions vary widely in all software activities**. The comparison between what the surveys research and what the **methods target reveals that the categories targeted by methods for UPI are similar to those targeted by the surveys**. The analysis of the validation context revealed **that most methods have been validated in a public sector environment**.

We also used an expert interview series to determine how and how well LSI projects support UDC. With regard to current communication structures in LSI projects, the results of the study indicate that there is **no direct communication between developers and users in most LSI projects**. However, the experts stated that there is a clear connection between communication gaps and increased implementation costs and a higher level of effort required in testing. **We classified the ideas from experts to overcome the obstacles** into **user-centered approaches** (e.g., show user prototypes), **developer-centered approaches** (e.g., developers must mediate between different user groups), and **organizational approaches** (e.g., use test data early in the project).

The **experts did not suggest a successful, sustainable solution to overcome the communication gaps in LSI projects, in particular to improve UDC in the design and implementation activities**, so there is a need to close that gap. Therefore, we targeted the next problem: *Designing a new method to enhance UDC in the design and implementation phase of LSI projects using traditional development methods.*

In order to define what are user-relevant decisions that should be communicated to the user, we developed a **descriptive classification of trigger points based on TORE**, which we extended through eighty-one examples of trigger points from the expert interviews. From these examples, we derived the **seven common discussion topics with users: license cost, staffing for the test, standard central processes, access rights and automation of approvals, manual vs. automated activities, infeasible user requirements, and support of user devices**. The participants considered the suggested **classification to be valid**.

We presented the **UDC-LSI method to enhance UDC in LSI projects that use traditional methods in the development of customer-specific software systems**. To design the method we first presented the problem context, that is, the targeted IT projects' challenges; a conceptual framework, which builds upon the hypothesis that an **increase in UDC improves system success**; and the design process based on practices of existing solutions.

The **UDC-LSI method has four parts**, each with several subtasks. The operationalization of the method **focuses on two central areas: documentation of user-relevant decisions and structural communication with users, so user-relevant decisions, formats, tools, traceability, user representatives, triggers, and means of communication must be defined**.

We also developed use cases for the descriptive classification and proposed deriving three artifacts—customized descriptive classification, classification structure, and checklist.

To find a solution to the third problem, *evaluating the new method's effects on system success*, we validated our method concept with experts and conducted a case study in the iPeople real-world LSI project.

The experts saw potential for our UDC-LSI method and **assessed the parts** (1 – setting up communication structures, 2 – training developers on capturing of decisions or changes, 3 – setting up the traceability of decisions, and 4 – defining the means of communication) **as useful in improving system success. In particular, it is important to get user representatives and traceability between system requirements and decisions**. The **benefits of the method** the participants named most often were **better preparation of the business organization and an increase in the transparency of the projects**. The results of our interviews showed that we should implement the UDC-LSI method only in a mature IT organization since the method requires stable processes. Furthermore, many of the experts believed that it would be difficult to motivate the developers to document decisions, to make them aware of the decisions, and to maintain the discipline needed for documentation throughout the project.

Finally, we did a case study of the UDC-LSI method's utility and usability in the real-world iPeople project. The as-is analysis revealed that the **iPeople project has issues that are due to the current development process and communication structures and that there is a need to improve UDC**.

The system success analysis showed the need for **improvement in ease of use and getting the project in time and on budget**. During the simulated instantiation, we analyzed each part with the corresponding subtasks of the UDC-LSI method. The as-is analyses showed the importance of **adapting the method to the project** and reusing as many communication structures and tools as possible. We had **to define two different processes for the design and implementation phases** since they differ in the nature of their decisions, documentation, and tools, so similar separation is needed in future implementations of the UDC-LSI method.

The evaluation with project participants resulted in a **clear, positive assessment of the method's utility (i.e., feasibility, effectiveness, and efficiency) and usability (i.e., acceptance by the future users)**. The participants saw the **feasibility** in terms of all studied perspectives (development process, system, and customer) **higher for the documentation part of the method than the communication part**. For **effectiveness,** we studied changes in the criteria for system success, and **the majority of participants** saw **an increase in each of these criteria**. However, a third believed that system success was unaffected by the method, although they still named advantages and suggested **that the method might have other effects**. The efficiency evaluation showed that **the all project participants agreed that the effort required to execute the method outbalances the benefits. For the acceptance** part we built on the TAM and asked project participants for their perceptions of the method's ease of use and usefulness, along with their attitude about using the method and their behavioral intention to it. The majority of participants evaluated **all four criteria for system success as positive**, so we concluded that the project participants accepted the USC-LSI method and would use it in the future.

10.1.1. Contribution to Theory

For the research community, the results of our meta-analysis showed that increased UPI improves system success, so research in the area of UPI in software development is beneficial and should be continued. We also increased the confidence that UPI is beneficial to system success, an important finding for researchers who develop methods to increase UPI in software development. In addition, the classification of the aspects of UPI can support researchers who study the aspects of UPI and could be used as a starting point from which to develop a common conceptual model for aspects of UPI and system success, as well as context factors.

Our analysis of existing methods showed that only a few methods focus on the design and implementation activities. This insight can support researchers in the identification of existing research gaps for methods that aim to increase UPI. The overview of proposed solutions can also be valuable to researchers by describing the state-of-the-art research of UPI methods in software development.

The definition of the UDC-LSI method broadens knowledge on methods to enhance UDC, and the descriptive classification can also be used in future research. Finally, the design validation and the evaluation of the UDC-LSI method in the iPeople project increases knowledge in the area of empirical studies in the software engineering community, which is currently not very well researched (Ramesh et al., 2004).

10.1.2. Implications for Practice

Our systematic mapping study shows that involving users in software development projects has a positive effect on system success. In particular, if users perform activities in the system development process (user participation), such as serving as project team leader or being responsible for selecting hardware or software, estimating costs, and requesting funds, the users' satisfaction with the system (and, thus, its use) increases. The same is true if users feel that the system is important and relevant to them (user involvement). Therefore, we encourage all practitioners to increase as much as possible UPI in all phases of their software development projects. The positive effects not only help improve the resulting system's quality but also increase the system's value for the user.

The overview of proposed solutions (see

Table 5) is also particularly helpful for practitioners who want to use existing practices and methods to increase UPI in software development projects. They can use those practices directly on projects.

The results from our expert interviews increase confidence for practitionneers that there is a need especially in LSI projects to increase UDC. Furthermore the examples of user-relevant decisions form the descriptive classification (see
Table 13) can be used to explain the relevant decisions to users and developers.

The UDC-LSI method itself is designed to solve a practical problem: to close the communication gap between users and developers in the design and implementation of LSI projects. Since our evaluation stated that the method has a positive effect on system success, we encourage all practitioners to implement the UDC-LSI method or parts of the method in their LSI projects. Especially the questions and criteria for operationalization (see **Table 15**) as well as the experiences of our case study (see chapter 9) are helpful for practitioneers, in case they want to implement the UDC-LSI method.

10.2. Limitations

Since we described the strengths and weaknesses and threats to validity in the subchapter for each research cycle (chapters 3.8, 4.7, and 9.7.), we explain only general limitations in this chapter.

Through the systematical approach of our mapping study, we covered a broad knowledge base, but it is possible that there is another method that also targets UDC in LSI projects.

Overall, we conclude that the systematic mapping study shows a positive correlation between various aspects of UPI and system success. However, there is still no common conceptual model with which to measure and validate this effect.

A possible limitation of the study is that the UDC-LSI method is designed for projects that use traditional software development methods, whereas the development process of our case study was a more agile approach. However, we believe that the issues in UDC within this project, still ensure a valid case study.

In addition, we could not directly ask users in our expert validation or in the case study, so future work should assess the UDC-LSI method from the users' perspective. This issue suggests another open issue that the case study revealed: we could not determine what the communication with user representatives should look like, especially how many representatives are required and what format (i.e., face-to-face or online meetings) is best.

10.3. Future Work

The analysis of the validation context revealed that most methods were validated in public environments, so we encourage other researchers to follow our approach and validate new methods also in private organizations.

Another interesting research field is the development of a common conceptual model to measure and validate effects of UPI and system success. We have begun developing a categorization of aspects with our categories and subcategories, but we encourage other researchers build upon this categorization to establish a standard model in order to enable the comparability of future studies.

In addition, we found that only a limited focus on the organizational factors and system attributes of UPI is available, so we encourage researchers to conduct studies to find out which context factors have influence of system success.

The large variation in the identified correlations calls for more sophisticated empirical studies on the effects of UPI. This would help to increase the research community's confidence in the positive effect of UPI on system success.

As we were not able to study the UDC-LSI method on a project using traditional method, a next step is to study the influence of the development process on the UDC-LSI method implementation. Nevertheless, the fact that the instantiation was possible in this project is an indication that the UDC-LSI method works also in agile development environments.

Furthermore, the concrete setting of communication with the users, as well as their interest in user-relevant decision is up for future research to determine. Thus we suggest another case study, with access to user.

Index of Tables

Figure 1: Characteristics of the Traditional Software Development Process 22
Figure 2. Structure and Contributions of the Thesis 27
Figure 3: Conceptual framework of the Technology Acceptance Model (Davis et al., 1989) 33
Figure 4. Research Cycles of the Thesis Based on the Design Science Approach 38
Figure 5: Research Method for the Systematic Mapping Study 50
Figure 6: Derived Search String for the Systematic Mapping Study 51
Figure 7: Sources and Hits in the Identification of Research Step 53
Figure 8: Excluded and Included Papers Based on Exclusion Criteria 56
Figure 9: Structural Equitation Model (SEM) of Surveys and Meta-Studies 65
Figure 10: Overview of Links in Studies with the Most Participants (on the Subcategory Level) 70
Figure 11: Methods Studies Classified by the Software Development Activities Affected 77
Figure 12: Development Methods of Case Studies 78
Figure 13: Historical Analysis of the Number of Surveys and Method Papers 96
Figure 14: Historical Analysis of Important Terms 97
Figure 15: Overview of the Experts' Educational Qualifications 109
Figure 16: Overview of the Experts' Industries 110
Figure 17: Overview of the Experts' Roles in their Companies 110
Figure 18: Conceptual Framework of the UDC-LSI Method 151
Figure 19: Exemplary Template for Documentation of Decisions 162
Figure 20: Conceptual Communication Process between User Representatives and IT Personnel 162
Figure 21: The Four Parts of the UDC-LSI method for User-Developer Communication 163
Figure 22: Use Cases for the Descriptive Classification 169
Figure 23: As-is Steps of the iPeople Project's Development Process 212
Figure 24: The Case Company's Standard Development Process 213
Figure 25: Example of a Scribble Doc Template from Other Projects 214
Figure 26: Workflow of Tickets using the JIRA Tool 215
Figure 27: Example of a Wireframe 221
Figure 28: Example of a Mockup 222
Figure 29: Established Communication Structures in the iPeople Project 224
Figure 30: New Process with UDC-LSI Method in the Design Phase 244
Figure 31: New Process with UDC-LSI Method in the Implementation Phase 246
Figure 32: Initial Requirement Related to Inactive Employees 246
Figure 33: Scribble Doc 1.0 of Inactive Employees 248

Figure 34: Course of Action in the First Workshop that Addresses the Requirement Related to Inactive Employees 248
Figure 35: Updated Scribble Doc 2.0 of Inactive Employees 250
Figure 36: Example of Three Types of Decisions Relevant to Customers 250
Figure 37: Example JIRA Ticket for a Customer-Relevant Decision 251
Figure 38: Exemplary JIRA Report for Jour Fixe 252
Figure 39: Exemplary Course of Action in Jour Fixe 252
Figure 40: Exemplary Presentation of Customer-Relevant Decision in Workshop with Users 253

Index of Figures

Figure 1: Characteristics of the Traditional Software Development Process............ 22
Figure 2. Structure and Contributions of the Thesis... 27
Figure 3: Conceptual framework of the Technology Acceptance Model (Davis et al., 1989) 33
Figure 4. Research Cycles of the Thesis Based on the Design Science Approach 38
Figure 5: Research Method for the Systematic Mapping Study 50
Figure 6: Derived Search String for the Systematic Mapping Study 51
Figure 7: Sources and Hits in the Identification of Research Step.............................. 53
Figure 8: Excluded and Included Papers Based on Exclusion Criteria...................... 56
Figure 9: Structural Equitation Model (SEM) of Surveys and Meta-Studies 65
Figure 10: Overview of Links in Studies with the Most Participants (on the Subcategory Level) 70
Figure 11: Methods Studies Classified by the Software Development Activities Affected 77
Figure 12: Development Methods of Case Studies.. 78
Figure 13: Historical Analysis of the Number of Surveys and Method Papers 96
Figure 14: Historical Analysis of Important Terms 97
Figure 15: Overview of the Experts' Educational Qualifications 109
Figure 16: Overview of the Experts' Industries... 110
Figure 17: Overview of the Experts' Roles in their Companies 110
Figure 18: Conceptual Framework of the UDC-LSI Method 151
Figure 19: Exemplary Template for Documentation of Decisions........................... 162
Figure 20: Conceptual Communication Process between User Representatives and IT Personnel 162
Figure 21: The Four Parts of the UDC-LSI method for User-Developer Communication 163
Figure 22: Use Cases for the Descriptive Classification 169
Figure 23: As-is Steps of the iPeople Project's Development Process..................... 212
Figure 24: The Case Company's Standard Development Process........................... 213
Figure 25: Example of a Scribble Doc Template from Other Projects..................... 214
Figure 26: Workflow of Tickets using the JIRA Tool 215
Figure 27: Example of a Wireframe 221
Figure 28: Example of a Mockup 222
Figure 29: Established Communication Structures in the iPeople Project.............. 224
Figure 30: New Process with UDC-LSI Method in the Design Phase 244

Figure 31: New Process with UDC-LSI Method in the Implementation Phase 246
Figure 32: Initial Requirement Related to Inactive Employees 246
Figure 33: Scribble Doc 1.0 of Inactive Employees 248
Figure 34: Course of Action in the First Workshop that Addresses the Requirement Related to Inactive Employees 248
Figure 35: Updated Scribble Doc 2.0 of Inactive Employees 250
Figure 36: Example of Three Types of Decisions Relevant to Customers 250
Figure 37: Example JIRA Ticket for a Customer-Relevant Decision 251
Figure 38: Exemplary JIRA Report for Jour Fixe 252
Figure 39: Exemplary Course of Action in Jour Fixe 252
Figure 40: Exemplary Presentation of Customer-Relevant Decision in Workshop with Users 253

References

Abelein, U. et al. 2012. A proposal for enhancing user-developer communication in large IT projects *In*: *Proceedings of the 5th International Workshop on Cooperative and Human Aspects of Software Engineering (CHASE 2012) at the ICSE 2012 Zurich, June 2nd* [online]. IEEE, pp. 1–3. Available from: http://ieeexplore.ieee.org/xpls/abs_all.jsp?arnumber=6223014 [Accessed September 19, 2012].

Abelein, U. and Paech, B. 2013a. A Descriptive Classification for End User -Relevant Decisions of Large-Scale IT Projects *In*: *Cooperative and Human Aspects of Software Engineering (CHASE), 2013 6th International Workshop on Cooperative and Human Aspects of Software Engineering*

Abelein, U. and Paech, B. 2014. State of Practice of User-Developer Communication in Large-Scale IT Projects Results of an Expert Interview Series *In*: *20th International Working Conference on Requirements Engineering: Foundation for Software Quality (REFSQ'14), Essen (Germany)*.

Abelein, U. and Paech, B. 2013b. Understanding the Influence of User Participation and Involvement on System Success - a Systematic Mapping Study. *Empirical Software Engineering* [online]. (Iivari 2004),p.in press. Available from: http://link.springer.com/10.1007/s10664-013-9278-4 [Accessed November 4, 2014].

Aladwani, A.M. 2001. Change management strategies for successful ERP implementation. *Business Process Management Journal* [online]. 7(3),pp.266–275. Available from: http://www.emeraldinsight.com/10.1108/14637150110392764.

Alleman, G.B. 2002. Agile project management methods for ERP : how to apply agile processes to complex COTS projects and live to tell about it *In*: D. WELLS and L. WILLIAMS, eds. *Extreme Programming and Agile Methods: XP/Agile Universe*. Springer Verlag, pp. 70–88.

Al-Rawas, A. and Easterbrook, S. 1996. Communication problems in requirements engineering: a field study *In*: *Proceedings of the First Westminster Conference on Professional Awareness in Software Engineering* [online]. Citeseer, pp. 1–12. Available from: http://citeseerx.ist.psu.edu/viewdoc/download?doi=10.1.1.30.4408&rep=rep1&type=pdf [Accessed September 29, 2011].

Amoako-Gyampah, K. 2007. Perceived usefulness, user involvement and behavioral intention: an empirical study of ERP implementation. *Computers in Human*

Behavior [online]. 23(3),pp.1232–1248. Available from: http://linkinghub.elsevier.com/retrieve/pii/S0747563204002201 [Accessed July 12, 2011].

Amoako-Gyampah, K. and White, K. 1993. User involvement and user satisfaction: An exploratory contingency model. *Information & Management* [online]. 25(1),pp.25–33. Available from: http://www.sciencedirect.com/science/article/pii/037872069390021K [Accessed December 6, 2011].

Amoako-Gyampah, K. and White, K. 1997. When is user involvement not user involvement? *Information Strategy: The Executive's Journal* [online]. 13(4),pp.40 – 45. Available from: http://www.redi-bw.de/db/ebsco.php/search.ebscohost.com/login.aspx?direct=true&db=buh&AN=9706306538&site=ehost-live.

Austin, R.D. and Nolan, R.L. 1998. *How to manage ERP initiatives*. Boston: Division of Research, Harvard Business School.

Bai, H. and Cheng, J. 2010. The Impact of Organizational Culture on ERP Assimilation: The Mediating Role of User Participation *In*: *2010 2nd International Workshop on Database Technology and Applications* [online]. IEEE, pp. 1–5. Available from: http://ieeexplore.ieee.org/lpdocs/epic03/wrapper.htm?arnumber=5658977 [Accessed April 12, 2012].

Bano, M. and Zowghi, D. 2013. User involvement in software development and system success: a systematic literature review. *EASE '13 Proceedings of the 17th International Conference on Evaluation and Assessment in Software Engineering* [online],pp.125–130. Available from: http://dl.acm.org/citation.cfm?id=2461017 [Accessed August 14, 2013].

Barki, H. and Hartwick, J. 1994. Measuring User Participation, User Involvement, and User Attitude. *MIS Quarterly* [online]. 18(1),p.59. Available from: http://www.jstor.org/stable/249610?origin=crossref.

Barki, H. and Hartwick, J. 1994. User Participation, Conflict, and Conflict Resolution: The Mediating Roles of Influence. *Information Systems Research* [online]. 5(4),pp.422–438. Available from: http://isr.journal.informs.org/cgi/doi/10.1287/isre.5.4.422.

Basili, V.R. et al. 1994. The Goal Question Metric Approach *In*: D. H. G. R. CALDIERA, ed. *Encyclopedia of Software Engineering*. New York, NY, USA: John Wiley & Sons, Inc., pp. 528–532.

Beck, K. et al. 2001. Manifesto for agile software development. *The Agile Alliance*.

Begier, B. 2010a. Evolutionally Improved Quality of Intelligent Systems Following Their Users ' Point of View *In: Advances in Intelligent Information and Database Systems.*, pp. 191–203.

Begier, B. 2010b. Users' involvement may help respect social and ethical values and improve software quality [online]. Springer Netherlands. Available from: http://www.springerlink.com/index/10.1007/s10796-009-9202-z [Accessed December 16, 2011].

Berger, H. 2011. *Reframing Humans in Information Systems Development* [online] (H. Isomäki & S. Pekkola, eds.). London: Springer London. Available from: http://www.springerlink.com/index/10.1007/978-1-84996-347-3 [Accessed April 17, 2012].

Bjarnason, E. et al. 2011. Requirements are slipping through the gaps — A case study on causes & effects of communication gaps in large-scale software development *In: 2011 IEEE 19th International Requirements Engineering Conference* [online]. IEEE, pp. 37–46. Available from: http://ieeexplore.ieee.org/lpdocs/epic03/wrapper.htm?arnumber=6051639 [Accessed January 18, 2012].

Bragge, J. 2009. Engineering E-Collaboration Processes to Obtain Innovative End-User Feedback on Advanced Web- Based Information Systems. *Journal of the Association for Information Systems.* 10(March 2009),pp.196–220.

Carmel, E. et al. 1993. PD and joint application design: a transatlantic comparison. *Communications of the ACM* [online]. 36(6),pp.40–48. Available from: http://portal.acm.org/citation.cfm?doid=153571.163265.

Cavaye, A. 1995. User participation in system development revisited. *Information & Management* [online]. 28(5),pp.311–323. Available from: http://www.sciencedirect.com/science/article/pii/037872069400053L [Accessed December 6, 2011].

Chang, K. et al. 2010. User commitment and collaboration: Motivational antecedents and project performance. *Information and Software Technology* [online]. 52(6),pp.672–679. Available from: http://linkinghub.elsevier.com/retrieve/pii/S0950584910000169 [Accessed October 17, 2011].

Cherry, C. and Macredie, R. 1999. The Importance of Context in Information System Design: An Assessment of Participatory Design. *Requirements Engineering* [online]. 4(2),pp.103–114. Available from: http://link.springer.com/10.1007/s007660050017.

Cohen, S. et al. 2010. A Software System Development Life Cycle Model for Improved Stakeholders ' Communication and Collaboration. *International*

Journal of Computers Communications & Control, [online]. 5(1),pp.20–41. Available from: http://75.98.171.106/opcat/docs/ASoftwareSystemDevelopmentLifeCycleModelforImproved.pdf.

Curtis, B. et al. 1988. A field study of the software design process for large systems. *Communications of the ACM* [online]. 31(11),pp.1268–1287. Available from: http://portal.acm.org/citation.cfm?id=50089 [Accessed October 6, 2011].

Davis, F. et al. 1989. User Acceptance of Computer Technology: A Comparison of two Theoretical Models. *Mangagement Science* [online]. 35(8),pp.982 – 1002. Available from: http://www.jstor.org/stable/10.2307/2632151 [Accessed July 11, 2012].

Dean, D. et al. 1998. Enabling the Effective Involvement of Multiple Users : Methods and Tools for Collaborative Software Engineering. *Journal of Management Information Systems*. 14(3),pp.179 –222.

Dennis, A. et al. 2008. Media, tasks, and communication processes: A theory of media synchronicity. *MIS quarterly* [online]. 32(3),pp.575–600. Available from: http://dl.acm.org/citation.cfm?id=2017395 [Accessed August 22, 2013].

Dennis, A.R. and Valacich, J.S. 1999. Rethinking media richness: Towards a theory of media synchronicity *In: System Sciences, 1999. HICSS-32. Proceedings of the 32nd Annual Hawaii International Conference on* [online]. IEEE, p. 10–pp. Available from: http://ieeexplore.ieee.org/xpls/abs_all.jsp?arnumber=772701 [Accessed December 22, 2011].

Doll, W. and Torkzadeh, G. 1991. A Congruence Construct of User Involvement. *Decision Sciences* [online]. 22(2),pp.443–453. Available from: http://dx.doi.org/10.1111/j.1540-5915.1991.tb00358.x.

Doll, W.J. and Torkzadeh, G. 1989. A discrepancy model of end-user computing involvement. *Management Science* [online]. 35(10),pp.1151–1171. Available from: http://www.jstor.org/stable/10.2307/2631983 [Accessed December 22, 2011].

Dörner, C. et al. 2008. Fostering user-developer collaboration with infrastructure probes. *Proceedings of the 2008 international workshop on Cooperative and Human Aspects of Software Engineering - CHASE '08* [online],pp.48–44. Available from: http://dl.acm.org/citation.cfm?id=1370126 [Accessed August 21, 2012].

Eckhardt, A. 2010. Lost in Translation ?! – The Need for a Boundary Spanner between Business and IT *In: SIGMIS-CPR'10, May 20–22, 2010, Vancouver, BC, Canada.*, pp. 75–82.

Emam, K. El et al. 1996. User participation in the requirements engineering process: An empirical study. *Requirements Engineering* [online]. 1(1),pp.4–26. Available from: http://www.springerlink.com/index/10.1007/BF01235763.

Esteves, J.M. et al. 2003. A goal/question/metric research proposal to monitor user involvement and participation in ERP implementation projects *In*: *Information Resources Management Conference (IRMA)* [online]., pp. 325–327. Available from: http://www.jesteves.com/IRMA_2003.pdf [Accessed October 18, 2011].

Evans, D.M. 2008. *Structural Equation Modeling and Natural Systems*.

Finck, M. et al. 2004. Using Groupware for Mediated Feedback *In*: *Proceedings of the eighth conference Biennial Participatory Design Conference 2004: Artful integration: interweaving media, materials and practices - volume 2, July 27 - July 7, 2004, Toronto, Canada*.

Fowler, M. and Highsmith, J. 2001. The agile manifesto. *Software Development* [online]. 9(August),pp.28–35. Available from: http://andrey.hristov.com/fht-stuttgart/The_Agile_Manifesto_SDMagazine.pdf.

Fruhling, A. et al. 2005. Collaborative usability testing to facilitate stakeholder involvement. *Value Based Software Engineering* [online],pp.201–223. Available from: http://scholar.google.com/scholar?hl=en&btnG=Search&q=intitle:Collaborative+Usability+Testing+to+Facilitate+Stakeholder+Involvement#0 [Accessed December 15, 2011].

Fuentes-Fernández, R. et al. 2009. Understanding the human context in requirements elicitation. *Requirements Engineering* [online]. 15(3),pp.267–283. Available from: http://www.springerlink.com/index/10.1007/s00766-009-0087-7 [Accessed September 1, 2011].

Gallivan, M.J. and Keil, M. 2003. The user-developer communication process: a critical case study. *Information Systems Journal* [online]. 13(1),pp.37–68. Available from: http://doi.wiley.com/10.1046/j.1365-2575.2003.00138.x [Accessed September 14, 2011].

Gefen, D. et al. 2008. Leadership and justice: Increasing non-participating users' assessment of an IT through passive participation. *Information & Management* [online]. 45(8),pp.507–512. Available from: http://linkinghub.elsevier.com/retrieve/pii/S0378720608001031 [Accessed May 4, 2012].

Hallows, J.E. 2002. *The project management office toolkit*. New York; London: AMACOM.

Hansson, C. et al. 2004. Agile Processes Enhancing User Participation for Small Providers of Off-the-Shelf Software. *World*. (April 2000),pp.175–183.

Hansson, C. et al. 2006. How to Include Users in the Development of Off-the-Shelf Software: A Case for Complementing Participatory Design with Agile Development *In: Proceedings of the 39th Annual Hawaii International Conference on System Sciences (HICSS'06)* [online]. IEEE, p. 175c–175c. Available from: http://ieeexplore.ieee.org/lpdocs/epic03/wrapper.htm?arnumber=1579648 [Accessed April 18, 2013].

Harris, M. and Weistroffer, H. 2009. A New Look at the Relationship between User Involvement in Systems Development and System Success Development and System Success. *Communications of the Association for Information Systems*. 24(1),pp.739–756.

Hartwick, J. et al. 2001. Communication as a dimension of user participation. *IEEE Transactions on Professional Communication* [online]. 44(1),pp.21–36. Available from:
http://ieeexplore.ieee.org/lpdocs/epic03/wrapper.htm?arnumber=911130.

Hartwick, J. and Barki, H. 1997. Delineating the dimensions of user participation: A replication and extension. *Review Literature And Arts Of The Americas* [online]. Available from:
http://www.computer.org/portal/web/csdl/doi/10.1109/HICSS.1997.661571 [Accessed November 11, 2011].

Hartwick, J. and Barki, H. 1994. Explaining the Role of User Participation in Information System Use. *Management Science* [online]. 40(4),pp.440–465. Available from:
http://mansci.journal.informs.org/cgi/doi/10.1287/mnsc.40.4.440.

Heinrich, R. 2014. Validation *In: Aligning Business Processes and Information Systems,*., pp. 151–194.

Hendry, D. 2008. Public participation in proprietary software development through user roles and discourse. *International Journal of Human-Computer Studies* [online]. 66(7),pp.545–557. Available from: http://linkinghub.elsevier.com/retrieve/pii/S107158190700170X [Accessed September 21, 2011].

Hevner, A.R. et al. 2004. DESIGN SCIENCE IN INFORMATION SYSTEMS RESEARCH. *MIS Quarterly*. 28(1),pp.75–105.

Hope, K. and Amdahl, E. 2011. Configuring designers? Using one agile project management methodology to achieve user participation. *New Technology, Work and Employment* [online]. 26(1),pp.54–67. Available from: http://dx.doi.org/10.1111/j.1468-005X.2010.00257.x.

Huang, Y. et al. 2008. Designing a Cooperative Learning System: A Scenario and Participatory Design Based Approach. *2008 International Symposium on Computational Intelligence and Design* [online],pp.334–337. Available from: http://ieeexplore.ieee.org/lpdocs/epic03/wrapper.htm?arnumber=4725520 [Accessed April 18, 2013].

Humayoun, S. et al. 2011. A Three-Fold Integration Framework to Incorporate User – Centered Design into Agile Software Development M. Kurosu, ed. *Human Centered Design, HCII* [online]. 6776,pp.55–64. Available from: citeulike-article-id:10346931.

Hunton, J. 1996. User Participation in Defining System Interface Requirements: An Issue of Procedural Justice. *Journal of Information Systems*. 10(1),pp.27–47.

Hunton, J. and Beeler, J. 1997. Effects of User Participation in Systems Development: A Longitudinal Field Experiment. *MIS Quarterly* [online]. 21(4),pp.359–388. Available from: http://www.jstor.org/stable/249719?origin=crossref.

Hwang, M. and Thorn, R. 1999. The effect of user engagement on system success: A meta-analytical integration of research findings. *Information & Management* [online]. 35(4),pp.229–236. Available from: http://linkinghub.elsevier.com/retrieve/pii/S0378720698000925 [Accessed November 29, 2011].

Igbaria, M. and Guimaraes, T. 1994. Empirically testing the outcomes of user involvement in DSS development. *Omega* [online]. 22(2),pp.157–172. Available from: http://www.sciencedirect.com/science/article/pii/0305048394900760 [Accessed November 2, 2011].

Iivari, J. et al. 2010. The user - the great unknown of systems development: reasons, forms, challenges, experiences and intellectual contributions of user involvement. *Information Systems Journal* [online]. 20(2),pp.109–117. Available from: http://doi.wiley.com/10.1111/j.1365-2575.2009.00336.x [Accessed August 25, 2011].

Ives, B. and Olson, M. 1984. User involvement and MIS success: a review of research. *Management science* [online]. 30(5),pp.586–603. Available from: http://www.jstor.org/stable/10.2307/2631374 [Accessed December 22, 2011].

Jalali, S. and Wohlin, C. 2012. Systematic Literature Studies: Database Searches vs. Backward Snowballing *In: Proceedings of the International Conference on Empirical Software Engineering and Measurement, ESEM'12* [online]., pp. 29–38. Available from: http://dl.acm.org/citation.cfm?id=2372257 [Accessed May 17, 2013].

Jorgensen, M. et al. 2005. Teaching evidence-based software engineering to university students *In*: *11th IEEE International Software Metrics Symposium* [online]. IEEE, p. 24. Available from: http://ieeexplore.ieee.org/lpdocs/epic03/wrapper.htm?arnumber=1509286 [Accessed September 13, 2012].

Kabbedijk, J. et al. 2009. Customer Involvement in Requirements Management: Lessons from Mass Market Software Development *In*: S. BRINKKEMPER et al., eds. *IEEE International Conference on Requirements Engineering* [online]. Ieee, pp. 281–286. Available from: http://doi.ieeecomputersociety.org/10.1109/RE.2009.28 [Accessed June 30, 2011].

Kamal, M. et al. 2011. *Analyzing the role of stakeholders in the adoption of technology integration solutions in UK local government: An exploratory study.* [online]. Elsevier Inc. Available from: 10.1016/j.giq.2010.08.003.

Kanungo, S. and Bagchi, S. 2000. Understanding User Participation and Involvement in ERP Use. *Journal of Management Research*. 1(1),pp.47–64.

Kautz, K. 2000. Customer and User Involvement in Agile Software Development. *Agile Processes in Software Engineering and Extreme Programming*. *10th International Conference, XP*,pp.168–173.

Kautz, K. 2011. Investigating the design process: participatory design in agile software development. *Information Technology & People* [online]. 24(3),pp.217–235. Available from: http://www.emeraldinsight.com/10.1108/09593841111158356 [Accessed April 11, 2013].

Kawalek, P. and Wood-Harper, T. 2002. The Finding of Thorns : User Participation in Enterprise System Implementation. *Data Base For Advances In Information Systems*. 33(1),pp.13–22.

Kensing, F. et al. 1998. MUST: A method for participatory design. *Human-Computer Interaction* [online]. 13(2),pp.129–140. Available from: http://www.tandfonline.com/doi/full/10.1207/s15327051hci1302_3 [Accessed April 18, 2013].

Kitchenham, B. and Charters, S. 2007. Guidelines for performing systematic literature reviews in software engineering. . (EBSE 2007-001). Available from: http://www.mendeley.com/research/guidelines-performing-systematic-literature-reviews-software-engineering-2/ [Accessed March 6, 2012].

Korkala, M. et al. 2006. A Case Study on the Impact of Customer Communication on Defects in Agile Software Development . *In*: P. ABRAHAMSSON and P.

KYLLONEN, eds. *AGILE 2006 (AGILE'06)* [online]. IEEE, pp. 76–88. Available from: http://doi.ieeecomputersociety.org/10.1109/AGILE.2006.1 [Accessed August 31, 2012].

Korkala, M. et al. 2010. Combining Agile and Traditional: Customer Communication in Distributed Environment *In*: D. ŠMITE et al., eds. *Agility Across Time and Space* [online]. Berlin, Heidelberg: Springer Berlin Heidelberg, pp. 201–216. Available from: http://www.springerlink.com/index/10.1007/978-3-642-12442-6 [Accessed October 25, 2011].

Kristensson, P. et al. 2011. Collaboration with Customers - Understanding the Effect of Customer-Company Interaction in New Product Development *In: 2011 44th Hawaii International Conference on System Sciences* [online]. IEEE, pp. 1–9. Available from: http://ieeexplore.ieee.org/lpdocs/epic03/wrapper.htm?arnumber=5718704 [Accessed April 13, 2012].

Kujala, S. 2008. Effective user involvement in product development by improving the analysis of user needs. *Behaviour & Information Technology* [online]. 27(6),pp.457–473. Available from: http://www.informaworld.com/openurl?genre=article&doi=10.1080/01449290601111051&magic=crossref||D404A21C5BB053405B1A640AFFD44AE3 [Accessed August 21, 2012].

Kujala, S. et al. 2005. The Role of User Involvement in Requirements Quality and Project Success. *13th IEEE International Conference on Requirements Engineering (RE'05)* [online],pp.75–84. Available from: http://ieeexplore.ieee.org/lpdocs/epic03/wrapper.htm?arnumber=1531029.

Kujala, S. 2003. User involvement: a review of the benefits and challenges. *Behaviour & Information Technology*.

Lin, W.T. and Shao, B.B.M. 2000. The relationship between user participation and system success: a simultaneous contingency approach. *Information & Management* [online]. 37(6),pp.283–295. Available from: http://linkinghub.elsevier.com/retrieve/pii/S0378720699000555.

Lu, H.-P. and Wang, J.-Y. 1997. The relationships between management styles, user participation, and system success over MIS growth stages. *Information & Management* [online]. 32(4),pp.203–213. Available from: http://www.sciencedirect.com/science/article/pii/S0378720697000219 [Accessed October 18, 2011].

Maalej, W. et al. 2009. When users become collaborators: towards continuous and context-aware user input *In: Proceeding of the 24th ACM SIGPLAN conference companion on object oriented programming systems languages and applications* [online]. ACM, pp. 981–990. Available from: http://portal.acm.org/citation.cfm?id=1640068 [Accessed September 28, 2011].

Maalej, W. and Pagano, D. 2011. On the Socialness of Software *In*: *2011 IEEE Ninth International Conference on Dependable, Autonomic and Secure Computing* [online]. IEEE, pp. 864–871. Available from: http://ieeexplore.ieee.org/lpdocs/epic03/wrapper.htm?arnumber=6118890 [Accessed April 13, 2013].

MacLean, A. et al. 1991. Questions, options, and criteria: Elements of design space analysis. *Human-Computer Interaction*. 6(3, 4),pp.201–250.

Majid, R. et al. 2010. A survey on user involvement in software Development Life Cycle from practitioner's perspectives *In*: *5th International Conference on Computer Sciences and Convergence Information Technology* [online]. IEEE, pp. 240–243. Available from: http://ieeexplore.ieee.org/lpdocs/epic03/wrapper.htm?arnumber=5711064 [Accessed April 12, 2012].

Mambrey, P. et al. 1998. User Advocacy in Participatory Design: Designers' Experiences with a New Communication Channel. *Computer Supported Cooperative Work (CSCW)*. 7(3-4),pp.291–313.

Marczak, S. et al. 2008. Information Brokers in Requirement-Dependency Social Networks. *2008 16th IEEE International Requirements Engineering Conference* [online],pp.53–62. Available from: http://ieeexplore.ieee.org/lpdocs/epic03/wrapper.htm?arnumber=4685652.

Marczak, S. et al. 2007. Social Networks in the Study of Collaboration in Global Software Teams *In*: *International Conference on Global Software Engineering (ICGSE '07).*, pp. 7–8.

Martin, A. et al. 2010. An Ideal Customer: A Grounded Theory of Requirements Elicitation, Communication and Acceptance on Agile Projects *In*: *Agile software development: current research and future directions*. Berlin: Springer, pp. 111–141.

McGill, T. and Klobas, J. 2008. User developed application success: sources and effects of involvement. *Behaviour & Information Technology* [online]. 27(5),pp.407–422. Available from: http://www.tandfonline.com/doi/abs/10.1080/01449290601110715 [Accessed February 13, 2012].

McKeen, J. et al. 1994. The Relationship between User Participation and User Satisfaction: An Investigation of Four Contingency Factors. *MIS Quarterly* [online]. 18(4),pp.427–451. Available from:

http://www.jstor.org/stable/249523?origin=crossref [Accessed February 13, 2012].

McKeen, J. and Guimaraes, T. 1997. Successful Strategies for User Participation in Systems Development. *Journal of Management Information Systems* [online]. 14(2),pp.133–150. Available from: http://www.redi-bw.de/db/ebsco.php/search.ebscohost.com/login.aspx?direct=true&db=buh&AN=33359&site=ehost-live.

Mohr, J. and Nevin, J. 1990. Communication strategies in marketing channels: a theoretical perspective. *The Journal of Marketing* [online]. 54(4),pp.36–51. Available from: http://www.jstor.org/stable/10.2307/1251758 [Accessed July 4, 2013].

OMG 2009. *Business Process Modeling Notation (BPMN) Version 1.2.*

Paech, B. and Kohler, K. 2004. Task-driven requirements in object-oriented development *In*: J. LEITE and J. DOORN, eds. *Doorn, Jorge H. Perspectives on Software Requirements.* Boston, MA: Kluwer Academic, 2004. Print., pp. 1–25.

Palanisamy, R. and Sushil 2001. User Involevemnt in Information Systems Planning Leads to Strategic Success: An Empirical Study. *Journal of Services Research* [online]. 1(2),pp.125 – 150. Available from: http://www.redi-bw.de/db/ebsco.php/search.ebscohost.com/login.aspx?direct=true&db=buh&AN=9893579&site=ehost-live.

Pekkola, S. et al. 2006. Towards Formalized End-User Participation in Information Systems Development Process: Bridging the Gap between Participatory Design and ISD Methodologies. *In the proceedings of the Participatory Design Conference 2006,* pp.21–30.

Pérez, F. et al. 2011. Towards the Involvement of End-Users within Model-Driven Development *In*: *International conference on End-user development.* Berlin, Heidelberg: Springer-Verlag, pp. 258–263.

Pries-Heje, L. 2008. Time, attitude, and user participation: how prior events determine user attitudes in ERP implementation. *International Journal of Enterprise Information Systems* [online]. 4(3),pp.48–65. Available from: http://scholar.google.com/scholar?hl=en&btnG=Search&q=intitle:Time,+Attitude,+and+User+Participation+How+Prior+Events+Determine+User#3 [Accessed November 3, 2011].

Pries-Heje, L. and Dittrich, Y. 2009. ERP implementation as design. *Scandinavian Journal of Information Systems* [online]. 21(2),pp.27–58. Available from: http://iris.cs.aau.dk/tl_files/volumes/Volume21/no2/21-2 Pries-Heje.pdf [Accessed April 17, 2013].

Ramesh, V. et al. 2004. Research in computer science: an empirical study. *Journal of Systems and Software* [online]. 70(1-2),pp.165–176. Available from: http://linkinghub.elsevier.com/retrieve/pii/S0164121203000153 [Accessed November 10, 2014].

Rouibah, K. et al. 2008. Effect of management support, training, and user involvement on system usage and satisfaction in Kuwait. *Industrial Management & Data Systems* [online]. 109(3),pp.338–356. Available from: http://www.emeraldinsight.com/10.1108/02635570910939371 [Accessed July 22, 2011].

Runeson, P. et al. 2012. *Case Study Research in Software Engineering*. Wiley-Blackwell, New Jersey.

Runeson, P. and Höst, M. 2008. Guidelines for conducting and reporting case study research in software engineering. *Empirical Software Engineering* [online]. 14(2),pp.131–164. Available from: http://www.springerlink.com/index/10.1007/s10664-008-9102-8 [Accessed July 23, 2011].

Saldana, J. 2009. *The Coding Manual for Qualitative Researchers (Google eBook)* [online]. Available from: http://books.google.com/books?hl=de&lr=&id=3TeojNqEbxkC&pgis=1 [Accessed March 20, 2013].

Singh, S. and Kotzé, P. 2003. An Overview of Systems Design and Development Methodologies with Regard to the Involvement of Users and Other Stakeholders In: *Proceedings of SAICSIT 2003.*, pp. 37 – 47.

Sommerville, I. 2007. *Software engineering* [online]. Addison-Wesley. Available from: http://books.google.de/books?id=B7idKfL0H64C.

Sommerville, I. 2004. *Software Engineering 7* 7th ed. Amsterdam: Addison-Wesley Longman.

Stapel, K. et al. 2011. FLOW Mapping: Planning and Managing Communication in Distributed Teams. *2011 IEEE Sixth International Conference on Global Software Engineering* [online],pp.190–199. Available from: http://ieeexplore.ieee.org/lpdocs/epic03/wrapper.htm?arnumber=6063167 [Accessed August 22, 2013].

Stapel, K. and Schneider, K. 2012. Managing knowledge on communication and information flow in global software projects. *Expert Systems* [online]. 00(00),p.n/a–n/a. Available from: http://doi.wiley.com/10.1111/j.1468-0394.2012.00649.x [Accessed June 4, 2013].

Sutcliffe, A. et al. 1999. Tracing Requirements Errors to Problems in the Requirements Engineering Process. *Requirements Engineering* [online]. 4(3),pp.134–151. Available from: http://www.springerlink.com/openurl.asp?genre=article&id=doi:10.1007/s007660050024.

Takats, A. and Brewer, N. 2005. Improving Communication between Customers and Developers N. Brewer, ed. *Agile Development Conference/Australasian Database Conference* [online]. 0,pp.243–252. Available from: http://doi.ieeecomputersociety.org/10.1109/ADC.2005.30.

Teixeira, L. et al. 2011. Using Participatory Design in a Health Information System. *Conference proceedings : Annual International Conference of the IEEE Engineering in Medicine and Biology Society* [online]. 2011,pp.5339–42. Available from: http://www.ncbi.nlm.nih.gov/pubmed/22255544.

Venkatesh, V. 2000. Determinants of Perceived Ease of Use : Integrating Control , Intrinsic Motivation , and Emotion into the Technology Acceptance Model. *Information Systems Research.* 11(No 4),pp.342–365.

Wagner, E. and Piccoli, G. 2007. Moving beyond user participation to achieve successful IS design. *Communications of the ACM* [online]. 50(12),pp.51–55. Available from: http://portal.acm.org/citation.cfm?doid=1323688.1323694 [Accessed October 26, 2011].

Wieringa, R. 2012a. *A Unified Checklist for Observational and Experimental Research in Software Engineering (Version 1)* [online]. Available from: http://eprints.eemcs.utwente.nl/21630/.

Wieringa, R. 2012b. Designing technical action research and generalizing from real-world cases. *Advanced Information Systems Engineering* [online],pp.697–698. Available from: http://link.springer.com/chapter/10.1007/978-3-642-31095-9_46 [Accessed June 17, 2013].

Wieringa, R. 2007. Observational Studies *In print*, pp. 137–157.

Wieringa, R. and Moralı, A. 2012. Technical action research as a validation method in information systems design science. *Design Science Research in Information Systems.* ... [online],pp.220–238. Available from: http://link.springer.com/chapter/10.1007/978-3-642-29863-9_17 [Accessed June 12, 2013].

Wixom, B. and Todd, P. 2005. A Theoretical Integration of User Satisfaction and Technology Acceptance. *Information Systems Research* [online]. 16(1),pp.85–102. Available from: http://isr.journal.informs.org/cgi/doi/10.1287/isre.1050.0042 [Accessed July 25, 2011].

Wu, J. et al. 2006. THE IMPACT OF OPERATIONAL USER PARTICIPATION ON PERCEIVED SYSTEM IMPLEMENTATION SUCCESS: AN EMPIRICAL INVESTIGATION University of Kansas. *Journal of Computer Information Systems.* 47,pp.127–140.

Yetton, P. et al. 2000. A model of information systems development project performance. *Information Systems Journal* [online]. 10(4),pp.263–289. Available from: http://onlinelibrary.wiley.com/doi/10.1046/j.1365-2575.2000.00088.x/full [Accessed October 16, 2012].

Zeffane, R. et al. 1998. Does user involvement during information systems development improve data quality? *Human Systems Management* [online]. 17(2),pp.115 – 121. Available from: http://www.redi-bw.de/db/ebsco.php/search.ebscohost.com/login.aspx?direct=true&db=buh&AN=866259&site=ehost-live.

APPENDIX

APPENDIX I: Further Data to Systematic Mapping Study

Table 53: List of Selected Survey, Meta-Study, and Method Papers

Survey and Meta Studies	Method Papers
Amoako-Gyampah, 2007	Amoako-Gyampah & White, 1997
Bai & Cheng, 2010	Begier, 2010
Barki & Hartwick, 1994	Berger, 2011
Cavaye, 1995	Bragge, 2009
Chang et al., 2010	Cherry & Macredie, 1999
Emam et al., 1996	Cohen et al., 2010
Gefen et al., 2008	Dean et al., 1998
Harris & Weistroffer, 2009	Eckhardt, 2010
Hartwick & Barki, 2001	Finck et al., 2004
Hartwick & Barki, 1997	Fruhling et al., 2005
Igbaria & Guimaraes, 1994	Fuentes-Fernández et al., 2009
Iivari & Igbaria, 2011	Hansson et al., 2004
Ives & Olson, 1984	Hansson et al., 2006
Kanungo & Bagchi, 2000	Hendry, 2008
Kristensson et al., 2011	Hope & Amdahl, 2011
Kujala, 2003	Huang et al., 2008
Kujala et al., 2005	Humayoun et al., 2011
McGill & Klobas, 2008	Kabbedijk et al., 2009
McKeen et al., 1994	Kamal et al., 2011
Rouibah et al., 2009	Kautz, 2000
Subramanyam et al., 2010	Kautz, 2011
Wixom & Todd, 2005	Kawalek & Wood-Harper, 2002
	Kensing et al., 1998
	Korkala et al., 2006
	Korkala et al., 2010
	Kujala 2008
	Martin et al., 2010
	Mambrey et al., 1998
	Pekkola et al., 2006
	Pérez et al., 2011
	Pries-Heje, 2008
	Pries-Heje & Dittrich, 2009
	Takats & Brewer, 2005

	Teixeira et al., 2011 Wagner & Piccoli, 2007

Table 54: Overview of Researched Aspects of System Success with Sources

	Source
User Satisfaction	Amoako-Gyampah, 2007
	Cavaye, 1995 (Allingham & O'Connor 1992; Baronas & Louis, 1988; Baroudi et al. 1986; DeBrabander & Thiers, 1984; Doll & Torzadeh, 1989; Franz & Robey, 1986; Hirschheim, 1985; Kappelmann & McLean, 1991; Tait & Vessey, 1988)
	Emam et al., 1996
	Gefen et al., 2008
	Harris & Weistroffer, 2009 (Blili et al., 1998; Choe, 1996; Doll & Deng, 2001; Guimaraes & Igbaria, 1997; Guimaraes et al., 2003; Hsu et al., 2008; Hunton & Price, 1997; Lawrence et al, 2002; Lin & Shao, 2000; Lu & Wang, 1997; Palanisamy, 2001; Saleem, 1996; Santhanam et al., 2000; Yoon et al. 1998)
	Igbaria & Guimaraes, 1994
	Ives & Olson, 1984 (Edstrom, 1977; Gallagher, 1974; Guthrie, 1972; Kaiser & Srinivasan, 1980; Maish, 1979; Swanson, 1974)
	McGill & Klobas, 2008 (Amoako-Gyampah & White, 1993; McKeen & Guimaraes 1997; Doll & Torkzadeh, 1988; Doll & Torkzadeh, 1991; Hartwick & Barki, 1994; Hawk, 1993; Lawrence & Low, 1993; Seddon & Kiew, 1996; Torkzadeh & Doll, 1999; Torkzadeh et al., 2003)
	McKeen et al., 1994 (Kappelman & McLean, 1991; Olson & Ives, 1981; Powers & Dickson, 1973)
	Rouibah et al., 2009
	Wixom & Todd, 2005
System Quality	Amoako-Gyampah, 2007
	Bai & Cheng, 2010
	Cavaye, 1995 (Baroudi et al., 1986; Jarvenpaa & Ives , 1991; Kim & Lee, 1986)
	Harris & Weistroffer, 2009 (Choe, 1996; Hunton & Price, 1997; Lynch & Gregor, 2004; Wu et al., 2006)
	Igbaria & Guimaraes, 1994

	Ives & Olson, 1984 (King & Rodriquez, 1978; Lucas, 1975; Swanson, 1974)
	Kanungo & Bagchi, 2000
	Kujala, 2003 (Barki & Hartwick, 1991)
	McGill & Klobas, 2008 (Barki & Hartwick, 1991; Hartwick & Barki, 1994)
	Rouibah et al., 2009
	Wixom & Todd, 2005
	Harris & Weistroffer, 2009 (Butler & Fitzgerald, 1997; Discenza et al., 2008; Doll & Deng, 2001; Foster & Franz, 1999; Guimaraes & Igbaria, 1997; Kirsch & Beath, 1996; Santhanam et al., 2000; Yoon et al., 1998; Zeffane et al., 1998)
Project in Time and Budget	Ives & Olson, 1984 (Boland, 1978; Gallagher, 1974)
	Kristensson et al., 2000
	Kujala et al., 2005
	McGill & Klobas, 2008
	McKeen et al., 1994 (Franz, 1979; Olson & Ives, 1981)
	Wixom & Todd, 2005
	Chang et al., 2010
Ease of Use	Harris & Weistroffer, 2009 (Jiang et al., 2002; Wu et al., 2006; Yetton et al., 2000)
	Kujala et al., 2005
	Kujala, 2003 (Heinbokel, 1996)
	McKeen et al., 1994 (Edstrom, 1977; Ginzberg, 1979)
	Amoako-Gyampah, 2007
Data Quali	Igbaria & Guimaraes, 1994
	McGill & Klobas, 2008 (Torkzadeh & Doll, 1999)
	Wixom & Todd, 2005

	Harris & Weistroffer, 2009 (Zeffane et al., 1998)
System Use	Amoako-Gyampah, 2007 Bai & Cheng, 2010 Cavaye, 1995 (Jarvenpaa & Ives, 1991) Cavaye, 1995 (Kim & Lee, 1986) Harris & Weistroffer, 2009 (Choe 1996) Harris & Weistroffer, 2009 (Hunton & Price, 1997) Harris & Weistroffer, 2009 (Lynch & Gregor, 2004) Harris & Weistroffer, 2009 (Wu et al., 2006) Igbaria & Guimaraes, 1994 Ives & Olson, 1984 (King & Rodriquez, 1978, 1981) Ives & Olson, 1984 (Lucas, 1975) Ives & Olson, 1984 (Swanson, 1974) Kanungo & Bagchi, 2000 McGill & Klobas, 2008 (Barki & Hartwick, 1991) McGill & Klobas, 2008 (Hartwick & Barki, 1994) Rouibah et al., 2009 Wixom & Todd, 2005

Table 55: Overview of Positive and Negative Surveys Structured on a Category Level

Category 1	Category 2	Positive studies	Negative studies
Development Process	Development Process	Barki & Hartwick, 1994 Harris & Weistroffer, 2009 (Hunton & Price, 1997) Harris & Weistroffer, 2009 (Wu et al., 2006) Hartwick & Barki, 2001 Hartwick & Barki, 1997 Kanungo & Bagchi, 2000	
	Human Aspects	Cavaye, 1995 (Robey et al., 1989) Gefen et al., 2008 Harris & Weistroffer, 2009 (Hunton & Price, 1997) Harris & Weistroffer, 2009 (Pries-Heje, 2008) Harris & Weistroffer, 2009 (Wu et al., 2006) Ives & Olson, 1984 (Alter, 1978) Kanungo & Bagchi, 2000 McGill & Klobas, 2008 (Amoako-Gyampah & White, 1993) McGill & Klobas, 2008 (Barki & Hartwick, 1991) McGill & Klobas, 2008 (Hartwick & Barki, 1994)	Barki & Hartwick, 1994; Cavaye, 1995 (Kim & Lee, 1986) Cavaye, 1995 (Robey & Farrow, 1982)
	System Attributes	McKeen et al., 1994	
	System Success	Bai & Cheng, 2010 Cavaye, 1995 (Allingham & O'Connor, 1992)	Cavaye, 1995 (Tait & Vessey, 1988); Harris & Weistroffer, 2009

		Cavaye, 1995 (Baronas & Louis, 1988)	(Zeffane et al., 1998); Kujala, 2003 (Heinbokel, 1996)
		Cavaye, 1995 (Baroudi et al., 1986)	
		Cavaye, 1995 (Jarvenpaa & Ives, 1991)	
		Cavaye, 1995 (Kappelmann & McLean, 1991)	
		Cavaye, 1995 (Kim & Lee, 1986)	
		Chang et al., 2010	
		Emam et al., 1996	
		Harris & Weistroffer, 2009 (Butler & Fitzgerald, 1997)	
		Harris & Weistroffer, 2009 (Discenza et al., 2008)	
		Harris & Weistroffer, 2009 (Guimaraes et al., 2003)	
		Harris & Weistroffer, 2009 (Hunton & Price, 1997)	
		Harris & Weistroffer, 2009 (Hunton, 1996)	
		Harris & Weistroffer, 2009 (Jiang et al., 2002)	
		Harris & Weistroffer, 2009 (Kirsch & Beath, 1996)	
		Harris & Weistroffer, 2009 (Lawrence et al., 2002)	
		Harris & Weistroffer, 2009 (Saleem. 1996)	
		Harris & Weistroffer, 2009 (Santhanam et al., 2000)	
		Harris & Weistroffer, 2009 (Yetton et al., 2000)	
		Kristensson et al., 2000	
		Kujala et al., 2005	
		Lin & Shao, 2000	
		Lu & Wang, 1997,	

		Harris & Weistroffer, 2009 (Santhanam et al., 2000)
		Harris & Weistroffer, 2009 (Wu et al., 2006)
		Harris & Weistroffer, 2009 (Yetton et al., 2000)
		Ives & Olson, 1984 (Boland, 1978)
		Ives & Olson, 1984 (Edstrom, 1977)
		Ives & Olson, 1984 (Gallagher, 1974)
		Ives & Olson, 1984 (Guthrie, 1972)
		Ives & Olson, 1984 (King & Rodriquez, 1978, 1981)
		Kristensson et al., 2000
		Kujala et al., 2005
		McGill & Klobas, 2008 (Amoako-Gyampah & White, 1993)
		McGill & Klobas, 2008 (Barki & Hartwick, 1991)
		McGill & Klobas, 2008 (McKeen & Guimaraes, 1997)
		McGill & Klobas, 2008 (Doll & Torkzadeh, 1988)
		McGill & Klobas, 2008 (Doll & Torkzadeh, 1991)
		McGill & Klobas, 2008 (Hawk, 1993)
		McGill & Klobas, 2008 (Lawrence & Low, 1993)
		McGill & Klobas, 2008 (Torkzadeh & Doll, 1999)
		McKeen et al., 1994

		McKeen et al., 1994 (Edstrom, 1977) McKeen et al., 1994 (Franz, 1979) McKeen et al., 1994 (Ginzberg, 1979) McKeen et al., 1994 (Kappelman & McLean, 1991) McKeen et al., 1994 (Olson & Ives, 1981)	
Human Aspects	Development Process	Chang et al., 2010 Iivari & Igbaria, 2011	
	Human Aspects	Harris & Weistroffer, 2009 (Wu et al., 2006) Barki & Hartwick, 1994 Chang et al., 2010 Harris & Weistroffer, 2009 (Lin & Shao, 2000) Harris & Weistroffer, 2009 (Pries-Heje, 2008) Ives & Olson, 1984 (Alter, 1978) Ives & Olson, 1984 (Igersheim, 1976) Kanungo & Bagchi, 2000 McGill & Klobas, 2008 (Amoako-Gyampah & White,1993) McGill & Klobas, 2008 (Hartwick & Barki, 1994)	
	System Success	McGill & Klobas, 2008 (Jackson et al., 1997) Cavaye, 1995 (Doll & Torzadeh, 1989)	Amoako-Gyampah, 2007; Harris & Weistroffer, 2009 (Zeffane et al., 1998);

		Cavaye, 1995 (Franz & Robey, 1986) Cavaye, 1995 (Tait & Vessey, 1988) Chang et al., 2010 Gefen et al., 2008 Harris & Weistroffer, 2009 (Blili et al., 1998) Harris & Weistroffer, 2009 (Choe, 1996) Harris & Weistroffer, 2009 (Foster & Franz, 1999) Harris & Weistroffer, 2009 (Guimaraes & Igbaria, 1997) Harris & Weistroffer, 2009 (Guimaraes et al., 2003) Harris & Weistroffer, 2009 (Hsu et al., 2008) Harris & Weistroffer, 2009 (Hunton & Price, 1997) Harris & Weistroffer, 2009 (Palanisamy, 2001) Harris & Weistroffer, 2009 (Yoon et al., 1998) Igbaria & Guimaraes, 1994 Ives & Olson, 1984 (Kaiser & Srinivasan, 1980) Ives & Olson, 1984 (Maish, 1979) Ives & Olson, 1984 (Swanson, 1974) Kanungo & Bagchi, 2000 McGill & Klobas, 2008 McGill & Klobas, 2008 (Barki & Hartwick, 1991) McGill & Klobas, 2008 (Hartwick & Barki, 1994)	McGill & Klobas, 2008 (Amoako-Gyampah & White, 1993); McGill & Klobas, 2008 (Doll & Torkzadeh, 1991)

		McGill & Klobas, 2008 (Seddon & Kiew, 1996) McGill & Klobas, 2008 (Torkzadeh et al, 2003) Rouibah et al., 2009 Wixom & Todd, 2005	
Organizational Factor	Development Process	Bai & Cheng, 2010 Iivari & Igbaria, 2011 Harris & Weistroffer, 2009 (Lu & Wang, 1997)	
	Human Aspects		McGill & Klobas, 2008 (Amoako-Gyampah & White, 1993)
	System Success	Cavaye, 1995 (Jarvenpaa & Ives, 1991) Harris & Weistroffer, 2009 (Guimaraes et al., 2003) Harris & Weistroffer, 2009 (Hsu et al., 2008) Harris & Weistroffer, 2009 (Lu & Wang, 1997) Harris & Weistroffer, 2009 (Santhanam et al., 2000) Harris & Weistroffer, 2009 (Yetton et al. 2000) McKeen et al, 1994 (Powers & Dickson, 1973) McGill & Klobas, 2008 (Amoako-Gyampah & White, 1993) Rouibah et al., 2009	
System Attribut	Development Process	Iivari & Igbaria, 2011 Harris & Weistroffer, 2009 (Lin & Shao, 2000)	

es	System Attributes	McGill & Klobas, 2008 (McKeen & Guimaraes, 1997) McKeen et al., 1994	
	System Success	Harris & Weistroffer, 2009 (Yoon et al., 1998)	Emam et al., 1996; Harris & Weistroffer, 2009 (Palanisamy, 2001); Harris & Weistroffer, 2009 (Yetton et al., 2000)
System Success	Human Aspects	McGill & Klobas, 2008 McGill & Klobas, 2008 (Hartwick & Barki, 1994) Wixom & Todd, 2005	
	System Success	Amoako-Gyampah, 2007 Harris & Weistroffer, 2009 (Yoon et al., 1998) Igbaria & Guimaraes, 1994 Kristensson et al., 2000 McGill & Klobas, 2008 Rouibah et al., 2009 Wixom & Todd, 2005	

Table 56: Aspects Influenced and Targeted by the Methods Papers

Study	Development Process				Human Aspects											System Attributes	Org. Fac	System Success					Total	Percent
	User Participation	User-Developer Communication	Mode of Development	User Involvement	Users' Belief about Developers	Users' Attitude towards System	Users' Ability in IT projects	Disagreement/Conflict	Developers' Attitude towards User	Users' Intention to Use	Users' Motivation	Complexity	Uncertainty	Top Management Support	Availability of Resources	User Satisfaction		System Use	System Quality	Project in Time and Budget	Ease of Use	Data Quality		
Amoako-Gyampah & White, 1997	1	1	0	1	1	0	0	1	1	0	0	0	0	1	0	0	0	0	1	1	1	1	12	55%
Begier, 2010	1	0	0	0	0	0	0	0	0	0	0	0	0	0	0	0	1	1	1	0	1	1	6	27%
Berger, 2011	1	1	1	0	0	0	0	0	0	0	0	1	1	1	1	0	1	0	0	0	1	0	9	41%
Bragge, 2009	1	0	0	0	0	0	0	0	0	0	1	0	0	0	0	0	0	0	1	0	1	0	4	18%
Cherry & Macredie, 1999	1	1	1	0	1	1	1	1	1	0	0	0	0	1	0	0	1	1	1	0	1	0	13	59%
Cohen et al., 2010	1	0	1	0	0	0	0	0	0	0	0	0	0	0	0	0	0	1	1	0	0	0	5	23%
Dörner et al., 2008	1	1	0	0	0	0	0	0	0	0	1	0	0	0	0	0	0	1	1	0	0	0	5	23%
Dean et al., 1998	1	1	1	1	0	0	0	1	0	0	0	1	0	0	0	0	0	0	1	1	0	0	9	41%

Study																								
Eckhardt, 2010)	0	1	0	0	1	0	0	0	1	0	1	0	0	0	0	0	1	1	1	0	7	32%
Finck et al., 2004)	0	1	0	1	0	1	0	0	0	0	1	0	0	0	0	0	0	1	0	0	5	23%
Fruhling et al., 2005)	1	0	0	0	0	1	0	1	0	0	0	0	0	0	0	0	1	1	0	10	6	27%
Fuentes-Fernández et al., 2009)	0	1	0	0	0	0	0	0	0	0	0	0	0	0	0	0	0	1	0	0	2	9%
Hansson et al., 2004)	0	1	0	1	0	0	0	0	1	0	0	0	0	0	0	1	0	0	0	0	12	55%
Hansson et al., 2006)	1	1	1	1	1	1	0	0	1	0	1	0	0	0	0	1	1	1	0	10	4	18%
Hendry, 2008)	0	1	1	0	0	0	0	0	0	0	1	0	0	0	0	0	0	1	0	0	6	27%
Hope & Amdahl, 2011)	1	1	1	0	0	1	1	0	0	0	0	0	0	0	0	0	0	1	0	0	7	32%
Huang et al., 2008)	1	0	0	0	1	0	0	0	1	1	0	0	0	0	0	1	0	1	0	10	5	23%
Humayoun et al., 2011)	1	0	0	0	0	0	0	0	1	0	0	0	0	0	0	0	1	1	1	0	6	27%
Kabbedijk et al., 2009)	1	0	0	1	0	1	0	0	0	1	0	0	0	0	0	1	0	1	0	0	7	32%
Kamal et al., 2011)	0	0	0	1	0	0	1	0	0	0	0	1	0	1	0	0	0	1	1	1	10	45%
Kautz, 2000)	1	1	0	1	1	1	0	0	1	0	0	0	0	0	0	1	0	1	1	0	9	41%
Kautz, 2011)	1	0	1	1	0	1	0	0	1	1	0	0	0	0	0	1	0	1	1	0	9	41%
Kawalek & Wood-	0	1	0	1	0	1	0	1	0	1	1	1	0	0	0	0	0	1	1	0	8	36%

Reference																							Count	%
Harper, 2002)																								
Kensing et al., 1998)	1	1	0	1	1	0	1	0	1	0	0	0	0	1	(	1	0	0	0	(	0		3	14%
Korkala et al., 2006)	0	1	0	0	0	0	0	0	0	0	0	0	1	0	(	0	0	1	0	(	0		7	32%
Korkala et al., 2010)	0	1	0	1	0	0	0	0	0	0	1	1	0	0	1	0	0	1	0	(	0		6	27%
Kujala, 2008)	0	0	0	1	0	0	0	0	0	0	1	0	0	0	(	1	1	1	0	1	0		13	59%
Martin, 2010)	1	1	1	1	1	0	1	1	1	0	1	0	0	1	(	1	0	1	1	(	0		8	36%
Mambrey et al., 1998)	0	1	0	1	0	1	0	0	1	0	0	0	0	0	(	1	1	1	0	1	0		7	32%
Pekkola et al., 2006)	1	1	1	1	0	0	0	0	0	0	0	0	0	0	(	1	0	1	0	1	0		6	27%
Pérez et al., 2011)	1	0	1	0	0	0	0	0	0	0	0	0	0	0	(	1	1	1	0	1	0		12	55%
Pries-Heje, 2008)	1	1	0	1	0	1	1	1	0	0	0	1	0	0	(	1	1	1	1	(	0		8	36%
Pries-Heje & Dittrich, 2009)	1	1	0	1	0	1	0	0	0	0	0	1	0	1	(	0	0	1	1	(	0		11	50%
Takats & Brewer, 2005)	1	1	0	1	1	0	0	0	1	0	1	1	0	1	(	1	0	1	0	(	0		8	36%
Teixeira et al., 2011)	1	1	0	1	0	0	0	0	0	0	0	1	0	0	(	1	1	1	0	1	0		7	32%
Wagner & Piccoli, 2007)	1	1	0	1	0	0	0	0	1	0	1	0	0	0	(	1	0	1	0	(	0		12	55%

Amount of paper per subcategory	2 5	2 5	1 1	2 1	1 9	2	6	7	1 4	1 4	2	9 2		2	8	2	19	1 3	3 3	1 2	1 23		
% per subcategory	6 9 %	6 9 %	3 1 %	5 8 %	2 5 %	3 3 %	11 7 %	3 9 %	1 1 %	3 3 %	2 5 %	2 6 %	1	2 2 %	€	%	53%	3 6 %	9 2 %	3 3 %	% 8%		
Amount of paper per category	34			29								10	1 3	36									
% per category	94%			81%								28%	5 0 %	100%									

Table 57: Summaries of the Method Papers

Study	Summary
Amoako-Gyampah & White, 1997	This paper discusses the value of user involvement at all stages in software development projects. It derives most of its insights from an information system development project at a large manufacturing firm. Traditional approaches to user involvement (including users on the project team, users on steering committees, using user sign-offs, and providing feedback to users) are good but not sufficient. The paper suggests that development projects ensure an interactive process, timely feedback on users' suggestions and input, minimizing semantic barriers between developers and users, keeping people informed about project changes, ensuring trust among project participants, ensuring effective communication, clarifying roles and expectations, and removing negative perceptions.
Begier, 2010	This paper introduces a method for integrating users during the evolutional development of an expert system (an AutoCAD system) applied in civil engineering. The suggestion is to get

	user feedback through a survey that developers can use to learn and improve the quality of software with regard to users need (e.g., ease of use and usability).
Berger, 2011	This paper looks into a case study in the public sector, where an in-house-developed agile development method was used in the development of an information system. Even though the methods implemented all principles for user involvement within agile methods, including colocation, an iterative process, and joint application development (JAD) workshops, system success was not achieved because of, as the authors explain, an organizational cultural mismatch that prevented a collaborative environment.
Bragge, 2009	This paper describes two cycles of continuing action research intervention that employed collaborative engineering with e-collaboration processes. The processes should motivates users to participate in feedback and suggest new development ideas during ongoing use of an advanced web-based student information system implemented in a university.
Cohen et al., 2010	This paper introduces a new software development methodology called "lean driven development." The method is suggested for vendors of "off the shelf" software for developing their products in line with customers and stakeholders. The authors adapted the software development life cycle model for the acquisition process of information systems.
Cherry & Macredie, 1999	This paper argues that strict requirements analysis is not very valuable in information system design, so it suggests PD approaches like cooperative prototypes, brainstorming, (future) workshops, and organizational gaming to specify the software system design.
Dörner et al., 2008	This paper defines the Collaborative Software Engineering Methodology, a framework for effective and efficient user involvement throughout the systems development process. This methodology includes mechanisms to support three layers of user involvement: selected user representatives, user groups (SMEs), and the entire user community. Specifically, it includes the intimate involvement of individual user representatives for development of preliminary models and prototypes; groups of SMEs to refine, validate, and prioritize requirements; and the broader user community during initial needs surveys and

	wide-scale beta testing. Participation by multiple SMEs is beneficial for both content and political reasons. Group meetings provide a useful mechanism by which to involve multiple SMEs. The methodology is validated and developed in projects in public administration and defense.
Dean et al., 1998	This paper introduces a new method for self-ethnographic methods, giving infrastructure probes (snapshot tool, USB stick, digital camera, Post-Its, etc.) to users and asking them to document software issues. The goal is to get a deeper understanding of the users' working context in order to help improve the collaboration between users and developers regarding requirements elicitation.
Eckhardt, 2010	This paper suggests using boundary spanners, that is, people who broker between business and IT people, to overcome the communication gap between IT and business. The authors interviewed two boundary spanners to derive reasons for this role and created a 25-item skill set for boundary spanners.
Finck et al., 2004	This paper proposes a special kind of mediated feedback through a web-based groupware system called Commsy. The goal is to enable a PD approach by combining the groupware's discussion forum with human facilitators. The first technique is a Facilitation-CommSy Project Room to exchange information and get feedback about the ongoing development and experience in facilitating Project Rooms with other facilitators and the development team. The second technique is feedback discussions using the discussion functionality in Project Rooms to get feedback from the working group and provide an incentive and a platform for expressing problems and ideas about CommSy usage. The facilitator also informs users about design decisions based on requirements from the discussion forum.
Fruhling et al., 2005	This paper presents a repeatable collaborative usability testing process supported by a Group Support System (e-CUP) that was developed to involve various stakeholders in software development in order to increase usability and, thus, system success. The process is evaluated in a series of workshops involving a real system called Secure Telecommunications Application Terminal Package (STATPack), which addresses

	critical health communication and bio-security needs. The results show that the collaborative usability testing process facilitates stakeholder involvement by stakeholders' expectations management, visualization and tradeoff analysis, prioritization of usability action items, the use of advanced groupware tools, and a simple business case analysis.
Fuentes-Fernández et al., 2009	This paper presents an analytical tool to elicit requirements related to the human context of systems. The Activity Theory Requirements Engineering (ATRE) is built upon a well-established theory from social sciences, the Action Theory (AT), and standard practices of software engineering. ATRE abstracts and formalizes the concept of social property. A social property presents knowledge from social sciences that can help to gain new insights into the human context of a system. A knowledge repository stores these properties, which are organized in areas that are related to dimensions of concern in AT and aspects of areas that refine them. This structure guides users to properties that are related to their current information interests. Validation in an enterprise system for a consulting firm leads to a knowledge repository that includes four areas that contain 38 aspectsof UPI with 185 properties but can be extended with practice. The result of using the ATRE framework is the identification of requirements specifications that are more complete regarding the human context and its influence in the design and behavior of the system to be.
Hansson et al., 2004	This paper describes a development method from a small but very successful Swedish company. The main product is a booking system developed with an agile-like development method. In order to keep the users satisfied, they have active support, hold user meetings throughout the country, and have a web interface for user requirements.
Hansson et al., 2006	This paper describes an approach from a small Swedish software company that mixes PD with agile processes. Therefore, it uses various channels (support calls, user meetings, courses, the website, and a newsletter) to obtain feedback on users' further development needs. The lessons learned include that it is important to (1) use a Customer Relationship Management tool to keep track of users' feedback, (2) develop a user community, and (3) use an agile-like development process.

Hendry, 2008	This paper addresses the question concerning how to engage users in design and development through communication and IT. The author develops a framework for user roles and discourse that makes two claims: (1) user roles and a social structure emerge after the introduction of a software application (role differentiation) and (2) different roles demand different kinds of discourse for deciding what to do and for reflecting upon intended and unintended consequences (role discourse demands). To validate the framework it is used to analyze the development of del.icio.us, a breakthrough application for social bookmarking that uses a mailing list for user participation.
Hope & Amdahl, 2011	This paper reviews the success of two projects that implement the agile method called Dynamic System Design Methods (DSDM) in a Norwegian software design company. DSDM aims to improve the collaboration between software designers and users and to develop other aspects of project management. The various activities of the DSDM-driven project include planning; mapping end-users' needs; describing the new system; selecting architecture; designing, modeling, coding, and testing; doing quality assurance; and providing project management. In one project the methods were not understood, so the method did not really improve user participation in design. The other project, with the help of an external IT consultant, had some success.
Huang et al., 2008	This paper proposes an integrated design method based on scenario and PD (DMSPD) for an Internet-based collaborative learning environment. The method has four phases. The first phase involves stakeholder analysis and task analysis to acquire system requirements. Methods like brainstorming, focus groups, interviews, and questionnaires are adopted. Scenario design, the second phase, consists of four sub-phases: activity design, information design, interaction design, and design specification. In design implementation, the third phase, sketches, mock-ups, and prototypes are used to conceive and represent design solutions. The last phase, usability testing and evaluation, consists of usability quiz and subjective evaluation. The total design phase is an iterative process. The authors

	testes the method with students in the art department of a university.
Humayoun et al., 2011	This paper presents a framework that incorporates user-centered design (UCD) philosophy into agile software development through a three-fold integration approach: at the process life cycle level suggestions for user involvement are for elicitation (focus groups and card sort methods) and evaluation (early design within paper based prototype's, later designs with evaluation experiments run from the development environment); at the iteration level for integrating UCD concepts, roles, and activities during each agile development iteration planning; and at the development environment level, suggestions include for managing and automating the sets of UCD activities through automated tools support. In addition the authors present two automated tools, UEMan and TaMUlator, which provide the realization of the development-environment level integration. The paper evaluated the methods as well as their two tool in two case studies from academia.
Kabbedijk et al., 2009	This paper describes a customer involvement method from an ERP company that develops products for the Dutch and Belgium small and medium sized companies. They ask their customer for requirements definition. The customers can either suggest through an incident report with the support staff, they can vote electronically on requirements suggested by the company (idea feedback) or suggest own ideas for features (suggestions), which then get voted on by all customers. The last two happen at so called customer participation session, where the customers get instant feedback and align with their follow customers.
Kamal et al., 2011	This paper argues for the use of stakeholder theory in Technology Integration Solutions (TIS) in local government authorities. It uses four cases to research the three areas of stakeholder analysis: stakeholder identification, stakeholder perception of the TIS adoption factors, and stakeholder involvement on the adoption life cycle phases.
Kautz, 2000	The paper presents a successful commercial agile development project of an operations management system with an underlying ERP system in a large German public sector organization. It analyzes the case in regard to user

	involvement. The formalized methods includes planning techniques called planning games; user stories and story cards to specify user requirements; onsite customers to support customer-developer communication; daily stand-up meetings of the project team to support team communication; pair programming; refactoring; collective ownership; continuous integration and testing to develop the software proper; and tuning workshops to improve the development processes regularly. The traditional XP methods are extended by some project management processes to cater to larger projects, such as an overall project plan, formal reporting mechanisms, and a formal contract based on a requirements specification called realization concept.
Kautz, 2011	This paper investigates how users participate in agile development, so it studies the methods of XP in regard to user participation. The analysis reveals that planning games, user stories and story cards, working software, and acceptance tests structure the participation and contribute to successful project completion.
Kawalek & Wood-Harper, 2002	This paper presents a study of a major, multinational program of Enterprise Systems (ES) implementation. The case study subject is a high-tech manufacturer. The investigation looks into the fact that the implementation methods espoused user participation even though the outcome of the project was already known. (Regardless of user input, the ES would be deployed as a standard system.) The paper reports that user participation was deployed to serve the interests of the project manager in reporting local circumstances as the implementation project moved across different sites. The users reported positively that they were involved, so the enhance communication prevented conflicts. The framework for this inquiry was Multiview2, the latest generation of the multi-view information systems methods. The structure of Multiview2 was used as a diagnostic device in order to inquire into the characteristics of the ES methods used at the case study sites.
Kensing et al., 1998	This paper describes a PD method called MUST, which was developed in the course of ten projects. MUST is based on five principles that suggest the five main activities—project

	establishment, strategic analysis, in-depth analysis of selected work domains, developing a vision of the overall change, and anchoring the vision. Some techniques for each activity, such as meetings, document analysis, and future workshops, are proposed.
Korkala et al., 2006	This paper uses a Mobile-D development approach inspired by several agile methods to compare the use of different communication media in four case studies. The authors found that, aligned with the Media Richness Theory, reliance on lean media (e.g., e-mail and telephone) led to a much higher defect rate. Therefore, they suggest using rich media (e.g., face-to-face meetings or videoconferencing) especially for requirements analysis with a light-weighted prototype, mid-iteration communication, and iteration planning. The telephone can be used for negations if the user is not on site. Rich media communication ensures a low defect rate and, therefore, higher-quality software.
Korkala et al., 2010	This paper looks into distributed development that combines traditional and agile methodologies with regard to customer communication. It provides practical guidelines for companies in distributed agile environments, including the advice to define a person to play the role of the customer; if face-to-face, synchronous communication is infeasible, to use an e-mail listserv to increase the chance of a response and encourage prompt, useful, and conclusive responses to e-mails; and to use globally available project management tools to record and monitor the project status on a daily basis. The key finding from a qualitative case study is that it might be difficult for an agile organization to get relevant information from a traditional type of customer organization even when customer communication is active and used via multiple communication media.
Kujala 2008	This paper suggests using field studies to improve early user participation in product development. Field studies appear to be a promising approach, but the analysis of the gathered user needs is demanding. Based on seven case studies, this study presents an early user-involvement process that consists of identifying stakeholders and user groups, visiting users and exploring their needs, describing the current situation, analyzing and prioritizing the problems and possibilities,

	redesigning the current situation, and defining user requirements. The process is evaluated using interviews and a questionnaire in two industrial cases of software managing infrastructures. The results show that the process supports early, effective user involvement; the resulting requirements were evaluated as being more successful and their quality as better than average in a company.
Martin et al., 2010	This paper extensively studies the role of the customer in agile XP projects. Based on eleven case studies from various industries, the authors derive roles for collaboration (Geek Interpreter, Political Advisor, and Technical Liaison), roles based on skills to support onsite customers (Acceptance Tester, UI Designer, and Technical Writer), and roles for direction-setting (Negotiator, Diplomat, Super-Secretary, and Coach). The author also identifies practices that primarily support real customer involvement by preparing the business representatives for their role (Customer Boot Camp) and providing opportunities for the business representatives to contribute to what to build (Big Picture Up-Front, Road Show, and Re-calibration). In addition, programmers should develop empathy for the customer team (Customer's Apprentice) and the end-user (Programmer On-Site).
Mambrey et al., 1998	This paper describes PD activities in a PoliTeam project. In this introduction of a groupware system to the German government, the project used user advocacy, where user advocates augment the interaction between users and designers, and osmosis, where a designer receives multi-level information by visiting the workplace and having contact with users, in an evolutional cycling process.
Pekkola et al., 2006	This paper suggests an iterative information system development process that uses PD (PD) elements. In particular, the use of prototypes in various forms leads to better requirements and, thus, more user orientation. The process has eight steps: 1. Decision to start the ISD process (gaining commitment to PD by all project participants) 2. Outlining preliminary user requirements (sharpening user requirements with scenarios, paper, and prototypes)

	3. Analyzing and designing prototype (testing system concept, components, and UI) 4. Implementing a full-feature prototype 5. Introducing a prototype into the organization 6. Gathering suggestions for improvements 7. Analyzing and verifying the requirements (selecting features for the next version) 8. Finishing the system or prototype
Pérez et al., 2011	This paper presents a method that involves users in Model Driven Development (MDD) approaches to ensure that the application fits the users' expectations. The method follows good practices and techniques in User Development and combines it with modeling techniques. The authors apply the methods of an existing MDD approach called PervML, which allows users to participate in the description of their smart home. Users can now participate in the software development by means of an appropriate Domain Specific Visual Language and a specific tool support for them.
Pries-Heje, 2008	This paper mainly reports on a large ERP project at the Danish headquarters of an international engineering company that used user participation during the whole implementation process. Even though the users of the consulting company were heavily involved (e.g., responsible for requirements definition) during the process, the dynamic switch that lead to "pseudo-participation," where users are asked to participate but not given the possibility to influence the design. Nevertheless, after "go-live" in the follow-up phase, quality and usability issues can be resolved. The author suggests having a thorough requirements specification as a basis for the contract, allowing necessary customizations to the system, choosing an implementation partner, recognizing the uniqueness of the organizational way of operating, and having users and consultants work as one team. The companies should also be aware who influences the design (standard system or organization) and should think about tools and techniques that will support the users' ability to gain knowledge about technical and socio-technical options.
Pries-Heje & Dittrich, 2009	This paper describes an in-depth case study of an ERP project and its challenges in regard to UPI. It suggests four PD approaches that could have prevented some of the

	misunderstandings that occurred during the project: mediating cooperative design, sharing representations, creating prototypes and using iterative design, and having an ERP competence center to mediate between users and external IT experts.
Takats & Brewer, 2005	This paper presents four patterns that help to improve the customer/user developer relationship by extending agile methods. As customers can rarely work full-time with developers, the authors include a workshop series into the iterative agile approach. The workshops were highly facilitated and focused on establishing a vision and high-level requirements (deliverables: program vision, logical architecture, executive briefing, operational concept diagram, and a capability timeline). They used pattern from the development company call group solve, be visual and forces rank.
Teixeira et al., 2011	This paper describes the development of an interactive health information system called Hemo@care with the help of user-centered design and PD practices. It suggests the three phases of exploratory (analysis of documentation, direct observation, and focus group), design (object-oriented system analysis (OOSA), hierarchical task analysis, and prototyping), and coding (eXtremProgramming).
Wagner & Piccoli, 2007	Based on a case study of an ERP system at a university that strictly followed the tenets of PD, this paper argues that users are interested only in real participation when the system affects their everyday lives after it goes live. Therefore, they suggest thinking differently about how to involve users (i.e., at the starting point asking users about their day-to-day work activities to elicit users' stories), broaden system analysts' skill sets (i.e., interpreting user's narratives), and enacting a modified system development life cycle (i.e., recognizing that implementation extends beyond "go-live").

APPENDIX II: Further Data to Expert Interview Series

Table 58: Base Data of Large-Scale IT Projects

	Development System	Industry	Project Duration [years]	Project volume [million EUR]	Number of Users	Roll out units	Development Method	Role/Task of Expert
1	Standard software + Customization	Pharma	5	n/a	n/a	>50	Waterfall	Developer
2	Standard software + Customization	Pharma	3	n/a	n/a	>50	Waterfall	Liaison officer
3	Individual Development	Pharma	10	n/a	n/a	>30	Agile	Developer, project manager
4	Standard software + Customization	Consumer Goods	8	>250	>50,000	>5	Waterfall	Business project manager (PMO lead)
5	Standard software + Customization	Public Sector	3	>200	>50,000	1	Waterfall	Business project manager (PMO lead)
6	Standard software + Customization	Service Company	6	>150	30,000	>30	Waterfall	Business project manager (PMO lead)
7	Standard software + Customization	Steel	2	30	400	3	Agile	Project manager
8	Standard software +	Automotive	2	5	3,000	10	Agile	Project manager

	Customization							
9	Individual Development	Insurance	<6	n/a	n/a	n/a	Agile	Developer/architect
10	Individual Development	Insurance	<5	n/a	n/a	n/a	Agile	Developer/architect
11	Standard software	n/a	n/a	n/a	50 - 100	n/a	n/a	Requirements engineer (Business side)
12	Individual Development	Public Sector	5	200 - 500	120,000	n/a	Waterfall	Business project manager (PMO lead)
13	Individual Development	Public Sector	5	200 - 500	120,000	n/a	Waterfall	Business Project Manager (PMO lead)
14	Standard software + Customization	Health Care	5	200	36,000	n/a	Waterfall	Business project manager (PMO lead)
15	Individual Development	Transport	n/a	n/a	n/a	n/a	Waterfall	Quality manager
16	Individual Development	Transport	n/a	n/a	n/a	n/a	Waterfall	Quality manager
17	Individual Development	Transport	n/a	n/a	n/a	n/a	Waterfall	Quality manager
18	Individual Development	Travel	n/a	n/a	n/a	n/a	Waterfall	Quality manager
19	Individual Development	Travel	n/a	n/a	n/a	n/a	Waterfall	Quality manager

	nt							
20	Standard software + Individual Dev.	Telecommunication	1	7	~ 7000	4	Waterfall	Project lead, requirement engineer
21	Standard software + Individual Dev.	Telecommunication	1.5	14	~ 7000	4	Waterfall	Business analyst, requirements engineer
22	Standard software + Individual Dev.	Telecommunication	2.5	80	~ 7000	4	waterfall	Business analyst, requirements engineer
25	Standard software	Insurance	4	n/a	n/a	5	n/a	Business project manager
26	Standard software	Insurance	n/a	n/a	>1,000	many	n/a	Business project manager
27	n/a	Insurance/banking	n/a	n/a	n/a	n/a	n/a	Business project manager
28	n/a	Insurance/banking	n/a	30	<1300	n/a	n/a	Business project manager
29	Individual Development	Public Sector	20	n/a	<10,000	n/a	V-Model	Requirement engineer (project manager)
30	Individual Development	Public Sector	n/a	n/a	n/a	n/a	V-Model	Requirement engineer (project manager)
31	Individual Development	Public Sector	18	n/a	30,000	n/a	V-Model	Requirement engineer (project

32	Individual Development	Public Sector	13	n/a	1,300	n/a	V-Model	Requirement engineer (project manager)
33	Individual Development	Insurance	10	100	1.000	>100	agile (iterative)	Head of requirement management
34	Individual Development	Insurance	1	<1	40	1	agile (iterative)	Project manager
35	Individual Development	Insurance	2	<10	40	1	agile (iterative)	Project manager
36	Individual Development	Insurance	4	<10	40	1	agile (iterative)	Project manager
37	Standard Software	Retail	8	300	200,000	8	Waterfall	Business project manager
38	Individual Development	Banking	n/a	n/a	n/a	3	Waterfall	Project manager
39	Individual Development	Public Sector	n/a	many millions	90,000	1	Waterfall	Project manager; requirement engineer
40	Individual Development	Health Care	2 to 3	n/a	<30,000	150	Agile (SCRUM)	Project manager
41	Individual Development	Banking	2 to 3	n/a	<100,000	1000	Waterfall	Project manager
42	n/a	Insurance	n/a	n/a	n/a	n/a	n/a	Project manager
43	n/a	Insurance	n/a	n/a	1,600,000	n/a	(Iterative) Waterfall	Project manager

| 4 4 | n/a | n/a | 3 | n/a | <1,000 | n/a | n/a | Project manager |

Interview questionnaire

Interview – Part 1 – Experience in large-scale IT projects
1. What is your role in your company? What is your education background?
2. In how many large IT projects (large number of users, multiple countries, or business units involved, large budget, project duration at least one year, such as ERP implementation) have you been involved?
3. What were the main characteristics of these projects (type of system, project duration, number of users)?
4. What were your role and tasks in these projects?
5. Would you classify yourself as being on the IT or the business side?
6. Was there communication between users and developers of the project? If yes, in what setup did the communication take place? In what software activities of the project did the communication take place?
7. Did you experience any issues/consequences in these projects that might be caused by communication gaps? If yes, please specify the issues. In what software activities did the issues occur?
8. What would you do to prevent those issues in your next project?

Interview – Part 2 – Trigger Points
9. Do you think the abstraction level helps to identify trigger points? Would you add/modify/delete any abstraction level?
10. Would you add/modify/delete any of the trigger points?
11. Do you have examples for trigger points?
12. Which of the trigger points have you used in projects to initiate communication with the user? Why?
13. Which of the trigger points would you never use to initiate communication with the user? Why?

Interview – Part 3 – Solution Idea

14. Do you think the structure of the solution idea is useful?
15. Do you have ideas for extending the solution idea?
16. Which parts of the solution idea would you use in your next project?
17. Which parts do you think will be hard to realize in your next project?
18. Do you think it is feasible to implement the solution in one of your projects?
19. What general obstacles do you see in using this solution in your next project?
20. Do you expect any benefits from this solution? If yes please specify.

APPENDIX III: Further Data to Case Study

Original interview questions of evaluation interviews (in German)
1. Was ist Ihre Rolle in der Firma?
2. Was ist ihre Rolle im iPeople Projekt?
3. Wie beurteilen Sie das iPeople System anhand der **vorgestellten Kriterien**?
4. Wie wichtig sind Ihrer Meinung nach die vorgestellten
5. Kriterien für das **iPeople System**?
6. Gibt es Ihrer Meinung nach andere wichtige Kriterien?
7. Wie stark stimmen Sie diesen Aussagen zu?

Kriterium	Sehr niedrig	Niedrig	Medium	Gut	Sehr gut
Benutzerzufriedenheit (User Satisfaction)					
Benutzerfreundlichkeit (Ease of Use)					
Systemverwendung (System Use)					
Projekt "on Time" und "on Budget"					
Systemqualität (System Quality)					
Datenqualität (Data Quality)					

Kriterium	Nicht wichtig	Eher unwichtig	Wichtig	Eher wichtig	sehr wichtig
Benutzerzufriedenheit (User Satisfaction)					

Benutzerfreundlichkeit (Ease of Use)			
Systemverwendung (System Use)			
Projekt "on Time" und "on Budget"			
Systemqualität (System Quality)			
Datenqualität (Data Quality)			

Aussage	Keine Zustimmung		Neutral		Völlige Zustimmung
Die systematische Dokumentation der Design Entscheidungen im Scribble Doc ist…					
…leicht für mich zu verstehen					
…leicht für mich anzuwenden					
…wichtig für meine Arbeit im Projekt					
… hilft dabei die Umsetzung der Benutzeranforderungen hinsichtlich des UI Designs/Konzepts transparenter zu machen					
…stärkt das gemeinsame Verständnis der Projektbeteiligten von UI Design und Konzept					
Ich denke es ist eine gute Idee die Designentscheidungen im					

Scribble Doc festzuhalten				
Ich werde in zukünftigen Projekten die Designentscheidungen im Scribble Doc festhalten				
Ich werde anderen empfehlen Designentscheidungen im Scribble Doc festzuhalten				

8. Wie schätzen Sie die Umsetzbarkeit ein? Bitte begründen Sie die Aussage kurz

Die systematische Dokumentation der Designentscheidungen im Scribble Doc ist...				Kurze Begründung
...ist innerhalb des internen iPeople Entwicklungsprozesses umsetzbar mit...	Wenig Aufwand	Mittlerem Aufwand	Großem Aufwand	Gar nicht
... ist für das iPeople System umsetzbar	Gut	Mittel	Schlecht	Gar nicht
...mit diesem Kunden umsetzbar	Gut	Mittel	Schlecht	Gar nicht

9. Sehen Sie noch andere Hinderungsgründe Designentscheidungen im Scribble Doc festzuhalten?
10. Haben Sie Ergänzungen oder Verbesserungsvorschläge zur Dokumentation der Designentscheidungen?
11. Welche Vorteile sehen Sie darin die Designentscheidung im Scribble Doc festzuhalten?
12. Wie schätzen Sie den Nutzen im Vergleich zum Aufwand ein? Bitte begründen Sie die Aussage kurz

Aussage	Trifft gar nicht zu	Trifft nicht zu	Triff eher nicht zu	Trifft eher zu	Trifft zu	Trifft voll zu	Kurze Begründung
Kompensiert Ihrer Meinung nach der Nutzen der Dokumentation der Designentscheid-ungen im Scribble Doc den Aufwand?							

13. Wie stark stimmen Sie diesen Aussagen zu?

Aussage	Keine Zustimmung		Neutral		Völlige Zustimmung
Die Abstimmung der Design Entscheidungen in Workshops mit Endbenutzern ist...					
...leicht für mich zu verstehen					
...leicht für mich anzuwenden					
... ist wichtig für meine Arbeit im Projekt					
... hilft mir die Anforderungen der Benutzer besser zu verstehen					

Ich denke es ist eine gute Idee die Designentscheidungen mit Endbenutzern abzustimmen				
Ich werde in zukünftigen Projekten Designentscheidungen mit Endbenutzern abzustimmen				
Ich werde anderen empfehlen Designentscheidungen mit Endbenutzern abzustimmen				

14. Wie schätzen Sie die Umsetzbarkeit ein? Bitte begründen Sie die Aussage kurz

Die Abstimmung der Design Entscheidungen in Workshops mit Endbenutzern ist…				**Kurze Begründung**
…ist innerhalb des internen iPeople Entwicklungsprozesses umsetzbar mit…	Wenig Aufwand	Mittlerem Aufwand	Großem Aufwand	Gar nicht
… ist für das iPeople System umsetzbar	Gut	Mittel	Schlecht	Gar nicht
…mit diesem Kunden umsetzbar	Gut	Mittel	Schlecht	Gar nicht

15. Sehen Sie noch andere Hinderungsgründe die Designentscheidungen in Workshops mit Endbenutzern abzustimmen?
16. Haben Sie Ergänzungen oder Verbesserungsvorschläge zur Abstimmung der Designentscheidungen mit Endbenutzern?
17. Welche Vorteile sehen Sie darin die Designentscheidungen in Workshops mit Endbenutzern abzustimmen?
18. Wie schätzen Sie den Nutzen im Vergleich zum Aufwand ein? Bitte begründen Sie die Aussage kurz

Aussage	Trifft gar nicht zu	Trifft nicht zu	Trifft eher nicht zu	Trifft eher zu	Trifft zu	Trifft voll zu	Kurze Begrün dung
Kompensiert Ihrer Meinung nach der Nutzen durch die Abstimmung der Designentscheidungen in Workshops mit Endbenutzern den Aufwand							

19. Wie stark stimmen Sie diesen Aussagen zu?

Aussage	Keine Zustimmung		Neutral		Völlige Zustimmung
Die Dokumentation der Anfragen innerhalb JIRA Tickets ist…					
…leicht für mich zu					

verstehen				
…leicht für mich anzuwenden				
… ist wichtig für meine Arbeit im Projekt				
… unterstützt bei der Kommunikation mit dem Kunden				
… erleichtert es Entscheidungen später im Projekt nachzuvollziehen				
Ich denke es ist eine gute Idee Anfragen innerhalb JIRA Tickets festzuhalten				
Ich werde in zukünftigen Projekten Anfragen innerhalb JIRA Tickets festzuhalten				
Ich werde anderen empfehlen Anfragen innerhalb JIRA Tickets festzuhalten				

20. Wie schätzen Sie die Umsetzbarkeit ein? Bitte begründen Sie die Aussage kurz

Die Dokumentation der Anfragen innerhalb JIRA Tickets ist…					Kurze Begründung
…ist innerhalb des internen iPeople Entwicklungsprozesses umsetzbar mit…	Wenig Aufwand	Mittlerem Aufwand	Großem Aufwand	Gar nicht	

... ist für das iPeople System umsetzbar	Gut	Mittel	Schlecht	Gar nicht
...mit diesem Kunden umsetzbar	Gut	Mittel	Schlecht	Gar nicht

21. Sehen Sie noch andere Hinderungsgründe Anfragen innerhalb JIRA Tickets festzuhalten?
22. Haben Sie Ergänzungen oder Verbesserungsvorschläge zur Dokumentation der Anfragen innerhalb JIRA Tickets?
23. Welche Vorteile sehen Sie darin die Anfragen innerhalb JIRA Tickets festzuhalten?
24. Wie schätzen Sie den Nutzen im Vergleich zum Aufwand ein? Bitte begründen Sie die Aussage kurz

Aussage	Trifft gar nicht zu	Trifft nicht zu	Triff eher nicht zu	Trifft eher zu	Trifft zu	Trifft voll zu	Kurze Begründung
Kompensiert Ihrer Meinung nach der Nutzen der Dokumentation der Anfragen innerhalb JIRA Tickets den Aufwand?							

25. Wie stark stimmen Sie diesen Aussagen zu?

Aussage	Keine Zustimmung		Neutral		Völlige Zustimmung
Die Abstimmung der Anfragen 1. im JF und 2. in Workshops mit Endbenutzern ist...					

…leicht für mich zu verstehen						
…leicht für mich anzuwenden						
… ist wichtig für meine Arbeit im Projekt						
…vermeidet Korrekturen der Entwicklung in der Testphase…						
Ich denke es ist eine gute Idee die Anfragen 1. im JF und 2. in Workshops mit Endbenutzern abzustimmen						
Ich werde in zukünftigen Projekten die Anfragen 1. im JF und 2. in Workshops mit Endbenutzern abzustimmen						
Ich werde anderen empfehlen die Anfragen 1. im JF und 2. in Workshops mit Endbenutzern abzustimmen						

26. Wie schätzen Sie die Umsetzbarkeit ein? Bitte begründen Sie die Aussage kurz

Die Abstimmung der Anfragen 1. im JF und 2. in Workshops mit Endbenutzern ist…					Kurze Begründung
…ist innerhalb des internen iPeople Entwicklungsprozesses umsetzbar mit…	Wenig Aufwand	Mittlerem Aufwand	Großem Aufwand	Gar nicht	

... ist für das iPeople System umsetzbar	Gut	Mittel	Schlecht	Gar nicht
...mit diesem Kunden umsetzbar	Gut	Mittel	Schlecht	Gar nicht

27. Sehen Sie noch andere Hinderungsgründe die Anfragen erst im JF und ggf. mit Endbenutzern abzustimmen?
28. Haben Sie Ergänzungen oder Verbesserungsvorschläge zur Abstimmung der der Anfragen 1. im JF und 2. in Workshops mit Endbenutzern?
29. Welche Vorteile sehen Sie darin die Anfragen 1. im JF und 2. in Workshops mit Endbenutzern abzustimmen
30. Wie schätzen Sie den Nutzen im Vergleich zum Aufwand ein? Bitte begründen Sie die Aussage kurz

Aussage	Trifft gar nicht zu	Trifft nicht zu	Trifft eher nicht zu	Trifft eher zu	Trifft zu	Trifft voll zu	Kurze Begründung
Kompensiert Ihrer Meinung nach der Nutzen durch die Abstimmung der Anfragen 1. im JF und 2. in Workshops mit Endbenutzern den Aufwand?							

31. Fallen Ihnen noch weitere Beispiele aus dem iPeople Projekt für die Design- oder Entwicklungsphase zur Diskussion mit den Endbenutzern ein?

32. Welche Auswirkungen hätten die vorgeschlagenen Maßnahmen in der Design und Entwicklungsphase auf Ihre Bewertung des IPeople Systems? Bitte begründen Sie kurz warum sich ihre Bewertung ändert?

Printed by Books on Demand GmbH, Norderstedt / Germany